WE KNOW NOTHING

Lockdown And The Spectacular Halfwittery Of The Human Race

BILL LECKIE

Published by BREAK THE ARROW

To Brian, Steven, Jane, Kasia, Annie, Wes, Gordon L, Lisa, Pam, Julie, Kat, Kylie, Nic, Ana, Karen, Jamie, Gordon C and Gary, for helping to open my mind and my heart just when they both needed it most.

Cover design by the amazing GARRY OLLASON

CONTENTS

INTRODUCTION

D O you know how much of the Universe the greatest minds in the human race have a clue about?

Four per cent.

All the planets, all the stars, all the galaxies. For all the awe their sheer scale fills us with as we look up and up into the skies, the truth is that they occupy about as much of Everything as a pile of potato peelings in the bottom of a wheelie bin. They're merely a dot in an unknown, impenetrable sea of blackness that scientists describe as Dark Matter and Dark Energy; names which mean nothing, but at least sound slightly more like something than if they'd called them .

Thing is, they *thought* they knew it all, that they'd plotted the whereabouts of all there was to plot. Until, that is, they realised that — in the simplest terms — the Universe was not the fixed mass they'd believed it to be, but more like a balloon constantly being inflated, a balloon covered with felt-pen dots that, the bigger the area they were dotted around swelled, grew further and further apart.

Question is, does it matter much that we know so much less about the universe than we thought? Probably not — at least not to you and I, who were born on this little speck in the middle of infinity and will die here. But it's important to scientists, because when it became clear in the 1990s that what they thought they know turned out to be 96 per cent off the mark, it forced them to rethink so many others things they thought they knew; if *this* was wrong, then it stood to reason *that* was wrong and so on, a never-ending chain of re-setting, re-calibrating, re-learning.

Far from dispiriting them, though, far from making them feel like failures, this new knowledge has inspired a new generation to find new ways of calculating distance and measuring mass, to create new theories of what holds all those stars and planets together, what keeps them moving.

These past few months, the rest of us on Planet Earth have had a taste of what life feels like for those scientists.

Because these past six months or so, we've been dealing with the global pandemic caused by coronavirus and its accompanying disease, COVID-19. And it appears for all the world that one the most important lessons humanity has to learn from the chaos this invisible, insidious enemy has wreaked is that we really *do* know nothing.

Seriously. We know nothing. We might reckon ourselves to be geniuses, that being able to watch live telly on a teeny-tiny mobile phone means we've cracked it. But ask yourself, what is it we're watching on them?

Love Island Australia.

Which is a bit like inventing a rocket capable of going to Mars then using it to keep our spare carrier bags in.

As I write this, it's 192 days since Britain went into lockdown, a Government-imposed state where all but the most essential shops and services were closed, all but the most essential travel was banned, when millions were told to work from or study at home, when we were allowed out to exercise for an hour a day and, even then, only if we weren't deemed an infection risk.

Reading that paragraph back, it could easily be from the synopsis of a 1970s science fiction novel. Yet this has been our science fact, our reality for a third of 2020 and counting, our New Normal; no sport, no pubs, no restaurants, no holidays, no commute to the office, no popping out for coffee, no hugging our family and friends, no visiting our parents. A massive test of our mental as much as of our physical health, a daily challenge for some to survive in isolation and for others to cope with the whole family being cooped up together for 23 hours a day rather than floating in and out of each other's lives.

In purely human terms, the immediate purpose of all this was to stem the spread of the virus and keep its effects to a minimum. It's a cause of huge sadness, frustration and anger that, no matter how hard the majority tried to stick to this task, the death toll at time of writing has still managed to rise beyond 42,000, although it would have been around 5,000 more had England's health chiefs not decided in August to recalculate what constituted a Covid-related corpse, as if it made them any less deceased.

The bigger picture, however, always seemed one of how we would cope with the overnight loss of our freedom, the sweeping changes to our accepted daily routines. You wondered whether we'd have the patience and the understanding to see lockdown through, how we'd deal with having to make our own entertainment; and, just as crucially, how badly an economy so heavily based on *offering* that entertainment would be damaged.

Most of all, though, what fascinated me was how we would re-set once the shutters finally clattered back up.

See, although it was clear from the off that coronavirus would bring pain and confusion and upset to our lives — the only unknown being how much of each — it felt like it also presented an opportunity. It felt like we'd been given time to think about our lives, to assess what we had and what we needed, to ask ourselves who and what really mattered; and I genuinely mean everyone, from you and I little in our little bubbles to the guy who runs the cafe on the corner to the corporate giants dealing in billions. The politicians, the religious leaders, the people who run sport and music and theatre. Newspapers, TV, radio, social media trolls. Surely no one could live through the virus and shrug that it didn't affect them either way? Surely, while the sight of people being so scared and mixed up that they were prepared to fight over the last toilet roll in Lidl was understandable the week before lockdown, there would be no excuse for the same selfishness once we came out the other side?

Surely, while the lack of urgency and the excess of complacency shown by our leaders in the run-up to the virus being declared a global pandemic was forgivable, for them not to learn from their mistakes by the time we came through the worst was not? You'd think so. Yet as what follows makes an attempt at documenting, it appears that to think the best of humanity's abilities in a crisis is to offer ourselves way more credit than we're due.

And yes, I'm the first to admit that this *is* no more than an attempt to document the coronavirus pandemic, because to fully document what we've been through in a single volume would have taken one man 37 hours a day and given the Amazon delivery dude a double hernia.

The optimist in me started writing what follows in the hope that when the all-clear finally sounded, we'd find ourselves less materialistic, less self-obsessed, less inclined to waste money, food and time, that we'd spend more of that time with our loved ones and less with our phones, that we'll work smarter, exercise harder and sleep better.

But then, that's why the title isn't *We Know Nothing (Apart From Me)*.

October 2020

1

1: LOCKDOWN'S BRILLIANT PARADE

10.45pm, Thursday June 25

OUTSIDE my window, not long before sleep arrives, they come with their sirens; and they sweep away all the boys slowly draining the joy from their lives.

Elvis Costello always was the master of capturing moments in time through his lyrics and these lines might well have been written with this very moment in mind. All it needs is a tickle of the song's title.

Because tonight, *London's Brilliant Parade* could be set in Glasgow, on Tyneside and Merseyside and even on the normally sleepy Dorset coast as well as down in The Smoke that inspired it.

I switch off the audiobook of David Mitchell's autobiography, open Spotify, scroll and click to hear the song's wistful opening chimes. I push up the volume to drown out the never-ending nee-naws floating on the oppressive night air, but all the hissing from the earphones does is wake Sonia - and, bugger it, now the puppy's up too, letting out squeaky little barks to protect us from the noise outside. We bring him up beside us, so now we're all lying there, bleary and grumpy, on the hottest night of the year, listening to those sirens as they scream towards Kelvingrove Park.

An all-too-inevitable end to a Venn diagram of a day, where Circle A was a set of mixed messages from rival politicians, Circle B was the shirts-off-and-get-pished weather and Circle C was the simmering frustrations brought ever nearer the boil by three months of pandemic-emonium. Each overlapping into D: *The Innate Stupidity of the Human Race.*

5

Because right now, after a day when temperatures had hit 93f, it wasn't just outside my window where cop cars and ambulances were hurtling around. Right now, the sorry sight of gangs of fours and fives morphing into masses staggering about at sixes and sevens after necking one over the eight was being replicated the length and breadth of Britain.

Along the beaches of Tynemouth and Cullercoats, the under-suncreamed and over-lubricated had been bawling and brawling since teatime. On the sands of Bournemouth, teeming crowds dispersed at nightfall to reveal 33 tonnes of litter and three bodies lying bleeding from stab wounds. On London's brilliant parade itself, mounted officers were pelted with missiles as they fought to break up the latest in an endless stream of illegal raves.

Meanwhile, live via our TV screens, thousands were defying all reasonable medical and scientific advice by charging head-long onto the streets the minute Liverpool were confirmed as English Premier League champions, bodies hanging off stadium balconies, the night turned scarlet by flares and fireworks being let off in every direction.

We lie in bed amidst it all, trying to decide whether to close the bedroom window and feel even hotter or throw it wider and to say to hell with the din. Eventually, we decide the din's more likely to let up sooner, so I get up and let in what atoms of air there are, leaning out to try and work out where it is in the neighbourhood they've spent the past three hours having what might well turn out to be a quiet back garden drink with a couple of pals but which, in the stillness, sounds like a party at Jay-Z's.

"Completely clueless..."

"*Who is?*"

"All of them. Not a fucking clue. They just don't get it, the selfish shites. They'll knacker it for themselves and for everyone else. Completely clueless."

Sonia laughs. She tells me I sound about 300 years old — and she's probably right, but what else is anyone with half a brain meant to think? We've all been warned that running around licking each other's necks the minute lockdown begins to ease is the easiest way to encourage a second wave that could force us all back indoors for another three months. Yet so many among us seem to think they know better.

When the sobering truth is that they really do know about half the square root of less than zero.

2: CERTAINTY DESTROYS

BEFORE last night, I'd been swithering over whether the title of this book was fair. After all, we must know *something,* or how could we have invented the quill pen, the printing press, this laptop?

How would we have the music playing in the background or the speaker it's wafting from, connected as it somehow is by invisible wires to the miraculous brain of a mobile phone? If we really *do* know nothing, how come one of us picked up a handful of sand one day and saw the possibility of creating the window that lets the sun shine in as I write this?

So no, I'm not claiming the human race isn't an incredibly developed species. All I'm throwing out for debate is...well, put it this way; watch anyone in a restaurant when the server warns them their plate's really, really hot. Then check the first thing they do the second that server walks away.

Correct - they touch it to check and burn their fingers.

By the way, I write 'they', but of course I mean 'we'. Because I do it and will continue to do it, just as you will.

That's what I mean by *We Know Nothing*, a title that, in the light of last night's mayhem, of those hyped-up, boozed-up, tooled-up crowds being herded away from parks and beaches and city streets up and down the land, once more seems perfectly legitimate. Because if any of us we knew anything about anything, if we had common sense to match our ingenuity, why would we still willingly choose to drain all the joy from gloriously sunny days like yesterday by burning our skin, by dehydrating ourselves, by poisoning our insides?

Why would we set out to have the time of our lives and

end up stabbing a stranger or hurling a rubbish bin at a police horse? Why would anyone listen to warnings that getting too close to people from outwith our own family was the easiest way to risk the spread of the deadliest virus in our lifetime, then charge out regardless into a baying mob?

Why do I bite my nails when all it ends up doing is hurting? Why do so many on social media have the strongest opinions yet the weakest grasp of their own language? Why do people not only allow friends to film them committing crimes, but then to post the evidence online?

Why do we drive drunk or on drugs or too fast or with dodgy eyesight when we know it could kill us or others? Why are there famines when the planet has more food than it can eat, poverty when it's awash with money, wars between nations whose populations have no quibble with each other?

How can all of these be products of the same world that gave us the wheel, penicillin, TV, plumbing, robots, aeroplanes, open heart surgery and potato scones?

Simple. Because for all the individual genius that has turned us from cavemen to spacemen, we're still pretty thick.

But don't take my word for it. Ask a Pope.

BACK in December, Sir Anthony Hopkins was doing the usual round of media glad-handing to publicise *The Two Popes*, in which he stars as Benedict XVI opposite Jonathan Pryce as Cardinal Bergoglio. One of these interviews, with BBC journalist Hasim Sam Asi, has stuck with me from the first day it was shared on my Facebook page. No matter how often I watch it, I'm never any less transfixed by the take Hopkins offers not just on his own life and career, but on the mindset that brings so many of us crashing down because we either cannot or will not get our ambitions and abilities in the correct order.

This constant wrestling match with the ego ruins lives and economies, it wrecks peace and reduces countries to rubble.

This belief so many cling to — whether in positions of power or drinking with pals in a park — that to come across as anything but 100 per cent sure of themselves in all they do is a sign of weakness, is in itself our *greatest* weakness. As a journalist myself, it's fascinating to watch this interview and see this misplaced self-confidence oozing out of Asi, who has clearly come to work convinced he has an opening question which will make the scales fall from his subject's eyes and allow him to reel in the biggest fish of his career.

Instead, if this was a riverbank, he would be a rookie angler trying to land a monster pike with a broom handle, a length of dental floss and a safety pin.

Asi and his killer question are poised as the titles fade and we open with a scene in the Vatican gardens, where Benedict berates Bergoglio's decision to resign as an Archbishop due to his disillusionment at the Catholic Church being racked by scandals over corruption and sex abuse.

Bergoglio was in line to replace Benedict as pontiff — and would, despite his misgivings, go on to become Pope Francis, the first South American to hold the post — but right then, Benedict demands to know if he even still wants to be a priest.

As we fade to the studio, its dark backdrop lit by the movie's title in neon red, Hopkins relaxes in brown jacket with matching scarf and open-necked cream shirt. Asi - glasses, intense, dark suit, shirt and tie all dark — takes his cue...

Asi: "You play a character who's pious and who exudes piety, but you've said before that you don't even believe."

Hopkins: "I didn't say that..."

Asi: "Agnostic, then..."

Hopkins: "Well, what *is* an agnostic? It's someone who sometimes has doubts and sometimes doesn't have doubt. Sometimes I have doubts and sometimes I don't, but I don't have doubts any more...well, of course you have doubts, that's being human. I don't know - I don't know *anything*. That's the greatest spiritual ethic of all; to know nothing."

Asi: *"But do you think he had doubts?"*

Hopkins: "Of course he had doubts. Any intelligent human being has doubts. In doubt lies...piety. In doubt lives humility. If you have certainty, you're dead. Certainty destroys people. Hitler destroyed 40 million people because he was certain, Stalin destroyed millions of his own people. Certainty. He knew. But no one knows. And the greatest way to live is to live constantly in doubt."

Asi: *"But is not the basis of faith not to have doubts at all?"*

Hopkins: "Not unless one is Torquemada in the Inquisition. Any human who has a faith in God...well, I don't know, but of course I have doubts. All I know is there's a mystery in my life greater than I can even comprehend. I don't what I am, I don't know where I came from, I don't know where I'm going. I have no idea *what* made me. I come from my mother, my father, my grandfather, but I don't know what I consist of - I have no idea, but I believe that something underneath is miraculous. I mean, all these years later...82?...and my heart is still beating, my body's still functioning as far as I know and I feel relatively sane, but all I really know is that I know nothing. I am completely clueless, I've lived to such an age that I realise my knowledge is meaningless and of myself I am nothing, that we are not special."

Asi: *"Hm-mm. -"*

Hopkins: "Once you begin to believe in terminal uniqueness, absolute specialness, then your life is not worth living, because we're not special...."

Asi: *"Mmm-"*

Hopkins: "We're just ashes at the end — that's the great feeling for me; to quote TS Elliot, *'I have seen the moment of my greatness flicker and I have seen the eternal footman hold me coat and snicker and in short I was afraid'*. That's the wonderful thing. Or Omar Khayyam: *'There was a door that had no key, a veil through which I could not see, some little talk a while of me and thee — and then, no more of me and thee...'*"

(Hopkins puts thumb and forefinger to his lips and blows,

like a conjurer making a playing card disappear. To the viewer, it's a mesmerising gesture; to the interviewer, the chance to shoehorn in a question...)

Asi: *"So, so you instil these values and beliefs in..."*

Hopkins: "In myself, yes."

Asi: *"...in your characters?"*

Hopkins: "Yes, that's why I do what I do."

Asi: *"But even when your character is a very religious...he is the authority, actually, on religion..?"*

Hopkins: "He is an authority, yes, an authority within the church, but..."

Asi: *"But you play him as a person with doubts and..."*

Hopkins: "Yes, because he says in the scene with Bergoglio..."

Cut to the two Popes side by side in an opulent Vatican chamber. Ratzinger speaks softly: 'The hardest thing is to listen. To hear his voice; God's voice...'

Then it's back to the studio...

Asi: *"But doesn't doubt breed fear in the hearts of religious people?"*

Hopkins: "No, no — who's the man 2000 years ago who when they were going to stone a woman to death for adultery, the man 2000 years ago who said: *'Cast ye the first stone who has not sinned.'?* He had no respect for the churchgoers, the humble ones. He liked sinners, drunks, prostitutes. He hung about with them, because he knew they were vulnerable human beings — and he would come along as the light and say: 'I'll give you light, not judgement'."

Asi: *"Hm-mm-"*

Hopkins: "That's what it's about. We live in such a world of such...such evil, such ignorant, bubble-thinking political correctness."

Asi: *"Mmm-"*

Hopkins: "We all have to *have* an opinion about something.

So people say to me, what do you think about this or that and I say, I dunno, I'm clueless, I'm just an actor, what do I know?"

Asi: "Ok, so let's talk about, then, morality. The Pope is the authority on morality, the moral authority, but you have played characters who had no morals at all - Hannibal Lecter for instance. How do you approach these characters? Does it make any difference if one guy has the authority and the other doesn't care at all?"

Hopkins: "No, no - I'm an actor. I know how to play them. I don't have to explain them, I don't have to analyse everything I do. I don't analyse how I get up in the morning. I don't analyse how I scrub my teeth. I don't analyse *anything* — who I am to analyse anything? I'm nothing."

Asi: "But what traits do you look for in a character in order to inhabit them?"

Hopkins: "It's in the script...it doesn't take a genius. To play Ratzinger was easy because I know parts of that personality; I have them myself, I like solitude, quiet, I don't like fuss — but that's as close as it gets. It's all in the script, Anthony McCarten wrote a very good script, I don't need to improve anything, rewrite anything. Actors always want to rewrite everything, because they're stupid, they think they're better than the writer. But if there's a good writer, then the actor should just turn up on set and say, let's do it."

Asi: "You are a voracious reader, you have vast knowledge, you have great erudition. That must seep into your characters..."

Hopkins: "Of course. I'm intelligent, but I'm not a brilliant intellect. I was intelligent enough to get into this business, to have survived this long — that's called native intelligence. But where I came from as a schoolboy, I was an idiot, I couldn't understand anything. I've no idea how I got here from there. I was doomed to failure, in school I was *told* I was doomed to failure, that I would amount to nothing; and I remember saying to my father: *'One day I'll show you.'* And who knows, maybe that *(snaps his fingers)* set a spark off. Maybe something divine happened inside of me. But whatever has happened to me happened despite myself, because of myself I am nothing.

That guy said it 2000 years ago: *'Of myself, I am nothing, it is the Father within it doeth the works, it is the Kingdom of Heaven within.'* Whether you're Christian, Catholic, Protestant, Muslim or Hindu or whatever, it's all the same. Life is a dream."

Asi: *"So how do you explain reaching the pinnacle of your craft?"*

Hopkins: "I have no idea. As I said, I cannot take credit for anything. See, the ego is the most dangerous part of us. Ego is the enemy. You have to have a little bit of it to keep moving, but you let it get out of control and then you have the power freak. You see it in the papers every day — the corruptness of corporations, the greed, the power, the belief that they are gods. And they all reach damnation in the end. But I'm not a religious person in that sense. I don't believe in the Devil, but I believe we have to pay the price for our actions. If I'm cruel or disrespectful to someone, I'm going to pay the price in the end. I've learned over the years, slowly — and I'm a sinner like everyone else - I've learned over the years to respect people, to be kind. And if I'm angry, fine, then I'm angry. I'm only human. I can't be anything else. I can't be a saint..."

(Cut to a scene in a Vatican garden where Ratzinger addresses Bergoglio...)

'You must remember that you are not God. You are only human...'

THAT young boy Hopkins speaks of, that idiot with no idea of how he got from there to here? That boy without any brilliant intellect, but with endless native intelligence?

How many of us must have read or heard those that description and seen ourselves? I did, that's for sure.

To hear him take life's complexities apart and reduce them to such a simple terms never fails to crystallise what's going on inside me at a time of life when everything seems up for question.

This feeling of re-evaluation is, of course, something we've all experienced via the virus, but the truth is that my own little orbit had been wobbling dangerously on its axis for a lot longer than these past few months of lockdown. At nearer 58 than 57, I've spent months giving far more time than is healthy to taking apart my existence like it's an ailing washing machine, then putting it back together only to find there's always a stray part left over.

I've earned my living as a journalist since Monday July 27, 1981, my first day on the *Clydebank Press* and two before Charles and Di got married; though in my head I'd been doing the job since the age of eight, when I found out my primary school headmaster, Sam McDougall, was also part-time St Mirren correspondent for the weekly *Paisley Pictorial* and it clicked that this was a fine way to get into the football for free.

Mr McDougall, amazing man that he was, found out through my teacher that I wanted to be a writer and persuaded his editor to let me do a match report from the next home game. The day it went in print, I was hooked — and from that day to this, I have had not the first, slightest Scooby Doo what I'd have done had it all not worked out — and neither, like Hopkins as he looks back over a fantastic career on stage and screen, am I any wiser on how or why it *has* worked out.

Best guess?

This same uncertainty applies to as many of us as it does not.

Yes, there will be plenty who had a plan, who applied themselves to that plan, who gave themselves targets and hit them bang on. The ones who found a job, worked their way through the ranks to a level where they were content, met someone and settled down, had kids and a mortgage and a pension and who can't understand why anyone would go through life without having a plan and sticking to it.

But for every one of them — and to each, I doff the chapeau in admiration — there will be someone else whose progress from kid to teenager to adult to mid-life crisis and on towards dotage will have felt more like...well, you know when you're driving and suddenly realise you've spent five, ten, 20 miles on autopilot, moving from A towards B without mishap, but also without consciously *avoiding* that mishap?

That's my life. And the trouble with leading a life this way is that you get away with it while autopilot's on, while you're happy to accept that this is the kind of person you are; spontaneous, take-a-chance, see-how-it-goes, pick-your-self-up-and-go-again. It's only when you stop and think about how you got here, when it dawns how easily you could have smashed head-on into a metaphorical juggernaut at any time that it all gets a little scary.

Like, you know when a cartoon character runs off the edge of a cliff and keeps on running in mid-air? Except that they suddenly *realise* they're running in mid-air and suddenly they can't any more? That beat of stillness between denial and the plummet into the Grand Canyon with a final, far-off *pffffft,* that's where I've been hovering these past few months.

ONE hour after my final exam - Higher grade German, May 23, 1979 — I left Camphill High School in Paisley and began getting very impatient to become a journalist for real.

I worked for a few months as petrol pump attendant, then come January went to Napier College in Edinburgh to begin a one-year journalism course, which I failed. For the next six months, my head was so locked into proving the examiners wrong (for something that was my own fault) and getting a job on a paper that it didn't even cross my mind to get out and earn some cash. Mum and dad really should have slapped me hard, but they were forever supportive to the point of wrapping me in cotton wool.

Finally, I got an interview over in Clydebank, got the job and since then I've reported, sub-edited, designed and written columns for, been Features Editor or Sports Editor of, battered out more than a thousand columns for, covered more than 2,000 football matches for, visited 76 countries on behalf of, commentated on football matches for, done the horoscopes and scripted cartoon strips for the *Clydebank Press*, *Renfrew Press*, *Clydebank Post*, *Renfrew Post*, *Govan Post*, *Paisley & Renfrewshire Gazette*, *Barrhead News*, *Johnstone Gazette*, *Paisley Daily Express*, *Sunday Mail*, *Daily Record*, *Evening Times*, *Daily Winner*, *Sunday Scot*, *Scotland On Sunday*, *7 Day Press*, *Scottish Football Today*, *The Sun* national edition, *Scot FM Radio*, *BBC Radio Scotland*, *BBC Radio 5 Live*, *talkSport*, *Setanta Sports* and, on and off for the past 32 years (23 of them consecutively since 1997), *The Scottish Sun*.

Between them, they've sent me to World Cups in Italy, France, Japan, South Korea, Germany, South Africa and Russia, European Championships in England, Belgium, Holland, Portugal, Austria, Switzerland and France, the Rio Olympics, nine Open Championships, five Wimbledons, three Australian Open tennis championships and too many Champions League, UEFA Cup and Europa League ties to keep track of.

And I'm tired.

Tired of being out in the cold on soaking-wet Tuesday nights, tired of departure lounges, tired of irritated managers answering irritating questions, tired of hanging around corridors in the bowels of stadium late at night hoping for vapid quotes from weary players. Tired - and bored beyond belief— of the sectarian bile that comes from being around Scotland's two biggest clubs, Celtic and Rangers. Or Rangers and Celtic, just so half of them don't take the huff at being put second. This aspect of the job was a prime mover in my mental health taking a dip that I only started to come out of after finally giving in and going for treatment in 2011 and then starting to work out how closely what happens in the head is linked with physical fitness.

(Feel free to break off at this point, go to Amazon and order The Six Inches In Front Of Your Face *to find out the full story. You'll laugh, you'll cry, you'll want to go and climb volcanoes in Ecuador.)*

There's been another side to this growing weariness, though; the ever-increasing toll on an ageing body. At the end of the 2004-05 football season, I had surgery on both wrists after years of typing and holding a phone brought on Carpal Tunnel Syndrome, where the nerves to the hands compress and stop the fingers working properly. Early in 2017, on a charity trek to the Arctic Circle, I developed frostbite in both my middle fingers - tip: never, ever go for a pee at -24F without gloves - which left them both gnarled as a gnarly thing and pretty much dead to the touch.

THAT summer, I needed a growth cut out from beneath a right eye that was already working on 40 per cent power thanks to damage caused by an attack of Shingles back in 1995.

By November 2018, the sight in that eye had deteriorated to the point where the docs recommended a corneal transplant; they cut out your dodgy one and replace it with a healthy one from a not-quite-as-healthy corpse, holding it in place with 36 teeny-tiny stitches until it decides whether it wants to adopt you permanently or not.

Meanwhile, my right knee — its medial ligament torn after a dust-up with a pothole 11 miles into the 2003 New York Marathon - was growling, especially when the weather got damp; which, for those of you who don't know Scotland, is every day apart from June 23 every second year. To be fair, 16 and a half years was a pretty fair length of time to keep hobbling along on without surgery, so it was hard to complain when in January of this year, a quarter of a mile into the first training run for April's London Marathon, it finally went ping.

Ouch, he hinted.

We were looking at six months minimum for an op on the NHS and so took what turned out be the smart decision of paying for an MRI, which told me within days it needed an op. Bang went the summer holiday fund as I paid for that too and, on Wednesday February 28, a consultant called Stuart Bell made a couple of holes under the kneecap and took away a strip of damaged meniscus, some floating cartilage, plus various other odds and sods of detritus picked up down the years. The following week, in for a regulation eye test, my friendly local optician announced that the dodgy right eye appeared to have grown itself a cataract.

Apart from all of which, I felt tickety-fuckedy-boo.

Since getting treatment for depression in 2011, just after coming back from covering the tenth anniversary commemoration of 9/11 in New York, I've climbed those above-mentioned volcanoes in Ecuador and picked up a fairly serious dose of altitude sickness, run four marathons to take my total to ten, trekked the Great Wall of China twice, cycled across Vietnam and Cambodia and up the French Pyrenees and done the frostbite-y thing in Finland, all while jumping from covering this sporting event in that corner of the globe to writing the next column on the hot topic of the day.

On top of this, I'd trained as an indoor cycling instructor and was teaching a minimum four classes a week as well as getting out on the road bike as often as the weather allowed, signed up for an online course in Mental Health Care followed by a week-long seminar that would hopefully qualify me to practice Neuro Linguistic Programming and was training to go up Kilimanjaro this coming September.

Oh, and in between knackering the knee and getting the op, I'd organised a 24-hour event at the cycle studio to raise money for a homeless charity's new cafe. It never ends. There's always something else to be done. And as much as it's all through my own choice and as much as I tell myself it's the only way I know how to live, there's no point pretending that it wasn't all getting too much. What to do about it, though? How should I know? Like Hopkins - like anyone who's honest about themselves - I know nothing. I knew nothing on my first day at college, didn't have the first notion about living away from home. Had no money either, because everything I earned from the petrol station — which, with tips, was plenty — went on clothes and nights out. On my first day at work, I knew nothing about how to help getting a newspaper out. First football match I covered, I didn't know how to get quotes from players and managers at time up.

First council meeting and first district court session, no idea what I was listening for and how to report it. First day of designing pages — on a local paper everyone does a bit of everything — first day moving from a weekly paper to a daily, first Saturday night shift as a casual sub-editor on the *Sunday Mail*, first day as a full-time sub-editor at *The Scottish Sun*, first trip to report on an away European match, first day as a Sports Editor, a Features Editor, a magazine editor, a radio and TV commentator, after-dinner speaker, husband, dad, brother, an uncle, indoor cycling teacher, marathon runner — you name it, I knew nothing about how to make any of it work.

Ask me to give a lecture on how to write a match report or a column and it would last as long as it takes to deliver a shrug, yet time after time, when the pressure's on and the presses are revving, it just happens. That bothers me. It makes me feel like I've got to this age and crammed more into the years than most and come away with more stories to tell — when did Alice Cooper ever phone *your* mum and dad's house? — yet it somehow I've never felt grown up.

Is it a comfort that there's no way I can possibly be alone in feeling this vague sense of whatever-the-fuck-it-is? Not really. After all, the thought that hundreds, thousands, millions of us are stumbling through time with the autopilot on, getting stuff done but not knowing how, doesn't say much for us as a species. Lions don't stumble across vulnerable gazelles. Bees don't make honey by accident. Then again, Lions don't try to branch out into the honey-making business and bees don't tend to take on second jobs hunting and killing members of the antelope family.

Both know their strengths and their limitations, they both know their place in the big scheme of things. And maybe that's our problem — we're not content to play our part in the maintaining the planet's natural balance, we think we know it all.

In some ways, our brains have expanded into the most astounding computers, allowing us to discover and invent and develop everything from the wheel to the internet; yet in others our intellect has closed in on us, because nights like this one, as the sirens blare and the missiles fly and the crowds scatter, prove over and over again that this belief we have that we're smarter than we are merely goes to prove our stupidity.

Or maybe it's just me.

EXCEPT that it isn't just me, is it? Surely I can't be the only one who touches the plate the waiter says is too hot to touch?

No, walk down any street, watch any news bulletin, reality show or panel game, go to any cinema or theatre, read any book or newspaper, listen to song lyrics or to the conversation on buses or trains or in a queue and you'll be reminded that we're sleepwalking though life.

Politicians rise to the top not by being the most knowledgeable among us or the fieriest debaters, but by being stubborn enough in arguments to wear their opponent down. That and having more patience than anyone around them to sit through endless round of excruciatingly dull meetings, being willing to volunteer for the most mind-numbing sub-committee or working party knowing they'll then talk themselves into chairing them and that each will become foundation stones on which they'll build power.

The comedians and actors you see on peak-time telly are rarely the ones regarded by peers or critics as the best in their fields. The singers and the bands who get to the top of the charts are rarely the best musicians. In every office, every factory, every school staffroom, every lawyer's office — every workplace you can imagine — there are people whose status and longevity is completely out of kilter with their ability. So what links all of these people? That plan they're able to focus on, to stick to like hairs on soap. Enough of what Hopkins calls native intelligence to know when to say yes, who never to say no to and how to play the game when someone throws them the ball.

The world has way more bullshitters, bullies, experts in keeping the head down, arse-lickers and back-stabbers than it does motivators, mentors and creative geniuses — which isn't to say that bullshitting, bullying, hiding, toadying and double-crossing aren't skills in their own right, because each are examples of that native intelligence. It's just that they happen to be the equivalent of the footballer who'd rather making himself hated by diving to win a penalty than a hero by beating the defender and scoring a glorious goal. Black arts are still arts.

From my experience, though, what this world has most of all amongst its teeming billions are people who not only refuse to accept the theory that we know nothing, but whose minds it has never even fleetingly crossed. People who have no doubts that their way is the right way, people who see debate as antagonism, people convinced that everyone else is either with them or against them.

My-way-or-the-highway kind of people. Doubt-is-a-weakness kind of people. What-you-see-is-what-you-get kind of people. I-speak-my-mind-so-get-used-to-it people. The kind of people who are certain. People who either don't get or don't care that certainty kills. For people like these, the world today might well be an even tougher place to live in than it is for the rest of us.

3: A CASE OF IDENTITY

"My dear fellow," said Sherlock Holmes as we sat on either side of the fire in his lodgings at Baker Street, "life is infinitely stranger than anything which the mind of man could invent. We would not dare to conceive the things which are really mere commonplaces of existence. If we could fly out of that window hand in hand, hover over this great city, gently remove the roofs, and peep in at the queer things which are going on, the strange coincidences, the plannings, the cross-purposes, the wonderful chains of events, working through generations, and leading to the most outré results, it would make all fiction with its conventionalities and foreseen conclusions most stale and unprofitable..."

Tuesday, March 24, 2020

TODAY feels like a right good day to start banging out that blockbuster novel. You know, the one that's been bubbling away under the surface for ages and whose monster sales will finally let you stick two fingers up at the world and retire to Hawaii.

If ever the time felt right to release all that pent-up creativity, this is it. The perfect day to knock up a couple of thousand words before lunchtime, to set the pace, to start drawing characters who'll morph from names into real people with recognisable features and believable characteristics, to be amazed by that feeling of a plot develop without you having consciously thought of what happens next. Maybe we find out that our hero has a sordid past, or that a villain might just have a triumphant future. Maybe love interests blossom or twists lurk round every corner. Maybe you decide enough's enough for now, that it's time to hit Command-S, to give it all a read over, to sit back and feel good, before rewarding yourself with a half-hour on the spin bike, followed by tea, a sandwich and an episode of *The Sopranos*.

Job done. Bada-bing and, furthermore, bada-boom.

Today also feels like a right good day for sticking a casserole in the slow cooker for a few hours, then for passing the time by scrubbing the loo and sinks to within an inch of their lives and YouTubing a video to help with fixing that skew-whiff kitchen cupboard door.

Hey, and while we're in the mood, why not gut the bedroom shelves and drawers, fill a bunch of black bags with gear you're never going to wear again and get them down the charity shop? Why not carry on from there and do the same with all the crap that's crammed in every spare corner of the house and get it ferried off to the dump?

Well, there's the fact that all the charity shops and council dumps and DIY stores are closed. The fact that day by day this past, ever-more-worrying week, pretty much all non-essential premises in the neighbourhood, the postcode, the city, the country and most of the planet have, with heavy hearts, pulled down the shutters. The fact that the pause buttons's been pressed on life as we know it from Stranraer to Sarajevo to San Francisco and back, offering at one turn the ideal opportunity to get on with all those tasks we're always moaning that we have no time for, yet at the next an understandable reason why so many of us are struggling to make a start on any of it.

This combination of opportunity and excuse goes by the name of coronavirus.

An infinitesimal organism we can't smell or taste or touch or hear. A bug that not so long ago was all on its lonesome, but which found a pal on Bug Tinder who introduced it to two more, who then hooked up with another four, then eight — and who, before long, was just one of an army beyond measure, sweeping from one stall in one meat seafood market in one street deep in the Chinese city of Wuhan to all points of the compass.

Or, if you wear a tin-foil hat to stop The Man reading your thoughts, a poison created in a Beijing lab in a joint mind-control programme with the CIA, but which Agent Clouseau dropped and smashed when he tripped over a loose paving stone on his way to the handover. Which theory you buy into, fact is that along the way, coronavirus has developed into a disease known as Covid-19 and it has changed all human life as we know it; maybe for a few more weeks, maybe forever.

It has closed all those charity shops and council dumps, every pub and cafe and restaurant, every fashion store and electrical warehouse, every hairdressing salon and nail bar, every school and college and university, every gym and football ground. It has silenced production at countless factories and halted commerce in even more offices. It has grounded planes and cancelled trains, it has changed the way we live and work and play.

What the long-term implications of all this upheaval are on the economy pretty much depends on what its short-term effect is on our collective health. Some fear the very worst — millions dead, a plague, mass graves — while others argue that it will pass like every winter's dose of the flu.

Yet already, on the cusp of what one of the most important social and medical crises in many generations, coronavirus has begun to bring out the best in good people and dredged up the worst in others. It has made some raid the supermarkets shelves in sheer panic and others offer their services to those regarded as most vulnerable should things turn nasty. Most of all, it feels like everything and everyone around us — the neighbourhood, the city, the country — is bracing itself for an attack of the likes previously only imagined in science fiction, this alien invader hungry to claim lives of anyone who refuses to respect its power.

And just to prove life really does sometimes imitate art, what do we find on the ITV schedule for two nights from now?

Contagion. The 2011 movie where Gwyneth Paltrow brings

home a mystery illness from a business trip to Hong Kong, sparking a pandemic that kills 26 million worldwide before a vaccine can be found.

Let's hope this time next year they're not re-running it as a documentary.

◆ ◆ ◆

LAST night at 8.30pm, Prime Minister Boris Johnson stared down the lens of a camera propped on the end of his Downing Street desk and announced that Britain was on Lockdown.

Ok, so in the interest of strict accuracy, he didn't actually use that word, but we all know it's what he meant. It had been a global buzzword ever since Tuesday January 23, when it was imposed on the Chinese city of Wuhan, whose Hunan Seafood Wholesale Market had been closed on 22 days earlier after the first recorded cases of a mystery, flu-like illness. Within a week of those first cases, scientists has identified the illness as a variant of the coronavirus family, which as long as 30 years ago had been transferring itself from bats to a host of live animals traded in Chinese markets; prime suspect as an initial smuggler was the pangolin, an ant-eating mammal which had become the most-trafficked creature on earth thanks to the Chinese having a taste for its meat and a medical use for the properties within its scales. Also pinned up on the operations room matrix board was a photofit of the palm civet, which looks like a cat who's gone a bit goth but which is actually related to the mongoose and who, like the pangolin, is a big deal in the dodgy critter-trading fraternity.

It's believed that back in 2002, a virus passed from civets to humans in the Guangdong region of China, close on 1000 km from Wuhan, caused a brief and thankfully more containable outbreak of an illness similar to today's coronavirus.

On January 11, Chinese reported their first death from this new strain. By January 22, there were 550 infection and 17 deaths. The following day, Wuhan was cut off from the world

— all road, air and sea transport suspended, no one allowed in or out. The day after that, 14 more cities were placed under the same restrictions, putting 50 million on lockdown. On February 11, the World Health Organisation announced that this new strain of coronavirus would be called COVID-19. On February 12, South Korea reported its first spike in reported cases. On February 20, authorities closed all schools and businesses in the whole of Hubei province, of which Wuhan is the capital and which is two-thirds the size of the UK.

By then, Italy was 20 days into a ban on flights to and from China and had declared a national emergency after two cases were confirmed in Rome. On February 19, a crowd of 44,236 watched Atalanta, from the city of Bergamo in the region of Lombardy, play Spanish side Valencia in Milan, a neutral venue used because Atalanta's stadium was being renovated. Next day, a man from Lombardy who had been in hospital but left without being tested for Coronavirus *did* test positive, by which times doctors feared he had spread his infection to countless others. On February 23, with cases at 150, small towns in Lombardy were quarantined, with carnivals and sporting events cancelled. That same day, South Korea implemented widespread testing, with as many as 10,000 carried out in a day at pharmacies and drive-through centres, while Iran closed all schools, universities, cinemas and theatres and even released 54,000 prison inmates to prevent infection after their cases reached 18,400.

On February 24 in Spain - its first case recorded on January 31 and its first death (a 69-year-man in Valencia who had visited Nepal) on February 13 - confirmed "multiple cases" originating from contact with a doctor from Lombardy who had holidayed on Tenerife. Entire hotels on the island were quarantined over the following days as more and more fell sick. On February 25, four news cases connected to Italy's outbreak were record by Spanish authorities; one was the wife of the doctor from Lombardy, while another two had been in Bergamo at the time of the Atalanta-Valencia match. On February

26, two more Italians who had been on holiday with the Lombardy doctor and his wife tested positive.

On February 29, the United States confirmed its first COVID-19 death at a Washington State hospital. Over the following two weeks, almost all US states declared a state of emergency. Come March 4, with cases at 3,089 cases recorded, Italy closed its schools and universities.

Within another four days, entire provinces in the north of the country were on lockdown as cases reached 7,375. Twenty-four hours later, that figure stood at 9,372 and Italy was in total isolation from the outside world — and within another 48, as it rose to 12,462, all its restaurants and bars were closed by order of the Government.

Meanwhile, Spain's case numbers grew day after day, with many of those affected either having been to Italy or been in contact with Italians. When a sportswriter in Valencia who had covered the Atalanta match fell ill, the club cancelled all media conferences. Yet despite having watched the acceleration of Italy's emergency footing, life went on as normally as possible — on March 11, despite Madrid already being in partial lockdown, a 3,000-strong battalion of supporters from the city's Atletico club travelled with the team and a horde of Spanish media for a Champions League fixture away to Liverpool. There were 52,000 inside Anfield that night, coming and going through the narrow streets around the stadium then drinking into the night in the city's bars and along its waterfront. That same day was the second of four at the annual Cheltenham Festival, which would attract a total of 251,684 horse racing fanatics, cramming every hotel room and pub in the town for the entire week.

It was also the day the World Health Organisation officially declared COVID-19 a pandemic, meaning it was classified as a disease for which there was no immunity and which has spread global beyond expectations.

Almost immediately, President Donald Trump banned all travel to the US from 26 European countries, though not from the UK or Ireland; exceptions which has nothing at all — nothing to see here, please disperse — to do with the fact that he has golf resorts in both.

Warning: Cynicism is a very dangerous side-effect of this virus.

On Monday March 17 — just as a report leaked to the *New York Times* claimed the pandemic could last 18 months or longer, Spain took the view that with cases beyond 6,000 and deaths at 190, an entire nation of 47 million should join Italy in quarantine.

In Italy itself, March 17 saw 475 deaths, the single-highest toll in any country on any one day since the outbreak began; the next two days would see this unwanted record rise to 627 and 793. They'd tried to keep manufacturing and other day-to-day services operating, but on March 22, as cases reached 59,138, the decision was taken to close down all but those deemed essential for a minimum of two weeks.

On Monday March 23, New York City confirmed it was dealing with nearly 21,000 cases. Globally, the figure stood at 375,000; 258,000 ongoing, 101,000 recovered and 16,370 deaths.

SO, no Boris Johnson didn't use The L Word during his address to the nation last night. He didn't have to, because we all know what he meant. Yet the strange thing is, an awful lot of people would have been an awful lot happier — if *happier* applies at a time like these — had he used it.

For days, I'd watched social media blare with calls for cops and troops to hit the streets in a bid to stop those who hadn't grasped the seriousness of situation from turning themselves into open goals for COVID-19 to tap into.

Then, at 5pm last Friday, the PM had announced the closure of all bars, restaurants and cafes to sit-in customers from that night, though they could stay open for takeaways. As it happened, the news buzzed on my phone while I was sitting in a place called Little Italy in the West End of Glasgow, having a beer with my pal David Smith to drown our frustrations at the indoor cycling studio we teach in having been closed for the duration. I showed a passing waiter and he simply shrugged: "*It was coming...*"

By now, most of us were at that stage, one of acceptance that this was a situation beyond our comprehension as well as our control. We'd gone from disinterest to vague concern to Googling the symptoms to wondering if it was safe to go to the gym to demanding a vaccine right now to batting around conspiracy theories about the Chinese having started it deliberately, but now most were ready to accept that it was what it was.

Along the way, we'd also welcomed a new buzz-phrase into our everyday vocabulary; self-isolation, the medical term for keeping the world at arm's length. The advice from on high was to stay indoors as much as possible. If and when we needed to venture out, we were told at first to keep one metre between ourselves and the next person from outwith our own household, a distance soon doubled. As one pal would later put it in a deliberately grim Facebook post: "*If you're not sure, think about as the length of a coffin.*"

Plus, all of the above only applied if we were fit and healthy and wanted to keep it that way. If, on the other hand, we were showing any symptoms of the virus, had other underlying health issues that made us more vulnerable to infection or if we were elderly, self-isolation basically meant going home and staying home to — another buzzword — shield.

Day by day, we came more to grips with what self-isolation meant and how it applied to us. For instance, the indoor cycling studio where David and I teach has 20 bikes, but as a precaution every second bike was being taken out of commission.

At my wife Sonia's hair salon, where six and seven clients were often in at once and where hugs and kisses came free with every cut and colour, bookings were down to one in, one out and affection reduced to the merest touch of elbows. We'd watched this menace come towards us from all point East, we'd seen the cases start to mount up on our doorsteps, watched first the universities and colleges and then the schools send everyone home indefinitely, sighed as our favourite sporting events fell one by one, stared slack-jawed at footage of fools ransacking supermarket shelves for everything from dried pasta to tinned beans to toilet rolls and, finally, we'd started listening to what our political leaders and their medical experts had to say about it all.

Or, like I say, most of us had.

Because, we humans being the halfwits we're capable of being, when Johnson said '*pubs must close tonight to help contain the virus*', what some heard was '*...so you'd better go out for one last kick at the ball that risks spreading it even faster*'.

And so, across that weekend, videos appeared on social media of bars defying the shutdown, packed to the gunnels with punters — mostly young — leaping about so smashed you'd think they'd just been told an asteroid was hours from smashing into earth. I'll never forget seeing one twonk showing off to the camera in a Dundee boozer by licking his palm and shaking hands with anyone who staggering past him. It was madness. But it was just what we are, it was just what we do. We are the most self-destructive, contrary, pig-headed mob in all of nature.

Not that it would be fair to pigeonhole everyone who acted like it was their last day alive as Jägerbomb-downing millennials. No, there were hordes of the supposedly grown-up and seemingly sensible Cabernet Sauvignon set who woke up, saw the sun was out and decided that self-isolating was something that only applied to everyone else.

All over Britain that Saturday and Sunday, every public park and every promenade, every countryside walking path and mountain hiking trail was mobbed. It was as if the moment they'd opened their curtains and squinted that early spring sunshine, they'd convinced themselves that no one else would notice and they'd have the open air to themselves.

But, like the football fan who thinks he'll beat the jams by heading for his car ten minutes before time-up, all they did was *create* those jams; this and rile up the vast majority for whom the penny had dropped and who had already holed themselves up whenever they didn't have to be anywhere. No wonder, then, that within minutes of the PM signing off last night, every pundit's analysis, every social media post and hastily clattered first edition newspaper story was calling it what it was.

Lockdown.

From this morning the closure of non-essential businesses is mandatory rather than precautionary. From this morning, outdoor gatherings of more than two, excluding families who live together, are prohibited. From this morning, we can go out for essential supplies, but as infrequently as possible. From this morning, we can jog, walk or cycle for an hour a day as long as we stay at least two metres from the next person.

Two metres? Boris Johnson has never been someone I've wanted to be within two miles of. Goodness knows I've caned him often enough in print for his fake buffoonery, his candy-floss hair and his Old Etonian bluster. His handling of the Brexit fiasco — remember when that was the only game in town, way pre-virus? — was appalling, his reach-out to the Working Class at the hurriedly cobbled Christmas 2019 General Election as fake as a chocolate Rolex. He embodies everything I loathe about modern politics, with his inability to debate, his snide asides to what we might loosely describe as the opposition and his oozing sense of entitlement.

Yet last night at 8.30pm, with the nation in crisis, he was impressive. He was calm and articulate, with a gravitas that seemed to spring from nowhere. Most comforting of all, he came across as someone who actually believed in what he was saying, someone who grasped the situation well enough to look us in the eye and give us it straight.

Compare this to the Scottish Government's health minister Jeanne Freeman, who I'd criticised in a column a week or so ago over a televised statement about the virus when she'd barely looked up from a speech that either had been written for her in a hurry or which had pictures of nudey women on it. Her halting delivery and lack of eye contact spoke of someone hugely ill at ease with her task and bred not a shred of confidence.

Johnson, on the other hand, was able in last night's highly-pressurised moment to deliver rotten news in a way that left you thinking he knew his stuff. Unlike so often when he addresses the nation, it felt like his words came from the heart; though even if it *was* all just an act, even if he was wearing Speedos beneath the desk and went straight back out to a pool party with 200 chums once the director yelled cut, fair play to him for getting the tone bang on when it mattered.

Though I reserve the right to whack the human Arctic Roll at any point in the chapters that follow should the mood take me.

THAT quote at the start of this chapter is from the opening lines of *A Case Of Identity*, the fifth adventure written by Arthur Conan Doyle about the great consulting detective Sherlock Holmes. The audiobook version of *The Complete Works* - all 58 hours and four minutes of it — is a constant go-to, the vocal dexterity of narrator Simon Vance bringing Doyle's characters and the Victorian era alike to wonderful life. Given the choice, these works would be my specialist subject on Mastermind; that or FA Cup Finals 1946-2000.

From the preamble of *A Study In Scarlet*, where a newly war-wounded and demobbed Dr Watson speaks of his lonely life in London — 'the great cesspool into which all the loungers and idlers of the Empire are irresistibly drained' — to the climax of *The Retired Colourman*, in which the scent of fresh paint in the hallway of the marital home helps Holmes trap a jealous husband who killed his wife and her lover, this compendium transfixes me.

And in those words about real life being infinitely stranger than fiction, how its 'strange coincidences, the plannings, the cross-purposes, the wonderful chains of events, working through generations, and leading to the most outré results' are beyond anything man could dream up, lies what this book makes some kind of stab at exploring.

In an ideal world, we'd see this as the perfect time to embrace how little we understand and to become better people because of it.

Wednesday, March 25
·Spain records 700 deaths in 24 hours as India locks down its 1.3b population.
·Olympics, due to start in Tokyo on July 23, postponed for at least a year
·NHS look for 250,000 volunteers as deaths reach 422 from 9,500 cases.

OR then again, we could stick to what we know; running around with our hair on fire, blaming anyone and everyone that moves for anything and everything that's going wrong.

Twenty-four hours in UK lockdown, fingers are already being pointed at politicians, doctors and scientists for not reacting sooner to what was heading our way and getting us into self-isolation earlier. Of course, we could have cut out the middleman and *chosen* to self-isolate. We could have Googled the word *coronavirus* and taken our own precautions to prevent it spreading. We could have used our initiative to cut off the bug at source, to look after our own little bubble and trust the people in the bubbles on either side of us to do the same.

We could have taken the strain off the NHS from Day One by being on our guard against infection in the same way as we tend to be on our guard again walking into speeding traffic. We could have done a whole lot of things of our own accord to make sure that, even if we were fearing the worst, we were preparing for something a lot better.

But we preferred instead to wait to be told, because then if we caught the bug it wasn't not our fault, it was Boris Johnson's or Nicola Sturgeon's, depending which of them we trust less.

Even this early in a period of self-isolation that might last another day, another week, another six month, a decent-sized minority of us — and by 'us', I mean in the human race as an entity, not just here in Britain - have clearly decided catching coronavirus is a gamble worth taking. Only time will tell if they'll lose their shirts, or worse. Take the situation in Spain, where a few days ago authorities were convinced they'd handled their response pretty well, but where today, the question is already being asked: *How did they get it so wrong?*

Yesterday, another 738 died there, leap-frogging them above the Italians to the top of the world's grimmest league table. From Wuhan and across the rest of China's gargantuan sprawl, to Iran, to Italy, an east-to-west advance no amount of tanks or cruise missiles could hope to halt has hit the Spanish so hard and fast the last set of ever-tougher Government orders broadcast before they're made redundant by the next.

No one in their right mind would volunteer right now to run the show in Madrid - or any capital city, for that matter. It must be like trying to direct an action thriller while it's already on screen. And yet, human nature being what it is, they're *still* getting it in the neck for getting it all wrong.

Today, we're reading reports claiming that as the Spanish could see what was happening in China, Iran and Italy, they should have acted sooner to impose lockdown and that failing to do so has cost thousands of lives. Critics point to the fact that nations surrounded by land borders - France, Switzerland, Austria, Slovenia and more — all have far lower rates of infection despite the traffic in and out. The general conclusion, in almost every paper and news website, is that Spain maybe thought it was far enough away from the epicentre to get off lightly; a conclusion backed by the claim on February 9 from Madrid's head of medical emergencies, Dr Fernando Simón, that 'Spain will only have a handful of cases'.

Six weeks on, Dr Simón is the modern-day town crier tasked with giving out daily figures of hundreds of deaths, his nation's losses per head already three times that of Iran and 40 times higher than in China.

And why? Seems it boils down to a couple of very mundane facts; an unusually mild spring and the love the people of Madrid have when the weather's decent than crowding their lovely city's pavement cafes, hugging friends and chattering non-stop in each other's faces.

Spain went into lockdown a week or so before the UK. A week before that, massive demonstrations were held to mark International Women's Day and the party political conference season played itself out alongside those of football and basketball. On March 11, as mentioned previously, those 3,000 Atletico Madrid crammed onto planes to watch their clubs Champions League victory away to Liverpool.

Today, all this dirty washing is being hung out like knickers from a backstreet window as hindsight kicks in on the counter-attack quicker than Atletico did that night at Anfield, the Socialist-led government of Pedro Sánchez being roundly accused of reacting too slowly and way too clumsily, a scandal brewing over a lack of ventilators, of protective clothing for doctors and of the failure to put a coronavirus testing system in place. Ironically, just weeks after the country's Chinese immigrant community were being blamed for bringing the virus in, it's Beijing which has ridden to the rescue, pouring these supplies in as fast as they can make it.

Yet the fear is that it won't be enough, thanks to endemic flaws in a Spanish care system where homes for the elderly are legally bound to turn a profit while keeping prices at levels residents can afford on a basic pension of around £8,500 a year. Because of this, critics say, many are understaffed, unprepared and were quickly overwhelmed, with death rates touching 20 per cent. Troops sent in to back up emergency services found some residents dead in their beds.

Spain has long been proud of its primary health care system, but since the global financial crisis of 2008 its hospitals have suffered from cutbacks, leaving them with a third of the beds available in Austria or Germany, though this remains more than in the UK or the USA.

But the key to the speed with which the virus has spread across Spain might well come down to the 24 hours between prime minister Sànchez announcing his intention to lock the nation down and it officially being imposed; time enough for huge swathes of Madrid to pack up and head to stay with families or in second home or in holiday resorts across the country. Add to this the fact that bars and parks had been overflowing for days after the capital's regional government had taken the unilateral decision to close universities and schools and we were talking one, huge petri dish.

Today, ministers are quietly suggesting the curve of fatalities should flatten soon and that the shackles could be loosened by April 11. The sound of cynicism at this from the Bernabeu to Benalmadina is deafening. Is this cynicism justified? Is the criticism being levelled at the Sànchez administration fair? Possibly. Maybe even probably. By the time you read this, perhaps even definitely.

Whether this cynicism and criticism are helpful in the current circumstances, however, is different question; and, yes, it's one which might sound a tad rich coming from someone like me who makes a living out of taking pops at those in positions of power. To be honest, I'm with Billy Connolly when he says the desire to become a politician should automatically bar them from becoming on, so I'm happy to cane any of them when they step out of line, no matter the colour of their rosette.

The Credit Crunch. The Commons Expenses Scandal. Phone Hacking. Independence. Brexit. These past dozen years, Britain has stumbled from one crisis to the next, with those elected to run the show permanently so far out of their depth their blazers should come with a light and a whistle for attracting attention. Throughout these huge stories and all the smaller, day-to-day balls-up that connect them, I've gone in studs-up week in, week out without a shred of regret.

But even for me, there's a key difference between all of these crises and the one we're caught up in today. *Complicity.*

Successive governments may have aided and abetted banks and City traders to turn our economy into the world's only failing casino. MPs may have played us for fools over their second homes and the cost of cleaning their duck ponds. Those same MPs may have taken revenge for being caught out over all this by standing by as scores of journalists were nicked on spurious charges while the police's role in the interception of phone calls was all but ignored. As for the divisive Scottish independence referendum and the Brexit fiasco that followed? Don't get me started. Coronavirus, though, isn't their fault. Their manifestos didn't include a pre-emptive promise to stop it in its tracks. And now it's here, they don't know from hour to hour, never mind day to day, what it's going to do next.

Yes, we can look at the situation in Spain, for example, and decide that they should have acted more decisively. But what would any of us have done in their PM's shoes?

Impose martial law when the first case was confirmed? Shut down the football, ban all air travel, quarantine thousands of pavement cafes?

My guess is that if it had been your call or my call and we had, the roof would have fallen in on us, we'd have been burned in effigy. Even if we'd been proved right in the fullness of time, the immediacy of mainstream and social media abuse would have killed our careers stone dead long before we got to say *Told You So.*

Governments are busking it here, they're making policies on the hoof. This isn't — despite some of the political rhetoric the contrary — a war, with tactics in place and troops drilled for years in advance. Neither is it a terrorist attack, where even if the secret service fail to prevent it, there's a process in place to react instantly and restore order.

Once the shutters come up, there will be plenty time to debrief and to debate, to point fingers and to call for heads to roll if need be. But even then, let's try and remember to ask ourselves what we'd have done differently; not with the benefit of hindsight, not with all the facts at our fingertips, but right there, in the moment, with world and its wife howling at us for decisions, decisions, decisions; every of which decision really could turn out to be a matter of life and death.

Hey, who knows? Maybe as lockdown unfolds, Downing Street or Holyrood will do something so crass and so destructive I'll give in and pull on the hobnail boots — and if so, feel free to kick me right back for being a two-faced ratbag. For now, though, I'm trying to have an open mind; and, as it happens, today I also have an optimistic mind.

Woke up to the sun shining through the blinds, had a magnificent breakfast, went for a lovely, long walk with Sonia, queued patiently with the socially distanced crowd for our turn to get into the supermarket, then went home and wrote down some good thoughts to make myself feel better.

ONE day soon, the shutters will clatter back up and we'll breathe in the air of a better world. Not a *perfect* world, not some new Eden - steady, I've not quite gone that stir-crazy yet.

A better place to live, though, a happier environment in which to work and play and love. A street, a neighbourhood, a town, a country, a planet where we'll have learned enough from adversity to reset and start doing what we do that little bit smarter, calmer, happier. This won't apply to everyone, of course. Today's hoarders and hoaxers and shysters will still be what they are once Coronavirus has run its course; they'll just be scratching around for new ways to project their inadequacies onto the most vulnerable and the most gullible. But as we react, day by day and restriction by restriction, to the gravest health crisis of our lifetime, I've seen and heard so much that offers hope for the future. So many stories of kindness and generosity, so many giving up time to make sure the neediest don't go short of the basics, so many offering others their talents for free.

From online exercise classes, virtual pub quizzes and dinner dates by FaceTime right through to armies of NHS veterans coming out of retirement to help man the barricades, this unprecedented situation is bringing out the very best in the those whose first instinct was always to do good. And if it's also brought out the worst in a minority whose first thought was always to do bad...well, sod them. We'll remember the bosses who used a pandemic as an excuse to cull staff or hike prices. We'll know which hotels to avoid, which airlines to swerve, which retailers to give the finger to.

That's all part of what I mean by a better world. One where we're that bit choosier about who gets our friendship, our custom, our trust. A world where it's no longer about the survival of the fittest, but of the fairest. The pubs who decanted beer kegs into milk cartons and handed them out round the doors. The cafes who didn't charge key workers for coffee. The businesses who put profit second by keeping laid-off workers on full pay.

We'll remember those who shared what they had rather than cramming their trolleys with stuff they didn't need. We'll want the generous ones to be the template for how we behave when life returns to some kind of normal. Some may find this unbearably drippy. They might sneer that we'll all just go back to how we were before. But just as it's our duty to self-isolate and help stem the spread of disease, so it is to emerge from our homes and prove we've learned from the experience.

I can't be alone in looking at our politicians as they cancel their normal yah-boo pantomime to actually work together, as they listen to each other's ideas and to get things done for the greater good and thinking: Why can't it *always* be this way? I can't be alone in watching Boris Johnson and Nicola Sturgeon, both speaking more from the heart than ever before and thinking: Why can't *they* always be like this?

If both Westminster and Holyrood could come out the

other side of this crisis with a fresh take on their role in society, realise how much more there is to achieve by burying divisions and pooling their knowledge, Britain really could be a better country. Johnson has to realise 'taking back our borders' means nothing to a virus. Sturgeon has to realise independence wouldn't have made us immune.

More than this, we ALL have to grasp that, when the bug hits the fan, none of the labels we define ourselves by mean a damn thing — religion, party politics, wealth, status, favourite football team. All the money and prayers and trophies in the world can't change a damn thing, all we have is each other. Forget that and we'll have thrown away a unique opportunity.

Right now, no one's quite prepared for the physical and mental effects of being stuck indoors 23 hours a day, for the toll on lives or the damage to the economy. While we adapt to the unknown, though, let's try to appreciate who and what we have in our lives. Ask how much of the way we live today is dictated by greed and how much by need. Talk to each other rather than staring at the telly in silence. Read those books gathering dust on the shelves. Spring-clean our homes, bodies, minds. Stay active, healthy, in touch.

Most of all, stay positive. Not just during lockdown, but for the rest of our lives.

Thursday March 26
·Nearly a third of the world's population is under restricted movement.
·New York the epicentre of USA outbreak, known cases doubling every three days.
·Prince Charles tests positive and is in self-isolation in the Highlands.

BUT just to prove that — guess what? — I know nothing, no sooner was this self-help passage saved than we found out that not only had the heir to the throne had been catapulted to the front of the testing queue after catching the bug, but he and wife Camilla had driven from London to Balmoral hours before you and I were ordered by No 10 to stay home.

So much for status and money not meaning a thing in the eye of the coming storm. So much for optimism.

Funny how the mind works. This morning, the sun was still shining through the blinds and Sonia and I still went for a post-breakfast wander. Yet unlike yesterday, I feel lousy. The head's cotton wool, the legs lead-heavy. Ribs feel like they've been battered with a baseball bat, chest's tight, neck's creaking and crunching. The knee griped every step of our walk.

Today's the kind of day everyone is either having, has had or will have during coronavirus, whether we catch it or not. The first low of self-isolation, one of those days when the easy thing would be to stay in bed, not or shower or shave or work or exercise. The kind of day when everything's an effort, when every step is taken in diver's boots.

The longer it's dragged — and we all know how they can drag right now — the deeper I've sunk into an armchair, flicking aimlessly through TV pap and the less my way better half has been able to get through to me.

"Three days down and this is how he is," she must be thinking. *"God help us when we're into the third week…"*

But then, something wonderful happened. Just on eight at night, we heard the sound of applause from outside and re-membered it was the first scheduled weekly ovation for the nation's key workers. The sound grew louder by the second, the banging of hands backed by the clang of ladles on sauce-pans, the clinking together of bottles.

We threw up a window and joined in as claps became cheers and whistles and roars. And, for the first time that low day, it dawned that I was smiling.

A two-line post on Facebook later saying what a fabulous five minutes it had been and, by half past, reactions were in three figures; from our neighbourhood, from around Glasgow, from Edinburgh and Dundee and Dumfries and London, from family in Newcastle and Gloucestershire, love hearts from the States and Italy and Spain and Russia.

Now multiply this reaction by a hundred, a thousand, ten thousand identical posts and the enormity of what just happened sinks in. It was the lead item on the news, for goodness sake. People clapping in the street was the biggest story in the nation.

It left you thinking that if this simple act of spontaneous gratitude to the people looking after us in our nation's time of need — the NHS staff, the emergency crews, the care workers, the teachers, the drivers, the shop assistants, the takeaway deliverers — lifted the heart of one man whose spirits had gone through the carpet, then surely it did the same in countless more homes where quarantine was taking its toll.

And if it had that effect on us non-key members of society…well, just think what music it must have been to the ears of those it was meant for?

It's only a gesture, of course; as one pal was quick to point out, doctors would happily have swapped that standing ovation for a warehouse-load of extra beds and a few lorries stuffed with up-to-date protective equipment. Come to think of it, they'd also prefer their salaries to be hiked to a level that matches their contribution to society rather than to be belated stuck on a pedestal by a Government who -— never forget — clapped and cheered in the Commons last time a health service pay rise was kiboshed.

Sadly, you and I can't sort that — and in any case, even those at the sharp end would agree it's an argument for another day, once this crisis has subsided. All they can do is keep putting themselves in danger of catching Coronavirus every day and all we can so is thank them as loudly and as publicly as possible. Should we avoid getting too close as we gather outside to offer these thanks, as TV pictures showed so many up and down the land doing? Course we should — our key workers must go spare at the mirthless irony of punters lining the pavements to praise the NHS for the amazing job they're doing in the most trying of circumstances, while simultaneously risking making their job even harder.

But the gesture itself works, that was obvious from about 20 seconds past eight tonight and it's something that hopefully be-

comes a fixture of however long we're stuck at home, not just some sort of #BeKind-style passing fad in the wake of a troubled celebrity's suicide.

Anyway, for what it's worth, we pulled the window back down when the applause faded and within the hour I'd made my first-ever rhubarb crumble from scratch; something I'd promised to do that afternoon, only to find all the ingredients were there bar motivation.

It was the best rhubarb crumble anyone had ever made.

That's the power of our collective positivity.

4: GET ISOLATION DONE

Friday March 27
·UK deaths rise by 181 to 759 in 24 hours.
·China reported no new locally transmitted cases for second day in a row.
·Prime Minister Boris Johnson has tested positive.

FIRST Prince Charles, now BoJo. The minute they displayed the symptoms, they were fast-tracked up the queue for testing — over the heads of NHS workers and an ever-multiplying horde of patients, past your granny and the bloke next door with underlying heart problems — and confined to barracks for the next seven days.

Bloody hell, it's barely half a dozen pages since I was writing that we should be trying not to judge the Government on its handling of this global whirlwind. But news like this really doesn't do them any favours. Even this early, it seems they can't resist reverted to type and pushing our buttons to see how much we can take.

One minute they're telling us we're all in it together and they're relying on our patience as we wait for mass testing that's nowhere near being delivered, the next it seems for all the world as if Those And Such As Those are eligible for VIP treatment; ok, maybe not VIP, since it's just a swab and a prick of the finger. But it's the principle that gets to you, the thought that while tens of millions of us wait for answers on when the promise of a testing centre in every branch of Boots and a kit with every Amazon delivery will be made good, the elite — and I really hate that word, but it's less offensive than calling them cunts — get looked after pronto.

Not the best way to instil a feelgood factor when the nation's spirits are through the floor, is it? Hardly the way to keep the oiks onside after last night's spine-tingling ovation for the nation's army of key workers. But hey, what can you do? Take to the streets in protest? In groups of no more than two? Don't be daft. Fact is, we are where we are and this is what it is. None of it's fair, but all we can do is suck it up then wash our hands.

So you get on with it, with adapting to being stuck indoors 23 hours a day, to making the most of your time out to shop and to exercise. You try not to vegetate on the couch too much, to glue yourself to social media too much, to raid the fridge too much. Then you think how long you've been doing it. Four days? Feels more like four weeks, especially when you don't get to be with people you love, to hug them, even just to meet them for coffee.

With Sonia, it's her mum. With me, it's my kids and big sister.

My son Kenny's 33 and lives with his partner Emily, 20 minutes drive away on the south side of the city. My daughter Georgia, 14 years to the day younger than her big brother and doing a Biochemistry degree at Glasgow University, is in a student flat about a mile from us. Big sis Anne still lives in Paisley, where we were born and grew up, her daughter Julie and grandkids Logan and Evie just a couple of miles from her.

Yet we might as well all be on different planets for all the help proximity does right now. This afternoon, I go down to G's place to see her from six feet away. We laugh about the daftness of it, but we're both sad at not being able to get close. Back home, Sonia's in from seeing her mum and she's as low as I was yesterday, mainly because they too have had to stay six feet apart when all they really want to do is hug. We talk and it helps, like talking always does with us, reminding each other that everyone's going through the same emotions, be they next door or on the other side of the world.

Fact is, all of us will have up days and down days as this weird, weird scenario plays itself out. We'll all get on each other's nerves or wish we had someone else's nerves to get on. We'll have days when we comfort eat, have a class of wine too many, when we won't be able to sleep properly, when we'll wake up tired and won't feel like doing a damn thing.

But as long as we have each other, either at the end of our fingertips, across the width of a pavement or merely on the end of a broadband signal, we'll get through it — and with any luck, enough of us might come out the other side of it as better people that it'll make a genuine different to the world we re-emerge into.

TONIGHT, I host my first online indoor cycling session. We hook up over the Zoom video app, me and 16 others missing their face-to-face fitness fix, the music plays and the sweat begins to pour.

There's a teeny-weeny crimp from my end, in that I don't have a bike at home. I ordered one when shutdown came, but delivery times have been pushed back and it might be another month before it gets here. Be just my luck if it arrives the day we're allowed back into the gym.

So, from the kitchen — a photo of the mighty Col de Tourmalet dropped in as a virtual backdrop rather than everyone seeing the extractor fan above the cooker - I talk the troops through their session while trying not to look like a jockey walking the Grand National as the gee-gees thunder around him. Here and there, I throw in a wee dad-dance. For one electronic track - *Daft Punk Is Playing At My House* by LCD Soundsystem - I duck off camera and come back wearing a white ceramic mask Sonia has for doing whatever it is she does to keep her skin looking like it's 21. They won't sleep tonight.

Saturday March 28
·Global cases pass 600,000, one in six in the USA.
·Spain records its highest daily death rate of 832.
·Domestic violence charities say cases up globally because of lockdown.

UP sharp for a big breakfast, on with plenty layers to keep out

47

the chill and away we go to see where the bike takes me and the newly-surgeried knee.

It's a perfect morning, both in its crisp, early spring sunshine and for how little traffic there is out there for my second turn of the legs since the op 29 days ago. From the off, every turn of the pedal feels magnificent.

I love my bikes. Couldn't even go one until I'd turned 50, but since buying something basic to learn on I'm already on my third upgrade; a black and day-glo green Cervelo C5 carbon work of art, super-light with electronic gears, 17-speaker stereo and built-in espresso-maker.

As Sonia's reading this, I can confirm it cost upwards of £350.

On it, I grew more confident going up hills — though still not so much coming down the other side — and, pushed on by a fantastic personal trainer called Neil Campbell - come September last year I was just about proficient enough to join a magnificent crew who raised close on £100,000 for Macmillan Cancer Support by riding up and over the French Pyrenees from west to east. A week and a bit of unbelievable freedom, of genuine achievement, that sapped every ounce of physical and mental energy but left me believing I could tackle anything.

This morning, that feeling came flooding back.

As I passed the Gothic beauty of Glasgow University, through Kelvin Way's canopy of trees, along Sauchiehall Street's new bike lane, down to George Square and its City Chambers, out beyond the Tennent's Brewery and into Dennistoun — half hard-bitten East End, half up-and-coming hipsterville — before swinging right at the red, white and blue of the Rangers oasis they call The Louden Tavern into Celtic territory where Parkhead rises like a chrome fortress, past the velodrome that bears Sir Chris Hoy's name with pride, past the dilapidated pile of Shawfield greyhound stadium, through the ever-regenerating Gorbals, into the South Side to tip the hat to Hampden Park, back down Pollokshields Road towards the city then up, York Street, Wellington Street and St Vincent

Street, along Argyle Street, onto Byres Road, Highburgh Road and home, it felt like the whole world was mine.

n no time — well, an hour and 49 — just under 18 miles had flown by. Cobwebs cleared, head energised, 1200 calories burned and, best of all, the knee none the worse. So, like any elite athlete, I celebrated with two square sausage sandwiches.

MEANWHILE, as Glasgow and every other British town and city got used to the feeling of doors clanging shut, Wuhan was waking up to its own finally re-opening. In the Chinese city where coronavirus first reared its head, lockdown was slowly being lifted, with people allowed in but not out.

As the day went on, pictures emerged of crowds coming off trains at its 17 stations, many returning to loved ones they hadn't seen in close on two months. In that time, Wuhan had dealt with more than 50,000 victims and China as a whole at least 3,000 deaths. But now, as numbers began to fall — they only reported 54 new cases yesterday — the authorities saw a chance to lift the spirits of hard-pressed locals, even if hugging is still banned.

At the same time, however, Beijing has announced a temporary nationwide ban on all foreign visitors, even those with visas or residence permits, to minimise the threat of fresh infections. All domestic and foreign airlines are limited to one flight per week, no more than 75 per cent full.

Anyone entering Wuhan for now has to show a green symbol on a traffic light-style health app to prove they're clear of symptoms. It will be April 8 at least before anyone is allowed to leave the city. It isn't quite the end of the nightmare for 11 million souls at the pandemic's epicentre.

But for now, the beginning of the end will have to do.

AND finally for today, over to BBC medical dramas Casualty and Holby City, where producers have proven truth really can be stranger than fiction — by donating protective equipment from its props store to the NHS.

How bizarre is that? The film sets for two fictional hospitals are better kitted out than most real ones. Though never mind bizarre — how *embarrassing* is it for Downing Street that it has allowed the health service to become so poorly stocked that it needs handouts from a couple of TV shows?

Health Secretary Matt Hancock has admitted there are "challenges" with the supply of PPE - personal protective equipment — to frontline NHS staff, but that on Tuesday the Government had 'shipped 7.5 million pieces, mainly masks, over 24 hours in literally a military effort'.

You got the feeling that with his boss suffering from the bug, Hancock would be discussing a whole raft of other 'challenges' — generally accepted as political code for 'fuck-ups' — over the days and weeks ahead. Only yesterday, we'd been looking on at the problems in Spain and the lack of joined-up leadership being blamed for them, yet today we're being confronted with a worrying picture of our own bed shortages, staff shortages, of confusion over if and when mass testing will be available.

As in Spain, we're now hearing a rising tide of accusations that our reaction as a nation was politically weak and individually stupid; our leaders saw the Spanish dither yet didn't learn from it, while ordinary people in the street saw the death toll in cities like Madrid and Valencia yet somehow decided to remain...well, as people in the street.

For every eight of us who've stuck to the guidelines of staying indoors unless to shop, exercise or go to a job that can't be done from home, another two are hugging on the pavement of sunbathing in the nearest park the second the clouds part. This has left many among the sensible eight yelling for police to get heavy with the idiot two, for fines to be imposed the way France has started to when citizens defy *their* lockdown laws.

Though the real test will come if this all drags out into summer. Or, as we Scots know it, the 17th of June.

Sunday March 29
·Global death toll passes 30,000, UK tally up by 209 to 1,228.
·Syria reports first death, New York medical supplies may only last a week.
·German state finance minister, Thomas Schäfer, commits suicide after becoming "deeply worried" by economic implications.

THERE'S something odd in the air this morning — you know, apart from the dreaded bug as it searches out more stray throats to invade. Something you can't quite put a finger on, but which everyone seems to be sensing.

I get this vibe from Sonia, from messaging the kids, from news bulletins and social media posts. Even birds in the trees seem to be holding their breath in anticipation of... what? That's the mystery. We've had no dire announcements from Downing Street, no overnight surge in fatalities. If anything, medical experts hint at an ever-so-slight slowdown in cases across Britain as social distancing begins to take effect.

So how come everyone's so obviously on edge?

Best guess, approaching the end of our first week in lockdown, the full impact of what we're involved in is biting. Individually and collectively, we're realising how helpless we are in the face of an invisible enemy, how little control we have over anything bar our own tightly limited movements; a sense of feeling trapped that claimed the life of a man who wasn't in the tiniest bit to blame for the situation affecting us, but whose head simply couldn't stop telling him he was.

THIS morning, the body of Thomas Schäfer, finance minister of the German state of Hesse, was found on a high-speed train line in the town of Hochheim between Frankfurt and Mainz.

Schäfer, a member of Chancellor Angela Merkel's Christian Democrat Party, had appeared regularly on TV in recent days to inform the public about financial assistance for those affected by the impact of the virus, but had admitted to those around him that he had 'considerable worries' about the effects on the nation once the pandemic was over.

Hesse's state premier, Volker Bouffier - who the 54-year-old Schäfer had been tipped to succeed — told the media: "His main concern was whether he could manage to fulfil the huge expectations of the population, especially in terms of financial aid. He clearly couldn't see any way out. He was desperate, and so he left us. That has shocked us, it has shocked me."

And if this situation can have such a terminal effect on the mind of such a highly intelligent, highly experienced, seasoned politician…well, maybe it's little wonder countless millions without a clue about the implications of what we're getting into are fretting, that we appear to be steeling ourselves for something nasty. What this is something us, I have no clue — after all, not even our sharpest scientific minds have managed to keep up with the virus. All I know is that whatever 'the worst' might turn out to be, this is the day when we all seem to be preparing for it.

It's a moment that calls for a spirit-lifting mind game and, as the kettle boils and the toast browns, an idea light-bulbs. Today, with it all portents of approaching doom, seems to call for a bit of nurturing, a bit of optimism, a bit of fun. So, tomorrow's column written, I log onto Zoom for my next virtual indoor cycling class. Today's theme? *Finding Our Happy Place.*

I've messaged the troops asking them to think of the one spot on earth they'd be if they could snap their fingers and escape self-isolation. The music's designed to let them disappear there, to carry them up imaginary hills and hurtle down the other side to race on flat, flawless roads.

My own bike still hasn't arrived, so I'm dad-dancing again, that and ad-libbing a commentary that — hopefully — goes with the playlist, reminds them that better times are coming, when we'll all be back out there again for real. Forty-five minutes flies by, from an eight-minute remix of Howard Jones' take on the ascent of man in *Hide And Seek* as our warm-up, through to a stringed version of the beautiful *Words* by The Christians as we warm down again.

Throughout the class, I can see all the troops in their little on-screen boxes — think *Celebrity Squares* with a few gallons more sweat — but have asked them to mute the sound at their end. Now, after the two-minute meditation I always like to end classes with, we unmute and share where we've been. My own Happy Place is there for all to see; I've used a virtual backdrop of Cascais, the gorgeous little resort half an hour's train ride along the coast from Lisbon, the one city where I could decamp to and settle down into old age. My fear was that few, if any, in the virtual room would give a virtual monkey's about some woolly suggestion about imaginary cycle routes.

I should have known better, because one by one, they smile into the lens and tell each other not just where they've been, but why — in Normandy because that's where their mum came from, the Kyle of Lochalsh because that was where they'd grown up, Calabria on the toe of Italy's boot, the sun-baked Majorcan mountains, the Philippines, a remote Highland beach.

It's lovely, utterly lovely. In the 16 months of so since qualifying to teach, I've never been part of such an uplifting class, one so committed not just to the workload but to an idea thrown at them ten minutes before they got on the bike; that bike not even in a hot, packed studio, but in their kitchen or their garage, their spare bedroom or their back garden. A day that began with such a feeling of foreboding was somehow blooming into something special. And, as the troops tour their Happy Places, that vague theory of creating something better that I'd written about in the paper the other day began to feel just a little more realistic.

I mean, what if those of us lucky to come out the other side of this safe and sound really *did* do so with fresh optimism, with a new sense of right and wrong? What if we did re-set our hard-drives back to the factory setting of our childhoods, when everything wasn't about possessions and money and being first all the time?

What if we used the time stuck indoors to think about our relationships not just with each other, but with ourselves, started appreciating what we had rather than constantly chasing stuff we barely wanted, never mind needed? If we learned the meaning of satisfaction, of contentment, of *enough*? Feel free to pause for a barf into the nearest poly bag at this point if it's all reaching Corden-level nauseating, but what if we *did* find our Happy Place? And better still, if we realised it had been under our nose all along?

It's a thought that gets me through the rest of Sunday.

Monday March 30
•Moscow and the Nigerian capital Lagos go into lockdown
•EasyJet grounds fleet for two months, British Airways asks Downing Street for urgent financial aid.
•The Mercedes F1 racing team is developing a breathing aid they hope to distribute 1,000 of a day.

CORONAVIRUS is today in self-isolation after contracting Boris Johnson's chief adviser Dominic Cummings. A spokesperson for the disease confirmed the symptoms began with a mild dislike of Europe, before developing into more serious and sustained desire to make disabled people work as scaffolders for their benefits.

The gag came to me as soon as the news flash came up on the phone. But then, it also came to roughly another half a million of us within the next 30 seconds. Some stories really are that much of an open goal.

Cummings, for those not clued up on their political organisms, was formed in a Whitehall test tube in the David Cameron era, grew arms and legs during his masterminding of the Leave campaign and, since Johnson's ascent to the Tory leadership, his influence had spread like...well, like a virus.

Within days of BoJo becoming Prime Minister thanks to

Theresa May coughing so hard she fell on her sword, the word on the street called Downing was that Cummings was already pulling the strings. By the time the Tories won a landslide in the pre-Christmas General Election called as a vote of confidence in their Brexit plans? If you believed the Westminster press pack, there might as well not have *been* a Cabinet any more, not once Johnson had scatter-gunned five ministers — including Chancellor of the Exchequer Sajid Javid, who'd refused to sack his advisers and work with a team picked by Cummings - in what became known as his St Valentine's Day Massacre.

Having said which, not everyone was convinced Cummings ran No10 single-handed; political columnist Yasmin Alibhai-Brown, for instance, preferred to argue that Johnson was controlled by an uneasy alliance of his chief spin doctor and his pregnant fiancée. On the eve of the reshuffle, she'd written in the online *i* newspaper:

> *"Believe it or not, the two biggest political players in Britain today are unelected insiders: Dominic Cummings and Carrie Symonds. The Prime Minister, it seems, cannot deny their whims and wishes...Symonds and Cummings were once co-conspirators and now, apparently, have fallen out, big time..."*

Symonds, the article claimed, messes with Johnson's mind and can be 'volatile', while Cummings has been various described as 'a career psychopath and 'a football hooligan with an Oxford First'. Between them, they're said to terrorise everyone they come in contact with. Half of those close to the PM are furious that Cummings 'acts like a tinpot dictator', while the other half snort about 'who the hell Symonds thinks she is'.

It's a situation that left Alibhai-Brown musing:

> *"All these years of disorder when millions in this country — aka 'the people' — rose against the 'colonising' and 'un-*

accountable' and 'corrupt' European Union; bonds of family, friendship, locality and nation cleaved by the referendum and the last election. What was it all for? Oh, of course, those mantras: to 'take back control' and 'make Britain great again'. That last wish was weaponised, used, and is now cynically disregarded...we should not care who is the victor. Our attention should be on the PM's careless disregard for rules of governance, propriety, trustworthiness and judgements. Would Symonds get to choose secretaries of state if she wasn't sleeping with Mr Johnson? Did the PM bring Cummings into the heart of government because he is scared of...the anarchic and catastrophising adviser? Is this the democracy you voted for and cherish?"

I QUOTE this to reiterate the point that however important anyone might think they are, no matter how influential they may be in the highest circles, coronavirus does not give one teeny-tiny toss. Last month, Cummings and Symonds were arm-wrestling to see who held more sway over the PM, but this morning, one's sick and the other in isolation to protect her unborn child because her lover is sick. Neither can spin or schmooze or bully their way out of this situation.

They have met their match in the shape of a bacteria. A bit like those five Cabinet ministers elbowed in the reshuffle.

Today, Cummings' wife, journalist Mary Wakefield, revealed he'd felt ill over the weekend and would be self-isolating. He joins Johnson himself, Health Secretary Matt Hancock, Scottish Secretary of State Alister Jack and England's chief medical officer Professor Chris Whitty in showing symptoms — the only surprise being that the numbers aren't higher, given how long the Cabinet have spent locked together these past few weeks. Some might see it as an irony that their attempts to thrash out a means of containing the disease have only served to expose them even more to its risks. Others might be a little less sanguine about the situation and ask why the hell they weren't meeting by video call long ago.

Me? I'm still trying to put myself in their shoes, still trying to compute how any of us would handle a situation that's flying by them on a conveyor belt that some joker's speeding up minute by minute.

I've got a conversation in my head right now, where Johnson calls in some top civil service bod and orders video conferencing screens to be set up in every minister's office, only to be told it'll take a day or two to get the system up and running, a lag-time that either leaves him reluctantly stuck with physical gatherings of his lieutenants or forcing them to shout through keyholes at each other while the IT bods get to work. Having said which, who knows when the first Cabinet victims contracted the virus? It could have been incubating for a week or more, from back when things weren't any like this critical.

Plus, the fact that so many of them have caught the bug kind or scuttles any thought that they know something we don't, because if so they'd have been broadcasting to the plebs from lead-lined bunkers 20 feet underground and stacked to the ceiling with a year's supply of truffles and Chablis, wouldn't they? While instead, Johnson has coronavirus. His chief spin doctor has coronavirus. Two cabinets ministers that we know of and the medical expert they rely on most have coronavirus. Sorry to disappoint the tin-foil hat-wearing community, but the boring truth is that they're all as clueless as the rest of us.

Tuesday, March 31
·Global cases hit 850,000
·France reports 500 deaths in the past 24 hours
·Boris Johnson hosts UK's first online Cabinet meeting from isolation.

WE thought this virus wouldn't trouble the young and the fit. But today, we heard the terrible news that a 13-year-old boy with no underlying health issues has become the pandemic's youngest British victim.

Ismail Mohamed Abdulwahab, from Brixton in south London, passed away in the city's King's College Hospital early yesterday. Worse still, he spent his final, painful hours without his loved ones by his side because of the danger of infection.

"He was put on a ventilator and then into an induced coma but sadly died yesterday morning," a family statement read. "We are beyond devastated."

Before Ismael, the youngest victim in Britain had been Luca Di Nicola, a 19-year-old Italian working in London as an assistant chief, who died on March 24, again with no underlying health conditions. As nationwide losses went past 2,500, BBC health correspondent Nick Triggle confirmed it was 'rare' for teenagers to become seriously ill from coronavirus.

"Just 0.3 per cent of those who show symptoms require hospital care and 0.006 per cent die," he said. "In other words, two out of every 30,000 infections among this age group will not survive. But it does happen, as these distressing cases show."

5: THE ASTONISHINGLY EXCELLENT MR TRUMP

Wednesday April 1
·Italy extends lockdown for at least 12 more days as Spain passes 9,000 deaths
·UK aims for 25,000 tests a day within two weeks
·Fundraising page for 13-year-old Ismael Mohamed Abdulwahab's funeral hits £51,000 inside a day.

TODAY feels like the perfect day to discuss Donald J. Trump. After all, every day since the good people of the US of A elected him as their 45th President has felt like April Fool's.

Remember his medical report during his campaign in 2015? The one he'd predicted in a Tweet weeks earlier would show 'perfection'? Well, the document with Dr Harold Bornstein's signature on it didn't quite go that far, but it did claim Trump's condition was 'astonishingly excellent' and he'd be 'by far the healthiest individual ever elected to the White House'.

No one laughed. Well, no one except anyone who'd ever seen him. And we're still laughing today, just like we laughed when he vowed to keep Mexicans out of the USA with a 2,000-mile-long wall that he was going to get those same Mexicans to pay for and build. We laugh when he stumbles through autocued speeches, tries to sound super-duper-intelligent while mangling every second word — witness his demands for a NATO probe into 'the oranges' of allegations that Russia meddled in the 2016 election.

"I hope they now go and take a look at the oranges," he said, "the oranges of the investigations, the beginnings. The Mueller Report, I wish it had covered those oranges."

How we laughed, just as we laughed when he wrote a Tweet about his wife Melania, but called her Melanie. How we howled when he described Puerto Rico as 'an island sitting in the middle of an ocean—a big ocean, a really, really big ocean'.

Oh yes, how we laughed and howled and chortled and sniggered. Even now, I'm watching a re-run of a Family Guy cartoon in which Peter Griffin goes to work for Trump, one of his first jobs being to walk ahead of the President into rooms and check for static electricity so his combover doesn't stand on end.

Every sketch show, every stand-up, every satirical magazine, every social media wit; how we grabbed every chance to rip the pure pish out of the Trumpkin, this fake-tanned, combed-over, tiny-handed, near-inarticulate sack of yoghurt on legs.

Yet all the time, the joke was on us, because he happily used the mirth as cover while the fantasy of him becoming president edged towards reality. He's a salesman, he's a wheeler-dealer, he's a serial putter-downer of his own failing businesses. He's a reality TV show host.

Most of all, he's a hypnotist.

Now, whether he's had actual training in this skill I'm not in a position to say. But he's brilliant at it, no question. With his endless stream of unverifiable statements—'We have the best science, the greatest science, the world envies our science'—and his ear-worm mantra of Fake News, chanted at anything which challenges his world view, he's kept us all, most sycophantic party ally and most vicious opponent alike, in a state of trance throughout his business and now his political careers.

"Every time I do this weird thing with my teeny-tiny thumbs in index fingers, you will laugh and it will distract you from all the bad shit I'm doing off-camera..."

IT'S a pity we didn't take a break from bamming Trump up long enough to listen to the warnings about him issued back in the day by a very clever man called Peter Wehner.

He's an author, was a speechwriter to Ronald Reagan and both George Bushes and is a lifelong Republican and, a full nine months before Trump went to the polls against Hillary Clinton, issued a dire warning to the American public should they choose to elect him.

Now, he's taken to *The Atlantic* website to refer back to that warning in relation to the five years gone by, writing:

> *"When, in January 2016, I wrote that despite being a lifelong Republican who worked in the previous three GOP administrations, I would never vote for Donald Trump, even though his administration would align much more with my policy views than a Hillary Clinton presidency would, a lot of my Republican friends were befuddled. How could I not vote for a person who checked far more of my policy boxes than his opponent?*

"What I explained then, and what I have said many times since, is that Trump is fundamentally unfit — intellectually, morally, temperamentally, and psychologically — for office. That is the paramount consideration in electing a president, in part because at some point it's reasonable to expect that a president will face an unexpected crisis — and at that point, the president's judgment and discernment, his character and leadership ability, will really matter.

"Mr Trump has no desire to acquaint himself with most issues, let alone master them...no major presidential candidate has ever been quite as disdainful of knowledge, as indifferent to facts, as untroubled by his benightedness. Mr Trump's virulent combination of ignorance, emotional instability, demagogy, solipsism and vindictiveness would do more than result in a failed presidency; it could very well lead to national catastrophe. The prospect of Donald Trump as commander-in-chief should send a chill down the spine of every American."

Disdainful of knowledge, indifferent to facts, untroubled by his own benightedness, a blend of personal choices that, according to Wehner —— and remember, this is a man who batted for the party whose rosette Trump wore — could lead to catastrophe if and when the person making those choices was faced with an unexpected crisis.

Well, here we are, right in the middle of that crisis. And there's really couldn't be a more beautiful summing up of the Trump has handled it. Over here, we have leaders who are making mistakes, but making them while attempting to do their very best only to discover that they're not quite well-enough equipped for the job.

Over there, they have a man who is deliberately making every contrary decision, statement, policy, you name it, to rile those who oppose him. No attempt to lead, to unite, to bring his doubters onside. No thought of becoming a hero, because he already firmly believes he is one, that he is the smartest and the bravest and the most in control and the most successful person in all of Covidom.

A man who, like every President since Oppenheimer invented his deadly toy, has his finger on a button that could vaporise us all; but who, unlike any before him, is more likely to spark Armageddon in 280 characters or less.

A man who, with his re-election campaign gaining some sort of weird, structureless momentum, already seems like he could be even more of a permanent annoyance if he loses than if he wins, seeing as he's likely to either allow himself to be turned into a martyr figure or will found and front Trump TV, beaming Fake News 24/7 while subliminally flashing the words Fake News over any story that the rest of us know isn't Fake News.

And, getting back to the subject at hand, a man whose most jaw-dropping soundbite to date on coronavirus may have escaped his lips eight days ago, but was tailor-made for April 1 - and which proved, as if proof were needed, that he was made to handle a crisis of this magnitude the way Boris Johnson was made for monogamy.

◆ ◆ ◆

ON March 24, as the World Health Organisation declared

America the looming epicentre of the Covid-19 pandemic, Trump defied all medical, scientific and generally sane opinion by declaring that he wanted 'the country open by Easter'.

Cases across the US were soaring, yet the President chose to look his citizens in the eyes and declare that everything would be 'back to normal within a couple of weeks'.

"I think it's possible, why not?" he said: "Look, Easter's a very special day for me. And I see it sort of in that timeline that I'm thinking about. Wouldn't it be great to have all those churches full? I think Easter Sunday and you'll have packed churches all over our country. I think it would be a beautiful time. And it's just about the timeline I think is right."

On March 24, global cases stood at 407,485 with 18,227 deaths. Now, on April 1, the USA itself has more than 200,000 cases and 4,300 deaths. Easter Sunday is just 11 days away.

Yet even those sums can't convince the man at the top that his prognosis might just be a teensy-weensy tad underplayed; or 'dangerous and immoral', as Florida Congresswoman Donna Shalala described it. Shalala - try saying the name without singing it — spat: "He defies ethical standards. No American believes we should choose the economy over human life. The president is putting lives at risk because he wants the economy to get back."

Los Angeles mayor Eric Garcetti said he would defy Trump by refusing to revoke restrictions until he was persuaded it was safe to do so, saying: "We can't wish coronavirus away. Some are putting out hope of us being back in churches by Easter, of restarting the economy in a couple of weeks. I think we owe it to everybody to be straightforward — and in Los Angeles, that means we won't be back to normality in that short a time. I've said to be prepared for a couple of months like this."

Joe Biden, vice-president to Barack Obama and the leading contender to oppose Trump for the presidency come November, added: "If you want to ruin the economy for a long time, go ahead and continue his way by having the virus burst out again. We haven't even flattened the curve."

Trump had spoken in a televised meeting of his frustrations at 'having to close the country to curb the spread', before claiming: "I gave it two weeks. We can socially distance ourselves and go to work."

Both he and vice-president Mike Pence said that, unlike in other countries, a widespread US lockdown had never been considered. Trump compared Covid-19 to seasonal flu, saying that despite thousands dying of it each year 'we don't turn the country off'. He then argued that more people die in car accidents, but nobody forces car companies to stop making wheels. He said: "It's a risk we accept so we can move about."

Now, at this point, I have to admit that in the early days of the virus, I was one of those who made the same point about seasonal flu, that thousands died of it every winter and Governments didn't panic. I'm an idiot, though. I know nothing. I write opinions for a living, some of which turn out to resonate or make a positive difference, while others are proved total cobblers; the one about coronavirus being no different to flu plopping firmly into the latter category.

But you know what? I'd like to think if I was the Leader Of The Free World® rather than some schmuck sitting typing at his kitchen table with an episode of *The Sweeney* on in the background and if I had every available medical, scientific and political expert at my beck and call, I'd have thought twice about coming out with something as crass and ill-judged.

Trouble is, Trump never thinks twice and sometimes not even once. Trouble is, whatever the experts tell is just so much noise drowned out by him telling himself how stupendous he is. Trouble is, as this nine-week berk-a-thon reminds us, he's been the one ripping the pish out of the world all this time.

The Donald's Timeline of Amazingness

January 22: "We have it totally under control. It's one person coming in from China. It's going to be just fine."

February 2: "We pretty much shut it down coming in from China."

February 24: "It is very much under control... Stock Market looking very good to me!"

February 25: "It's a problem that's going to go away... they have studied it. They know very much. In fact, we're very close to a vaccine."

February 26: "Within a couple of days, our 15 cases will be close to zero."

March 4: "We'll have thousands or hundreds of thousands that get better by, you know, sitting around and even going to work — some go to work, but they get better."

March 5: "I've NEVER said people who are feeling sick should go to work."

March 6: "Anybody right now, and yesterday, that needs a test gets a test, they're there. And the tests are beautiful...I really get it, people are surprised I understand it. I've spoken to so many doctors and every one is amazed I know so much. Maybe I have a natural ability. Maybe I should have done that instead of running for President. We have a perfectly coordinated and fine-tuned plan."

March 9: "The Fake News Media and its partner, the Democrat Party, is doing everything within its semi-considerable power [it used to be greater!] to inflame the Coronavirus situation, far beyond what facts would warrant."

March 10: "It will go away. Just stay calm. It will go away."

March 13: Declares a National Emergency.

March 17: "We're asking everyone to work at home, if possible, postpone unnecessary travel, and limit social gatherings to no more than 10 people."

March 24: "I'd love to have it the country open by Easter..."

March 25: "It's time. People want to get back to work. They're not going to be walking round hugging and kissing each other when they get there, even though they may feel like it."

March 26: As figures show USA now has 82,404 confirmed cases, more than any other country, Trump suggests social distancing rules could be relaxed 'within two weeks'.

March 27: "The first thing Boris Johnson said to me today was that Britain needs ventilators — and if the US makes more than it needs, we will share them with him."

Asked if every American who needed a ventilator would get one, he called the male journalist who posed the question 'a cutie pie'.

March 28: New York governor Mario Cuomo describes Trump's suggestion of placing parts of NY, New Jersey and Connecticut on quarantine as 'preposterous' and 'a recipe for mayhem'.

March 29: Trump extends social distancing measures until April 30, saying: "Nothing could be worse than declaring victory before victory is won. That would be the greatest loss of all."

March 30: "Our testing is better than any other testing in the world."

March 31: Trump warns America to brace itself for a 'very, very painful two weeks'.

ALL of which blustering and blundering brings us to tonight and a White House press conference at which Trump was asked by a journalist for his views on reports that the pressures of self-isolation had led to a spike in cases of domestic violence.

He looked for moment like a dog who's just been shown a card trick before replying: "Mexican violence?"

6: BALL OF CONFUSION

Thursday, April 2
•Global cases set to reach one million.
•UK Health Secretary Matt Hancock promises 100,000 tests a day by end of April.
•Britain turns out in force again to applaud key workers.

EVEN by 3.25am, this felt like a properly mixed-up kind of a day. For a start, I couldn't sleep, which almost never happens; normally I could doze on a razor blade, so I'm left wondering how badly all those who don't enjoy regular, restful zeds are toiling.

If and when I get that qualification in Neuro Linguistic Programming (keep up, it was in Chapter 2), the first plan is to set up group sessions and one-to-ones with the sleep-deprived and try to change the pictures in their heads that keep them awake just when the body needs to re-set.

So as I lay there in the pitch black, scrolling my ancient iPod for a book to listen to, the only sound Sonia's breathing — was it just my imagination, or was her chest rattly? — it bugged me why it should happen now.

Maybe I'd over-stimulated myself by working on Friday night's spin class playlist before turning in. Maybe it was down to one black coffee too many late in the day. Or who knows, maybe my system was just coming out in sympathy with a world more confused with every dragged-out, locked-down day. Check the BBC News and the top three items are questions:

•How many confirmed cases are there in your area?
•How deadly is the Coronavirus?
•How close are we to a Coronavirus vaccine?

The fourth is a prediction from the PM that 'testing will unlock Coronavirus puzzle'. As for the fifth, it suggests the world is close to its one millionth case. Wonder if there'll be a special prize for the victim, like they do with a supermarket's one millionth customer? Maybe they'll get a VIP day out* at a Testing Centre (*test refused without proof of family heritage).

Plus, people were still struggling to grasp that a social media post doing the rounds yesterday claiming the Scottish Government had banned the sale of alcohol. It was, thankfully, an April Fool's prank. But to a nation with its walls closing in, the very suggestion felt like an invitation to civil war.

When this over, whatever anti-social ratbag who came up with it should first against the wall, bop-bop-bop...

EVENTUALLY, to the sound of Sherlock unpicking another mystery in *The Valley Of Fear* - for me, Conan Doyle's finest hour - I fall back asleep, to be woken by the alarm at 7.50 then black out again until quarter to nine.

As I make breakfast before Sonia goes to walk her mum's dog, BBC Breakfast is on the box in the background and it's clear that the confusion of those wee small hours hadn't just been in my addled, snooze-deprived head.

They're talking about the effect on charities of their shops being closed for the duration as well of the huge collective amount of funds lost through the postponement of marathons in London. Edinburgh, Manchester and Brighton as well as countless other smaller events for countless causes; the question at hand is how and when the Government will step in and help make up at least some of the shortfall, yet I can't help thinking that this in itself presents a conundrum within a conundrum.

After all, charities only exist in the first place to plug the holes left in services by a lack of State funding, so it's a melon-twister to think that they themselves might only be able to stay afloat *through* State funding.

Then there's the NHS, creaking at the seams before the virus even approaches its peak effect. That nationwide ovation for key workers a week ago — to be repeated at eight tonight — has led to growing pledges of cash from individuals and companies alike. There are calls for the next telethon to be not for children in need or starving villagers in Africa, but for our under-funded, under-paid, overworked doctors and nurses.

But, for all that they come from a place of genuine kindness, these pledges of support are also the products of confused thinking — because the NHS isn't a charity. We already pay for it through our taxes. It isn't Macmillan Cancer Support or Help The Aged, it doesn't rely on donations to keep it ticking over. It may have been the most magnificent development of this country's twentieth century, but it isn't what we've come to know as 'a good cause' and we can't allow it to become one.

As happened in China a month and more back, this country is currently setting up temporary hospitals packed with thousands of beds to cope with demand. Thousands of retired NHS clinical staff are coming back to work. Exhibition centres in London and Glasgow as well as football stadiums all over the nation are being readied for an ever-greater flood of the sick.

This surely tells us we really need is to revisit the entire system when this is over, to learn from the mistakes — and mistakes is being kind, because it would be nearer the mark to say the greed — which have left our health service so short of wards, of beds, of staff, even of something as basic and as crucial in dealing with infection as disposable face masks. It just feels so wrong, it feels like such a dereliction of duty on the part of those we elect to run our public services and who we trust with our taxes that they've turned surviving a global pandemic into such a lottery.

IN the movie *Sophie's Choice*, Meryl Streep has to decide which of her children to send to a Nazi labour camp and which to condemn to the gas chamber. In *Armageddon*, Bruce Willis sacrifices himself to let his daughter's husband escape a nuclear blast that destroys an asteroid but saves Earth from oblivion. Luke Skywalker went through *Star Wars* tormented by his tug-of-war with his estranged dad and the lure of the Dark Side.

But fiction is concocted to play with our emotions, to stretch our heartstrings like piano wire. For two hours in a cinema, we willingly suspend disbelief. Our eyes well to the minor-chord shift in the soundtrack. We cry, cheer, drop our popcorn on the carpet, then go back into the real world.

Coronavirus, though, is very, very real. And the deeper we find ourselves immersed in its breakneck plot, the more our NHS faces up to the kind of dilemmas no scriptwriter can wangle them out.

Who gets tested and who doesn't. Who gets a hospital bed and who stays home. Who's put on a ventilator and who has to wait. Who should be their priority, the soul terrified they might have cancer or the latest batch of victims brought down by the pandemic — maybe even, as this crisis reaches its peak, who lives and who dies. It's an appalling position to put our doctors and nurses in, one I wouldn't do for Lionel Messi's wages.

Yet these are decisions which simply have to be made, without fear or favour, every single day, thanks to the severity of cuts to and the lack of frontline investment in our hospitals, a scandal which has left them held together by goodwill and sticking plaster as the greatest health crisis of our lifetime takes hold. The crushing pressure medics and administrators alike find themselves under could easily have been alleviated had successive Governments not chopped and chopped again at facilities, had they not demotivated workers to the point that there were 500 vacancies for consultants and 4,000 for nurses and midwifes in Scotland alone.

Had those same Governments, be they Tory or Labour, not

quietly hived off so many areas of healthcare to the private sector, had they not cared more about opening a Starbucks in every foyer than cutting waiting lists, we might have been so much better prepared for the crisis we find ourselves in today.

Hospitals would still be under the cosh. Sheer weight of numbers would still be testing them even if we had empty beds and clinical expertise falling out of every cupboard. But the fact that every time some pen-pusher sees an under-used ward offers an opportunity to shut it down to save money on lightbulbs and loo roll has brought us here — to a place where your doctor, my doctor, your granny's doctor, has to choose between screening this patient's bowel or that one's sore throat. To a place where those doctors have to tear up one of their profession's six core values: Everyone Counts.

Listen, we all knew and we all accepted — even if we did so reluctantly — that our hip replacement or cataract removal or nose job would have to be parked until coronavirus had done its worst. We've had to realise that whatever pain we're in, something else's need would always be more urgent.

Tell me this, though. How the hell does a consultant choose between the bowel cancer case and the coronavirus case? How does the clerk sleep at night after phoning one or the other to tell them they've lost the toss? A week ago tonight, it was wonderful to be part of that nationwide, five-minute ovation in appreciation of all our key workers. We applauded, we cheered, we whistled, banged pots and clinked bottles as our humble way of letting doctors and nurses, ambulance crews and paramedics, pharmacists and admin workers know how much their efforts mean to us. Yet today, as the full pandemic gathers itself for its greatest assault, it feels more like they're being slapped than clapped. And that's shameful.

Over these past few, crazy weeks, there's been so much around us to be optimistic about. The help we've offered each other, the upsurge in families exercising together, the armies volunteering to help the vulnerable; these thoughts and more should help us get through the worst and will hopefully stay with us when the world gets back to normality.

But try seeing the upside if you're working in a hospital where every morning brings a heavier workload and where once you finally come off shift you're scared stiff of infecting your own family.

A burden that might be worth it if your bosses had stocked your ward up to the gunnels with everything from beds to ventilators to cotton buds and you felt like you couldn't have treated your patients any better.

But we all know this is far from the case. Shamefully, the picture emerging makes a day in the life of our NHS seem more like an episode of *M*A*S*H*. Except without the laughter.

HOWEVER, as the second Thursday of lockdown unfolded, there was fresh confusion, this time of when, where and how mass testing was going to be introduced so we could get a clearer picture on numbers of confirmed cases and put as many minds at rest as possible.

On the BBC's non-stop morning coronavirus coverage, medical experts have linked up daily from their homes to answer questions from viewers about their concerns during the crisis. Today, almost all these questions are about the issue of test; or rather, the lack of it.

Sheffield-based public health consultant Rebecca Cooper said the issue is that Downing Street started out with a policy of protecting the old and others deemed vulnerable while allowing the bug to move freely among the rest of us, before moving belatedly to a policy of trying to suppress it on a mass scale. Then, she said, we looked at testing, but by this time we were bidding in a global market and dealing with that market's forces; after that, stepping up testing capacity depended on lab capacity. At this point, in came Professor Mark Harris from Leeds University to claim laboratory staff left twiddling their thumbs by the shutdown of universities are ready to help, that a database of names has been sent to the Department of Health, but 'the co-ordination doesn't seem to be there'.

Professor Cooper reckoned it would take as long as a year to perfect a vaccine, but that even then there would be issues persuading some to take it. In his opinion, a more practical — and more readily available — option would be the use of anti-viral drugs to treat symptoms. Trials were underway via a company called Gilead of one called remdesivir and 'signs are good', so this could let us treat while we wait to be able to prevent.

From there, they moved to a question about if and when frontline NHS are finally tested en masse and whether, even if they showed up negative today, they could still get it tomorrow. All Dr Cooper could shrug was that it was an excellent point, because there was nothing to say a negative test meant anything than that we had no symptoms at the time. Finally, Prof. Harris took one asking how we can be sure home delivery food isn't infected. With a barely-supressed sigh, he replied: *"If it's fresh, wash it. If it's packaged, wipe the packaging."*

At which point I was left more mixed up than ever; mainly over whether gluing ourselves to all this coverage helps us understand what we're dealing with or simply helps drive millions of us slowly up the wall.

On one hand, TV is the first point of contact with all the latest stats and advice. It would also be very odd if most of us didn't *want* to know what's going on around the country and the world. But on the other? Sitting there too long, absorbing too much, can't be good for our individual and collective mental state, not when it's this never-ending tsunami of bad news, of gloomy predictions. Of death.

I can usually manage about 20 minutes before it becomes white noise. Yet it's clear from social media that for others the telly coverage has become addictive, especially those in key-worker jobs forced to isolate from their loved ones when they come off shift. Many admit sinking into a debilitating pattern of work, worry, TV, worry, lack of sleep, worry and repeat.

They're eating the wrong things, maybe having a drink too many at night, getting down about their weight; in short, the opposite of what's good for their health.

Though then again, what IS healthy in the midst of all this?

COME teatime, the daily Westminster bulletin is given by Matt Hancock, the Health Secretary who has himself now recovered from the virus. It's the beginning of a long, long 18 hours for a man caught in the crosshairs of the testing issue. From behind a placard bearing the slogans *Stay Home, Protect The NHS, Save Lives* - surrounded by what's meant to represent red-and-yellow social-distancing tape, but which makes the podium look more like a TGI Friday's welcome desk - Hancock claims the UK hit its 10,000-tests-a-day target by the end of March.

I say 'claimed' because with the speed at which everything is changing it seems impossible to confirm anyone's figures.

For instance, a check at the Scottish Government website today claims 19,535 tests have been carried out here so far - 16,534 negative, 3,001 positive and with 172 deaths. Yet in *her* latest statement, First Minister Nicola Sturgeon admitted 'family liaison issues' had led to a further 40 fatalities being excluded from the total.

Hancock, meanwhile, was being quizzed over how many days his 10,000-tests-a-day figure stat applied to. He was asked whether these tests merely told if subjects had the virus at the time or also whether they'd had it previously. He tensed at mention of how he himself got tested after displaying symptoms when the majority of frontline NHS workers were still waiting. And then, of course, there was the PM's own promise the other day of 25,000 tests a day by the end of April.

Hancock's response to this was a belter.

Forget 25,000 tests a day, he said. By the end of April, we're aiming for 100,000.

Up and down the land, those charged with making this happen must have face-palmed so hard they'll still have five red finger-marks a month after all-clear. From maybe 10,000 tests a day to definitely 100,000? In under four weeks? When we still don't have the kits, testing centres or lab space? On a day when Scotland's chief medical officer, Dr Cathy Calderwood, admitted we could test everyone and everything, but that without self-isolation and social distancing we'd do nothing to stop the virus spreading even more rapidly?

No pressure, people.

Hancock would later go on BBC Question Time to defend his position. First thing next morning, he was booked to go on Radio 4's Today programme. In between times, the London edition of *The Sun* was preparing a front page showing a drive-through testing centre at the Chessington World of Adventures theme park in Surrey lying empty while NHS trusts were sending swabs to Germany because results come back quicker from there.

Today, Germany would also carry out 70,000 Coronavirus checks compared to 10,657 in the UK. Today, the UK death toll rose to 569, with 4,324 new infections on Thursday - a jump of more than 40 per cent from Wednesday's figure of 3,009.

Come 8pm, we stood at our front windows and on our doorsteps and we applauded the nation's key workers once more. Bottles clinked, pans were banged, the whistles and the cheers hung in the cool evening air.

As we settled back down to watch the news, the headlines told us that the world's one millionth case indeed had been recorded.

7: IT'S FOR THEIR OWN GOOD

Friday April 3
•Staying at home this weekend 'not a request' says UK Health Secretary.
•Global death toll passes 58,000.
•Donald Trump refuses to wear a protective mask outdoors, saying official medical guidance 'isn't for Presidents, Prime Ministers, dictators, kings and queens'.

JUST when we thought the tale of Britain's youngest virus victim Ismael Mohamed Abdulwahab couldn't get any more tragic, life twists its knife deep even deeper into a grieving family's wounds.

A family who had been denied access to the 13-year-old's hospital bedside as the virus sucked the life out of him in case they contracted it too. Yet who now, three days on from his passing, find themselves dealing with the quite unimaginable unfairness of being banned from his funeral because some of them had since developed symptoms anyway.

Can you imagine the heartache? The helplessness? The anger, the frustration, the depth of the despair?

Can we even try to put ourselves in their position as they sat at home, broken in pieces not only by the loss of a son and a brother, but by the stomach-churning frustration of not even being able to say one final goodbye? *Fuck you, coronavirus, fuck you to hell and back.*

I've gone back and scrubbed that last sentence out about a dozen times now only to keep on putting it back because it's as honest a reaction to this lousy news as I can muster. In the midst of what's happening to Ismael's family, it feels all too glib to go on about some greater purpose making these decisions for us, too pointless to nod sagely about how there's a reason for everything, too unbearably twee to sigh that whatever God we may or may not believe works in mysterious ways.

Listen, a faith-based coping strategy in times of trouble might work for some and if you're one of those people then I'm genuinely happy for you, because like an awful lot of others who don't practice religion but who can't abide the face-punchingly-smug certainty of atheism, I often feel it would be nice to have that faith to fall back on in tough times.

I grew up in a church-going family. My mum was an elder, she led the choir, she ran the Women's Guild and the Old Folks' Club, she was on every fundraising committee going and would rather have gone hungry than missed a Sunday service. Truth to be told, she wanted me to become a Church of Scotland minister when I grew up, even though my feeling was that she was only projecting her own disappointment at it not being a career for a females when she was of an age to take the vows.

There was a time in my early teens when it all resonated with me, but that was perhaps more down to who our minister was at the time, a wonderful man called Jack Fraser who quit as a bus mechanic to take up the cloth and whose working-man's touch packed the house every week. He came with us to the football on a Saturday and next morning would use the experience to help deliver sermon, before addressing the children in the congregation through a ventriloquist's dummy, the Reverend Abernathy. Whether he made the scriptures a joy or whether it was just the showman in him that had me looking forward to Sundays at 11am is debatable; all I know is that when he moved on, the succession of Weary Willies who followed killed not just my enthusiasm but that of half the community, who vanished pew by pew.

It wouldn't be fair to say that I made a conscious decision not to go to church in my 20s and 30s; it's nearer the mark to admit that Sunday mornings during that period were more about first nursing hangovers or then children. Come 40, though, I started to think far more deeply about beliefs and to doubt everything about the various Holy books; you know the argument, if oil and dinosaurs were real, then the concept of God creating everything in six days about 6,000 years ago was nonsense. I'm not whatever-the-opposite-of-evangelistic-is about it. If you think there was nothing before some higher being made it all happen and if that gets you through the days, who am I to argue? After all, no one and nothing will ever stop me believing in Santa Claus.

It would, no doubt, be easier to join in with those who see a hurricane hit Haiti or an earthquake devastate New Zealand and say prayers for the victims. It makes them feel useful and most genuinely believe God will, in his mercy, give them shelter in their hour of need. I just question why if he has it in his locker to make things all right after a catastrophe, he lets it happen in the first place? Why is He always reactive, rather than proactive? Wouldn't it be better for all of us if He chose prevention over cure?

But hey, this wasn't meant to turn into a discussion on whether or not any of the Gods exist, it just went this way as my mind wrestled with how the Muslim family of young Ismael could possibly have dealt with a hand dealt them from the most marked of decks. Last Wednesday their son, their brother, their cousin was fit and happy. On Thursday, he had a cough, began sweating and struggling to breathe. Next thing he was in an ambulance whisking him to intensive care and a waiting ventilator. They rush in behind him, but the door slams in their face; not through rudeness on the part of the nursing staff, but purely for their own good.

How those last four words must stick in their throats today.

For their own good? What bit of this has been even the tiniest bit for their own good? Between the youngster dying early on Monday and the funeral being arranged, two of his siblings developed symptoms. Because of this, none of the eight-strong family was allowed to the cemetery, his coffin carried by strangers in protective suits and masks while friends lined the way, six feet apart to comply with social-distancing.

It's a scenario that breaks your heart — and which should

make most of us feel grateful that our biggest gripe today is not being allowed to hug our family and friends.

Yet it isn't as simple as counting our blessings, is it? It's way more complicated than that when we look through our own individual prisms, stuck as we are in our own individual prisons. Ten days in lockdown have felt like months, a sort of Christmastime disorientation seeping in, that weird feeling of not being able to tell Saturday from Wednesday from a hole in the head. The only reason I know for sure what day this is comes via a reminder on my phone saying: *Virtual Spin 7pm.*

I'm teaching online and it's Friday Night Fever, a 45-minute session straight out of the days of Travolta's flares and of knock-backs at church hall discos, banged out by a dozen self-isolated cycling pals watching their teacher dad-dance because his own bike *still* hasn't been delivered. They sweat, they smile, offer thumbs-up and wave bye-bye before one by one clicking back to whatever another weekend of nothingness has to offer.

THE weather forecast looks great for this week. The prognosis for getting out and enjoying it? Not so much, says Westminster's killjoy-in-chief Matt Hancock, who took to the briefing podium this teatime remind us how sunshine isn't an excuse to take a break from social distance. This isn't a suggestion, he told us — and if we choose to ignore him, people will die.

At which point we're reminded that sometimes it's not the message we don't want to hear, but the messenger. Because with the nation still cursing his every word, the Health Secretary hands over to a lady who reminds us why, like it or not, working on our tans this weekend simply isn't worth it.

She's called Ruth May, she's wearing powder-blue scrubs and is England's Chief Nurse. She speaks sadly of the loss to the virus of two colleagues, Areema Nasreen and Aimee O'Rourke, both mothers-of-three in their 30s and both lost in the past 24 hours.

May stands at the briefing podium with its now-familiar red-and-yellow tape motif, clearly uncomfortable speaking to such a massed audience, but with a calmness and an honesty that overcomes any nerves. She says of Areema and Aimee: "They were both one of us, of my profession, of our NHS family. I worry that there are going to be more deaths like theirs and I want to recognise their service today. I am grateful to all our frontline staff, but also to all of us you help keep them safe.

"It's going to be very warm this weekend and it will be very tempting to go out and enjoy those rays. But I ask you, please, remember Areema and Aimee. I ask you, please, stay at home for them."

Areema, 36, was a nurse long before she worked at Walsall Manor Hospital in the West Midlands. The eldest daughter of immigrant parents from Mirpur in Pakistan, she grew up in Birmingham and spent much of her teens tending to her sick grandmother. After that, all she wanted to do was help others.

"Reema was a legend," her sister Kazeema told *The Observer*. "Me and her were like twins — we got married on the same day, into the same family. We even had the same due date. The day she went into intensive care, she just wanted to sit and talk. She called mum in Pakistan and told her not to worry. She had to hold her breath really hard because the coughing was so bad. She just said to her: 'I'll be fine, don't worry. Don't be upset otherwise I'll get upset'. Then we took her to hospital..."

Aimee was 39 and worked at The Queen Mother Hospital in Margate, Kent. A single mum who raised her three girls Megan, Mollie and Maddie, she qualified as a nurse in 2017 and her ward manager described her as having "a special relationship" with patients on the Acute Medical Unit.

Her daughter Megan wrote on Facebook:

"It was us 4 against the world! Now us 3 will pull together more than ever!!! Look at all the lives you looked after and all the families you comforted when patients passed away. You are an angel and you will wear your NHS crown forever

more...one day when I have children of my own I will tell your grandchildren about their Glamorous Gran, every single day! I can't believe one day I will have to go through labour without my mummy!!! Night night..."

◆ ◆ ◆

THE other news item that chimes today is about the Nightingale Hospital in London's docklands, the first of many emergency coronavirus units scheduled to open around the country as the NHS braces itself for the pandemic's peak. It's been put together in a fortnight in the 100,000 square metre ExCel Arena - right opposite the dome of the O2 and connected to it by cable car — stripped out 4,000 beds rushed in; beds which, if filled to capacity, will need 16,000 staff to deal with demand.

The first thing that strikes you about this is the sheer scale of the project, the thought that Britain's capital, one of the globe's great economic and social titans, is that far short of capacity in a crisis. Then there's the name; Nightingale, conjuring pictures from a war zone, of the Lady With The Lamp tending to horribly wounded soldiers with little more equipment than disinfectant, a saw and a smile. For me, though, it's the setting itself that really drives the ExCel's new purpose home; because exactly three weeks from now, I should have been going there with a bunch of pals to register for the 2020 London Marathon.

We've been doing it every year now since 2004, numbers swelling as the fundraising group Des McKeown and I set up the year before grew from a one-off attempt to help Macmillan Cancer Support in memory of my late dad into what today is a business in its own right, driven by Des and his amazing wife Carolyn. In those 17 years, we've raised more than £1.5m, new recruits signing up all the time to run round London, climb Ben Nevis, trek some of the world's most famous landmarks, cycle some of its most punishing peaks.

Yet when we walk into the ExCel around lunchtime on the last Friday of every April to collect our vest numbers and the timer chips we fasten to our shoelaces, to browse the stalls for last-minute gear and to felt-pen messages on our chosen charity's wall, our contribution shrinks down to a dot. Because here, milling under the echoing vaults of this concrete and steel warehouse, are another 40,000 runners and their families and friends, all of whom contribute to a pot which, since the first London Marathon in 1981, has swollen to an incredible £1billion for everything from Alzheimer's to the Zoological Society, from the kiddie next door who needs a transplant to a pan-African famine.

Yet let's pull the camera even further back and see an even wider perspective of the charity sector: Although this event is the biggest of its kind on the planet, it's still only one event.

Every day of every week of every month of every year, someone somewhere is doing something selfless to pull in a few quid for their pet cause. Coffee mornings, sponsored walks, dinners, football matches, golf tourneys, mountain climbs, bungee jumps, firewalks — if we'll donate to it, someone will do it. Except right now, no one's *allowed* to do it.

So, come the last Friday in April, not only won't our gang be at the ExCel to prepare]for those 26.2 miles of torture, but the truth is that this concrete shed which has become such a totem to us is the very last place we'd want *anyone* to be.

It's cost tens of millions to create the first Nightingale Hospital - plus another £3m a month in rent - and it'll take tens of millions more to replicate the project in Glasgow, Manchester, Birmingham, Cardiff and Belfast.

This isn't something we'll say often about taxpayers' money. But you can't help but hope every penny turned out to have been wasted.

Saturday April 4

·French total of 83,031 cases overtakes China.
·High Street chain Debenhams heads for administration with 22,000 jobs at risk.
·UK deaths rise by 708 to 4,313, including a five-year-old boy.

OUT on the bike first thing this morning, the fourth time since that knee op that might have been five weeks or five years ago the way this whole caper's messing with the melon. I pick an old favourite route — from the West End of Glasgow through Maryhill to Bearsden and Milngavie, pretty much a constant climb for the first eight miles until the village of Strathblane and a series of fast descents with little bumps along the way to keep you honest.

Down through Blanefield, past the Glengoyne Distillery at Dumgoyne - usually teeming with visitors, now deserted — round the roundabout at Oakfield Garden Centre and back, turning all those descents into climbs, but promising the luxury of a final few miles when the legs can relax a little. Door to door, it's what we locals describe as a bawhair under 30 miles and it takes me two hours 13 minutes 29 seconds, an average speed of just about 13 miles an hour, one mile an hour faster than the first ride after the op.

The sunshine feels good, the breeze feels good, the freedom feels good, the knee feels good. All in all, life feels pretty damn good when you're out of self-isolation and immersed in this other kind, the splendid kind. The traffic's light and those who do have somewhere to drive to seem way more considerate than usual, no one beeping or bullying, everyone hanging back before overtaking then offering plenty room on their way past.

If this caught on post-virus, it would hugely appreciated.

So too, for that matter, the purity of the air. With barely a plane in the air, hardly a lorry to be seen, with no twice-daily rush hour, with industry not spewing gunge into the air from its chimneys, the world's become a way cleaner place in no time at all. During lockdown in China and Italy, the pandemic's early twin breeding grounds, air pollution dropped by anything between 20 and 30 per cent. Venice reported its canals turning from browny-grey to blue, ducks paddling happily for the first time in decades.

In the north of India and Pakistan, locals have gazed in awe at the snow-capped Himalayas after 30 years of grime blocking the view. And here? Everything feels cleaner, fresher, brighter — not to mention so much quieter. If ever there was a time for climate change protestors to walk around looking even more self-satisfied than usual, this is surely it. You can't see it staying this way permanently; well, not unless we never want another new car, new telly or new iPhone, because none of these things we take for granted can be made or transported without industry and industry creates pollution.

If we want the convenience of super-dupermarkets offering low, low prices on all our everyday essentials, then until they all invest in electric-only fleets we'll have to put up with hulking artics churning up and down our motorways, belching out nasty fumes. Irony of ironies, those climate change protestors themselves, the ones who love to guilt the meat-eaters by ordering smashed avocados on spelt bread while you and I are at the next table having bacon rolls, might even have to accept that their breakfast is damaging the environment too, since it's racked up more air miles than Michael Palin.

But hey, we'll enjoy filling our lungs while we can. Then all we can do when all this is over is hope that, at very least, we might willingly take some of the excess out of our lives. By this, I mean being content with what we have for even a little longer, not changing our cars every time the air freshener runs out or ordering a new DVD player when the remote batteries go dead. Not wasting so much food we bought but didn't need. Not using as much packaging that ends up rotting on landfills.

Fewer lorries on the roads shifting all our consumer trinkets would mean less air pollution, as would airlines scrapping their offers of flights halfway round Europe for the same price as taxi to the airport, offers that have put the likes of FlyBe out of business as soon as their fleet's grounded and have so many of its rivals begging for handouts. As for business travellers? There must be millions of air miles and tens of millions more on the road racked up every year by men and women who in all honestly could get as much out of the same meeting if they held it online.

Yes, we'll always need face-to-face, physical contact to help establish relationships — but do we really need to shuttle from Glasgow or Edinburgh to London or Manchester, once, twice, three times a week just to touch base or discuss sales figures? Do we really need to fill the tank and drive hundreds of miles for chats that could be done free on Skype or Zoom or Microsoft Teams?

Not for me, we don't. And my guess is that, when this is all over and the Big Reckoning arrives — which it surely will — any business with half a brain will look at the money saved across however long their staff have worked from home, ask themselves whether productivity and customer service have suffered and decide that this is the way to go from now on.

More of us exercising together, more of us staying in touch more often, cleaner air, fewer traffic jams, more than a couple of minutes between every plane taking off, way fewer working hours wasted hanging around departure lounges or nights spent away from families in soul-less hotels, less crap we don't need cluttering up our drawers and cupboards and needlessly emptying our bank accounts...all of it sounds a lot healthier than the way we lived before coronavirus forced us into this new type of normal.

The two great unknowns are whether we have the courage and the patience to make it stick — but, more crucially, whether we have the leadership at the top of the house to make it happen in the first place.

As this first Saturday in April unfolded, a story was emerging that would sorely dent our faith in that leadership.

8: CATHY COME HOME

Sunday April 5
•Donald Trump urges Americans to fight Covid-19 with little-known malaria drug.
•Spain's 124,870 cases overtake total in Italy.
•UK PM Boris Johnson said to be 'ok' despite contracting the virus.

EVERY day and night of lockdown until now, Cathy Calderwood had been a fixture on Scotland's TV screens as she outlined the latest guidance on how to stop the spread of disease. Every day and every night, her No1 priority for all of us had been absolutely simple: Stay at home.

Go out for essential shopping as infrequently as possible, allow yourself one bout of exercise a day, go to work if it's not possible to do your job from home. And apart from these exceptions? There *are* no exceptions.

We're locked down, she told us over and over, so end of story.

Cathy Calderwood was Scotland's Chief Medical Officer, the most senior health adviser to the Holyrood government. Hers was one of the friendlier faces of the nation's fight against its greatest crisis since the Second World War, her soft Northern Irish tones and matter-of-fact delivery a welcome change from the relentlessly grim nature of news bulletins and the choppy hand gestures and stilted delivery of politicians are comfortable as Donald Trump at a rap gig.

A consultant obstetrician in the Lothians, she'd taken over the CMO's role five years and two months ago and had earned a terrific reputation among NHS staff — a reputation that couldn't help but be enhanced by photos of her outside her Edinburgh home three nights back, joining in the weekly 8pm ovation for those on the frontline. So quite what possessed her to throw it all away by nipping off the next day for a weekend at her second home in the Fife seaside town of Earlsferry will remain a mystery. But as the photo splashed across the front page of this morning's *Scottish Sun On Sunday* proved, that's exactly what she chose to do — and as the words that went with that damning snapped confirmed, she'd also been there the weekend before.

This attitude of Do As I Say, Not As I Do has long since come as standard with a political class who think voters button up the back. But even at that, rarely can I remember someone who appeared so rock-solidly dependable as Calderwood proving to have such feet of clay. Turning from that front page, headlined HOME & NO WAY, pages four and five scream HYPOCRITICAL OATH, with another shot of Calderwood and her family strolling on a golf course. Then, the story...

SCOTLAND'S chief medical officer takes her daily exercise near her seaside retreat — days after SNP bosses called for powers to stop second home owners travelling to rural areas.

Dr Catherine Calderwood, 51, was snapped strolling across a golf course with her husband and kids after flouting lockdown advice by heading to her coastal property this weekend. The top medic, who has become one of the key figures in the fight against the coronavirus pandemic, was spotted out and about in quaint Earlsferry, Fife – an hour and ten minutes drive from her home in Edinburgh. Wearing a turquoise jacket, Dr Calderwood looked like she didn't have a care in the world as she walked with her family and dogs near her bolt-hole yesterday. But locals in the quiet coastal town hit out over the seemingly unnecessary trip, which came after a working week in Edinburgh where she spoke at daily pandemic briefings alongside First Minister Nicola Sturgeon.

Residents accused her of failing to heed her own government's advice that people with second properties should stay at home to protect rural communities during the outbreak. One source said Dr Calderwood was among several high-flyers from Edinburgh who had second properties in the area and were putting locals at risk.

On Thursday, Dr Calderwood shared a photo of her family outside her £1.5m home in the capital as they took part in the nationwide Clap For Carers event, telling her 24,000 followers: "My family clapping my NHS and care colleagues — and me! Thank you all."

The following day the graduate of Cambridge and Glasgow universities attended an official Scottish Government press call where she delivered crucial public health advice alongside Ms Sturgeon. But yesterday the mum of three angered locals after she was seen heading towards the beach in picturesque Earlsferry, where she has a cosy bungalow. Dr Calderwood has given regular press conferences on the Covid-19 pandemic at St Andrew's House in Edinburgh where she has repeatedly urged the public to stay within their homes, but her second home in Earlsferry is 44 miles away from the capital.

This weekend's trip comes just days after Nats chiefs called for emergency powers to stop second-home owners self-isolating in rural areas. MP Ian Blackford said legislation should be used to protect areas with less health infrastructure from visitors trying to flee the coronavirus. He spoke out after a number of communities reacted angrily as tourists blocked lay-bys and swamped camping areas.

Mr Blackford, the SNP's leader at Westminster, said: "With Easter almost upon us it is worth reminding everyone of the emergency powers that restrict non-essential travel. That means no tourists should be coming to the Highlands and Islands. If anyone owns a second or holiday home they should not be using the Highlands to self-isolate and powers exist and must be used to stop this."

Similar warnings have also been issued in England and Wales, with. UK Health Secretary Matt Hancock saying he did not consider people going to their holiday homes as an essential trip during the crisis. His plea followed concerns that rural health services could be overwhelmed by those leaving cities who then end up suffering from Covid-19. Mr Hancock said: "We've said people should not take unnecessary journeys and I don't regard going to your holiday home as necessary."

Yesterday it was revealed that a further 46 people have died from coronavirus in Scotland, bringing the total number of deaths to 218, while the UK-wide total increased by 708 to 4,313. The latest deaths including a child aged just five — the youngest UK victim so far. The Scottish Government said 3,345 people had now tested positive for the virus, an increase of 344 from Friday. In total, 20,798 patients have been tested across the country.

Belfast-born Dr Calderwood has pleaded with Scots to stay at home to protect the NHS and "help save lives" — including on TV and radio ads and at daily press briefings on the pandemic with Ms Sturgeon.

When asked to explain the official view on travelling to a second home last night, a Scottish Government spokesman said: "We strongly advise against any travel to second homes. It runs the risk of adding pressure to services in more remote and quieter areas, from food supply to health care."

The Scottish Sun on Sunday then asked why the Chief Medical Officer was ignoring official advice. An SNP spokesman replied: "Since the start of this epidemic, the CMO has been working seven days a week preparing Scotland's response. She took the opportunity this weekend to check on a family home in Fife as she knows she will not be back again until the crisis is over. She stayed overnight before returning to Edinburgh. In line with guidance she stayed within her own household group and observed social distancing with anyone she was in passing in the village."

EXCEPT that the official quote at the end of the report didn't quite tell the full story. Nor, for that matter, did the statement Cathy Calderwood herself issued at 11.05 this morning.

Yes, she apologised unreservedly. Yes, she admitted failing to follow her own advice. No, she didn't want her 'mistake' to detract from the job at hand. Yes, it was confirmed around noon by Police Scotland chief constable Iain Livingstone, officers has spoken to the Chief Medical Officer about her actions, warning about her future conduct and reminder her that 'individuals must not make personal exemptions bespoke to their own circumstances'.

However, it wasn't until 2.30pm, as she and the FM co-hosted Holyrood's daily briefing, that Calderwood admitted to also having been at her second home the weekend before she was caught out by the camera. She told of her embarrassment at a barrage of tweets and emails branding her a hypocrite, a disgrace and — social media being social media — far worse. She admitted letting the country down, at which point the country counted the minutes until her resignation.

Yet next thing, Sturgeon was again defending her adviser, admitting her actions were 'wrong', but that her expertise was invaluable. She asked the public 'not to be angry' and revealed that while Calderwood had 'offered to do whatever was in the best interests of the country, that would not be resignation'.

Maybe they both thought that would be that; a ten-minute wonder, tonight's chip wrappers. Or maybe there were just trying to convince themselves they'd made it all go away. Either way, they didn't have long to wait for reality to bite hard and deep.

Within an hour, the backlash was so severe Sturgeon had to issue a statement revealing Calderwood was being withdrawn from all broadcasts with immediate effect. Again, it seemed inevitable that resignation would follow pretty much immediately. While we waited, I posted this on Facebook:

"Mixing up your hair gel and toothpaste is a mistake. Putting salt in your coffee is human error. Going to your second home in Fife two weeks in a row when you're on telly every night telling everyone else to stay home is taking the piss. Trust me. If the rest of us end up banned from exercising outside because of selfish sods like Cathy Calderwood, this won't end well..."

Yet as the internet turned white-hot this afternoon with reaction to the story and the fallout from it, all went quiet for a while on the government front. Friends in the NHS were telling me what a mistake it would be to get rid of their boss, that maybe she'd have to pay the price once coronavirus had been and gone, but that for now she was too crucial to the organisation to be let go.

They liked her, they trusted her and these qualities meant more to them right now than any knee-jerk reaction to a public scandal that would be forgotten about soon enough. Meanwhile, there were growing accusations from Nationalist diehards that *The Scottish Sun On Sunday* was the real guilty party here, that whoever took the photographs was breaking lockdown guidelines by travelling to Fife on what wasn't a key worker mission; not true, but since when did social media subscribe to the fact-checking it demands of the mainstream?

By mid-evening, Cathy Calderwood's second home wasn't even top of the national news agenda any more, not once it broke that PM Boris Johnson had been rushed into hospital after his symptoms worsened. As the first editions of Monday morning's Scottish papers went to press, most led on how she was hanging on, but the story really hadn't moved on.

Then, at 9.45pm, she quit. And suddenly, every newsroom — actually, make that every *living* room, since just about every editor, sub-editor, designer and reporter was by now working from home with only a skeleton staff going into offices to pull everything together for the printers — went into overdrive to update as quickly as humanly possible. By the early hours, *The Scottish Sun* was running with FLOUT ON HER EAR. The *Daily Record* roared: STAY AT HOME FOR GOOD. At *The Scotsman*, they liked Sunday's *Sun* headline so much their cover also tutted about THE HYPOCRITICAL OATH. The Scottish edition of *The Times* stuck with Boris as its lead, a second story headlined CHIEF MEDIC QUITS AFTER CRITICISM OVER TRAVEL.

Meanwhile, over at *The National* - the pro-SNP paper launched after the 2014 referendum by the owners of unionist stalwart *The Herald* - the front page thundered: 700 YEARS ON WE STILL FIGHT FOR INDEPENDENCE.

For them, the anniversary of the Declaration of Arbroath, which asked the Pope to recognise Scotland's independence, was more important than the downfall of their pet party's medical guru. Back in the real world, though, the hastily re-vamped second edition of *The Scottish Sun* used pages two and three to describe Calderwood as An Unhealthy Risk, the story outlining how the day before unfolded and how a reputation had unravelled with it, with pages four and five given over to a withering overview by columnist Andrew Nicoll. Its headline read: *Hypocrisy, lies, public disgust..why did Nicola try to save her?* Beneath this, the subdeck: FM AT ODDS WITH SCOTLAND ON SHAMED DOC.

Then, the hounds were released...

YESTERDAY'S coronavirus press conference with First Minister Nicola Sturgeon and the disgraced Chief Medical Officer Catherine Calderwood made only one thing clear: Your government lied to you.

On Saturday night the Scottish Government issued two statements.

First they said trotting off to one's country place for a spot of weekend relaxation was a very bad thing. Then they were confronted by our story revealing that Catherine Calderwood had done exactly that.

After another exhausting day recording public information films stressing the importance of staying indoors, Dr Calderwood went out.

It took the government another two hours and 26 minutes to come up with an explanation. Apparently, after working seven days a week, Dr Calderwood had taken the rare opportunity of travelling to her holiday home to check on its security, knowing she wouldn't be able to get back perhaps for weeks at a time.

Of course, it didn't stand up to a moment's examination. Even if she had been concerned that she might have left the gas on, why would she need her husband, her kids and her dog to help her check? As an explanation it was implausible. It was also jaw-dropping in its sense of self entitlement. Were we all supposed to melt because the Chief Medical Officer was working seven days a week in the middle of the biggest national crisis since Dunkirk? Dr Calderwood earned six times more than the nurses she has been sending into the front line without so much as a paper mask. Those of them who survive this will never be able to afford a weekend place on the beach in Earlsferry but we were supposed to feel sorry for her. It was a ridiculous attempt to wriggle out of an appalling act of hypocrisy — and we know now for sure it was a lie.

Dr Calderwood opened her statement of apology with an admission that she took the family to her weekend hideaway in Earlsferry this weekend and was there 'with my husband' last weekend.

Not once, but twice.

That isn't a dreadful mistake, as she claimed. That isn't 'human error.' It was a sustained pattern of behaviour that blew a hole in the 'seven days a week' claim. Anybody could see the thinking behind yesterday's briefing. Despite the public disgust, despite totally destroying the message on social distancing and essential travel, despite condemnation from the Chief Constable and even Earlsferry Community Council, despite demands for her sacking from every opposition party, the First Minister decided Calderwood should keep her job. Ms Sturgeon clearly believed that, if the Chief Medical Officer survived the ordeal of an on-camera apology, it would all go away. Everybody would forgive and forget and we could all get on with the business of fighting the bug again.

But yesterday's broadcast was far, far worse than car-crash television. It wasn't a car crash and not even a train wreck. This was the TV equivalent of a jumbo jet loaded with endangered rhinos crashing on an orphanage.

Every question but one was focused on the integrity of the Chief Medical Officer – and the one that wasn't was about the constantly changing messages we have all been getting from government. None of the questions was answered. After Dr Calderwood had made her apology — including the interesting little revelation that she has been driving round the country without a care for weeks — she was completely shielded. Journalist after journalist posed questions directly to her but she was barely allowed to speak. The camera stayed fixed right on Nicola Sturgeon. We were not permitted even to look at Catherine Calderwood, far less listen to her latest, made-up justification.

Instead of seeing the Health Secretary and Chief Medical Officer flanking the First Minister, almost every shot was squarely fixed on Nicola Sturgeon looking straight down the camera and repeating: 'Nothing to see here, move along.'

On those brief occasions when she was allowed to speak, Catherine Calderwood had nothing to say. Instead she stuck to the script, just as she had been told: 'I can't justify being away from my home. No reasons justify that. I have let the public and my NHS colleagues down and I apologise unreservedly.'

Nobody could be bothered to answer the actual questions. Not Dr Calderwood and certainly not the First Minister. Did Dr Calderwood offer to resign? The First Minister refused even to say if she'd be removed from TV advertising. But *after* the press conference the Scottish Government issued a statement from Ms Sturgeon saying the ads fronted by Calderwood were being 'withdrawn' and a 'revised' campaign would take its place.

Catherine Calderwood did not simply destroy her own credibility in all of this, she has deeply damaged her colleague Jason Leitch, the Scottish Government's clinical director, who loyally defended her on TV yesterday. Catherine knows the rules on social distancing, he said. She kept herself safe. But by yesterday afternoon he was back-pedalling like crazy, tweeting: "I agree she broke the rules and I am glad she has apologised."

Nobody doubts Catherine Calderwood has worked hard and she damn well should for the money and because it is her duty. But there are thousands and thousands of people not working at all right not, people who don't have a charming holiday home to hide away in.

There are people who have been separated from loved ones for weeks. People who have been kept away from dying parents. There are people who have gone to their graves alone, without a funeral, nurses, paramedics and doctors at breaking point. There are others who are already desperately ill.

Catherine Calderwood spat in the faces of all those people and, for some reason, Nicola Sturgeon completely failed to understand the depth of public anger. So who knows what sparked Calderwood's belated resignation? Twitter abuse? Worldwide disbelief? It doesn't matter.

She's gone and it's right that she's gone. But the most remarkable thing is that Nicola Sturgeon tried to save her.

Tuesday April 8
•Foreign Secretary Dominic Raab at helm of UK as PM Boris Johnson spends second night in intensive care.
•First train leaves Chinese city of Wuhan after 11 weeks of lockdown.
•Donald Trump threatens to withdraw US funding from World Health Organisation for being 'China-centric'.

WHEN the pandemic finally becomes yesterday's news, all of us will have to reflect on the decisions we'd change if we could have our time again.

Today, Scotland's First Minister is surely wishing she could go back and start Sunday's press conference with Cathy Calderwood all over again — and read the room more accurately before trying to defend the indefensible. Because judging by her reaction 36 hours after the Chief Medical Officer's resignation, it's clear Nicola Sturgeon's judgement of the situation was as far removed from that of the nation as Earlsferry is from Edinburgh. Today, she told how a barrage of messages from the public and colleagues alike had made her 'reflect' on keeping Calderwood in her post. She told how she feared a loss of trust in her Government if she continued to back her key health adviser. In other words, how a key adviser had become toxic.

As two more Coronavirus deaths took Scotland's total to 222, Sturgeon told her daily media briefing: "At an earlier point of the day I perhaps thought when she apologised and made clear her actions were unacceptable then the importance of her continued advice would be the priority. But it was clear as the day developed this would be a risk to the public message.

"It wasn't so much new information, it was my reflection on the course of the day. Certainly people had been contacting me through email and other means and it became clear to me that Dr Calderwood remaining in office was going to be a risk to the confidence in and trust in the government's message.

"That was not a risk I or — to be fair to her — she was prepared to take. That is the reason for the change in my view and it was based on an honest assessment of the balance. We had a conversation and my view, having reflected on developments, was that it was not possible for her to remain in office."

By now, it was crystal clear that Scottish Sun columnist Nicoll's claim yesterday that 'your Government had lied to you' was bang on. He wrote in this morning's edition:

IT'S been one revelation after another since we broke the story of Dr Calderwood and her curfew-busting jaunts to a seaside second home. After a toe-curling briefing where the First Minister condemned the Chief Medical Officer's visits to her holiday home, but defended her place in the campaign, she let her go. Why is far from clear.

Seemingly it took a 12-hour social media barrage to persuade Ms

Sturgeon.That won't have been helped by the fact that I'm told she couldn't persuade a single MSP to bat for Dr Calderwood. Public demand for a sacking was irresistible. So she buckled. She bowed to public anger after failing to understand instinctively how fierce it was.

Amid all this she still can't answer how many picked up this sickness in hospital or whether care workers have the kit they need. It looks wobbly. She must steady the ship quickly before public confidence starts to evaporate.

THIS wasn't how Sturgeon put it, of course — she said their response to the paper's inquiry on Saturday night had 'reflected the information we had at the time, up against a deadline, of the reasons for her visit to her house in Fife that weekend', before adding: "Dr Calderwood later clarified to her deputy Dr Gregor Smith that she had been there the weekend before. She made that clear at the briefing yesterday morning and was open about that."

Sturgeon, who today appointed Dr Smith to take over in the interim, denied attempting to 'spin' the situation and insisted her defence of Calderwood had been made 'in good faith' and 'for the best of reasons'.

Meanwhile, there were now 3,961 confirmed Coronavirus cases in Scotland, 255 up on the day before. A total of 1,599 are being treated in hospital, 199 in intensive care with the First Minister saying: "Unfortunately there is almost certainly still worse to come before we turn the corner."

In terms of the virus, this was beyond all doubt. In terms of her Government's reputation, she could only hope for the best.

And then...well, and then it all went awfully quiet again. Normally a tale as juicy as this would be squeezed until its pips squeaked. But nothing about now is normal, not even the way newspapers work.

Fact is, every day right now is one roaring, foaming river of a story deeper and wider than the Nile and the Amazon combined, a torrent into which the Cathy Calderwood scandal, for all that it was massive at source, really only fed as a tributary.

Yesterday morning, she was all anyone was talking about. By this afternoon it would all be about Boris being in intensive care. Come tomorrow, who knows what where the surging current of affairs will carry humanity's rickety raft.

So for now, let's dock at a dilemma bugging me far more than where some doctor sneaks off to at weekends.

Why aren't my own Saturdays feeling empty?

9: THE BALL'S BURST

FORGIVE me, readers, for I have sinned.
It's been 46 days since my last football match.
And I don't miss it one little bit...

IT'S the first Saturday of February in 1973, it's coming up to one o'clock and we're due to get picked up in an hour to go to the game. On any other Saturday, we'd be chatting, excited, making predictions and airing our fears.

But today? Today, dad's in a major league huff.

Why, I have no idea, just as I have no idea why any of this has stayed with me for close on half a century. But it's there all the same, a reminder of just how unthinkable not being at the football used to be.

We'd have been watching telly that morning, probably some Laurel & Hardy or *The Virginian* in those pre-Swap Shop days. We must have had our lunch of Heinz Pork Sausages and Beans on big, floury, thickly buttered McMillan's rolls and washed down with builder's tea, because that's what we always did and it's what I still always do. But after that? All I know is something happened to make dad bark the most appalling, stomach-churning sentence imaginable:

"That's it — we're not going."

It was Partick Thistle at Love Street in the Third Round that day, the visit of a top flight side and last season's League Cup winners to our sprawling, crumbling, once-proud oval of a Second Division ground. But it wouldn't have mattered had we been playing Cowdenbeath Reserves, because all the ten-year-old me cared about when Saturday came was watching his team with his dad. It was our day, our ritual, our special time of the week. Yet something, presumably something I'd done, had managed to wreck it.

As I write this, it's struck me for the first time that we were always actually going to go to the game, because dad hadn't phoned my Uncle Sam to tell him not to bother picking us up. At the time, though, the fear of missing a St Mirren game had clearly negated all logic.

Plus, when dad was in the huff I'd never, ever have been so complacent as to think *yeah, whatever.* He was the kindest, gentlest man alive, but he suffered from what today would undoubtedly be diagnosed as depression and when the fit took him his mood couldn't be shifted with a bulldozer.

So, once he'd made his announcement, we sat there, rolypoly anchorman Sam Leitch talking us through *Football Focus* but neither of us tuned in, the clock tick-ticking towards 2pm and every passing second another nail in the coffin of the day, *our* day. Yet then it was five to two, dad went to the loo, came back with his jacket on and told me to get ready. The car pulled up and off we went, this strained hour neither mentioned again nor ever explained.

We lost that cup-tie, 1-0, the game itself not registering much in the memory banks but the lead-up to it indelible. We'd come as close as we ever would to *not* going when we *could* have gone — and this was how my life had been ever since, as a fan and a sportswriter, one built around where and when the next match would be. One where the words *Game Off* cut like a knife, even if a glance out the window at three feet of snow dictated that indoors was the only place for any sane human being to be.

As a fan, I'd skip school to watch us play away in midweek. I can still recite the starting 11s, scores, scorers and crowds for meaningless fixtures from the 70s. As a sportswriter, I was always the one to put a hand up when the gaffer was short of a body to go to Dingwall on a Tuesday night or Stranraer on a Wednesday and occasionally both. I remember with some shame being gutted when a cup-tie between Brechin City and

East Fife came off second best to a heavy frost the day after my daughter was born.

The observant reader, however, will have noticed all this being described in the past tense, used quite deliberately, because right now - Wednesday April 8, 2020, 14 days into lockdown — that feeling of football being everything simply isn't there any more. After 55 years as a fan, the past 39 also as a sportswriter, owning up to this is a bit like Jacob Rees-Mogg confessing he's tired of being a Dickensian fruitcake. But that's how hard but football's response to coronavirus has hit me, this odious scramble for the strongest to survive and to hell with everyone else.

Forty-six days on from my last match, a rain-lashed 0-0 draw between Hamilton and Motherwell, I should be climbing the walls, bingeing on the retro-barrage being screened from Beeb One to Sky Sports 99, pining like a schoolgirl for her favourite pop star or Eamonn Holmes for attention.

Yet the truth is, I haven't missed it one teeny, tiny bit. Truth is, my obsessive, forensic love for the beautiful game had been ebbing for a long time before it was forcibly taken away from all of us.

What's happened between me and football is pretty much what happens in countless relationships all over the planet; one day, it's the most amazing thing in the world, it completes you, it can do no wrong. Its little flaws aren't annoying, they're endearing. You'd do anything for it, you simply can't imagine life without it. Then, overnight — don't know how, don't know why — you notice that it chews a little too loudly. That laugh you always thought was quirky suddenly starts to grate.

Its views begin to get to you, its politics get your back up. Sure, it always had friends who were a bit greedy, a tad obnoxious, maybe a bit bigoted — and, sure, you've had arguments with it about them. But you'd always kissed and made up, because what mattered most was that you loved each other.

But now, you find reasons *not* to go with it to Dingwall, just this once. You wake up one morning to a flurry of snow and hope — just fleetingly, not fervently — that it keeps on falling so you get an afternoon to yourself. Now, the buzz it always gave you fades to an irritating hum, the fantasies it conjured up pale, the willing suspension of disbelief it instilled in you to regard it as wonderful even though deep down you knew it was all-too-often bang ordinary feels a tiny bit ridiculous.

And suddenly, it's like you've been blind all this time. Suddenly, you don't have the energy to defend it against those who didn't fancy it much in the first place. Suddenly, you don't have it in you to hype up Wednesday night in Stranraer like you used to.

This was how I'd already been feeling about football for a long while before coronavirus hit us like a 1970s tackle from behind. It was the way too many fans had decided the real enjoyment wasn't in supporting their own team, but in hating everyone else's. It was the way too many players had gone from doing anything but show weakness when some bruiser booted them up in the air to sensing a tackle coming and deciding they were entitled to fall down and roll over.

It was the way wages at the top end of the game had got so obscene that one English Premier League superstar's weekly take-home would run an entire Scottish League Two club for a year, the way ticket prices had accelerated way beyond inflation while entertainment value was in a double-dip recession.

It was...well, call me an idealistic fool, but it was the sheer cynicism that had set in like wet rot, the way so few involved in it all — and I include myself in this — saw the best in anyone or anything any more. And now it had been taken away, albeit temporarily, all I felt was relief — a feeling that the response to the crisis of those who run the game at home and around the world has done nothing to alleviate.

Because, at a time crying out for leadership, cool thinking and togetherness, it was instead every man and woman for themselves and every one of them running round with their hair on fire.

IT WAS just before 8.55pm on Wednesday March 11 when Jon Obika cut through the driving rain to score the only goal of the game as St Mirren pulled four points clear of Hearts at the bottom of the Scottish Premiership.

A goal that would have been pivotal enough at this stage of a normal season, but which in the circumstances enveloping football like a pea-soup fog would turn out to be monumental.

Because 36 hours later, British football was in lockdown. And the Scottish end of it was heading for meltdown.

Who knows how different what happened over the next weeks and months might have been had Hearts won that game at Paisley and lifted themselves out of the one automatic relegation place just in time for the shutters coming down? Maybe we'd have avoided all the finger-pointing and back-stabbing, all the division and the derision, all the ruined relationships that might never be healed. Or maybe St Mirren would have taken the hump at how their fellow clubs reacted to the pandemic just as badly as the team they'd beaten that ugly, attritional night in Paisley. As a life-long fan and a season-ticket holder, I'd hope not. I'd hope that, when it went to the vote and the majority decided to end the campaign there and then, rather than wait and hope for a virus-free window in which to get it finished, we'd have taken our medicine.

That's certainly what I'd have been advocating, because right from the off it felt like this situation was so much bigger than who kicked a ball in which division once we'd come out the other side of this global health crisis.

Yes, it was unfair that Hearts — as well as Partick Thistle and Stranraer, bottom of the Championship and League One when the plug was pulled — ended up relegated on the basis of a show of hands. But their reaction to it, when held up against the genuine tragedies families were going through every single day, was outrageously disproportionate.

If you missed how it all unfolded...well, you're one of the

lucky ones, because it would dominate so much of what I wrote over the next few months and would leave me wanting to do anything but watch, read about or talk about football.

Actually, no, that's not strictly true. Had the chance been there to sit somewhere with some pals and a pint and reminisce about games gone by and the great characters involved in them, that would have been heaven.

But to be stuck at home, sifting through endless reams of accusation and counter-accusation about who'd done who wrong and who was in whose clique, listening to the latest self-serving, self-important statement from this chairman or that chief executive about how they were going to blow the whole business wide open — and then having to make some sort of sense of it all in the next column — was genuinely depressing. That ten-year-old boy, praying his dad would come out of his huff in time for them to go to a cup-tie against Partick Thistle, would be horrified to read those words. He thought football was the greatest thing in the world, sometimes the *only* thing.

He already knew he wanted to spend his life writing about it and knew for absolutely sure he'd never tire of it. Well, kiddo, I'm sorry. But back then, we didn't reckon on the world being full of so many half-witted spoilsports who'd have made Tigger quit bouncing.

THE morning after Obika's goal, I met my gaffer, Roger Hannah, to discuss getting back on duty following the op. Even in the hour we spent chatting in a cafe high up in a shopping mall behind our Glasgow city centre office, the world seemed to speed up like it was being spun by some hulking celestial bully.

Ireland closed all its schools, with the UK mainland almost certain to follow. Boris Johnson went from believing shaking hands with all-comers was perfectly safe to describing the virus as the greatest health crisis in our lifetime. Nicola Sturgeon was admitting we'd gone from containing the spread to merely delaying it. Stock markets suffered their heaviest one-day loss since 1987.

Next thing, an email pinged in from our editor, Alan Muir, advising that as of now we would be running trials of staff being rota-ed to work from home in a bid to minimise the potential of infection.

Just before that email, we'd been talking about how short-sighted it seemed that, amidst all this ramping up of threat levels, that night's Europa League tie between Rangers and German side Bayer Leverkusen was going ahead. Crazier still, there was still no suggestion that Sunday's league game between Rangers and Celtic would be called off.

There would be 47,494 inside Ibrox for that European tie, including 2,000 who'd travelled with the visiting team. Had the Old Firm clash gone ahead that weekend, there would have been the same numbers again, plus ten times as many crammed into pubs. In that moment, it almost felt like a First Minister who'd already announced a ban of public gatherings larger than 500 from the following Monday was trying to find a way to let both go ahead so as to avoid any fuss, like she was negotiating a temporary ceasefire with a virus. As we drained our coffee, I floated the idea of a piece for the next day's paper pleading with all concerned to call an immediate halt.

Within hours of the piece being published, that's precisely what happened; all UK football was suspended indefinitely. I'd argued that, if we went by China's graph of cases, we'd peak in three to four weeks time, get players back into training a couple of weeks after that and be ready to restart the season sometime in June, before taking a short break once it was done and getting 2020-2021 up and running in September or October rather than August as planned.

Even by the Monday, however, things were moving on at such a pace I was beginning to doubt this, suggesting in that morning's column that although there was no need to rush into decisions and that if come the end of April it didn't look like we'd be able to get this season going again, that would be the time to cut our losses and start planning for August.

Above all, however, my feeling was that it was no time for anyone to panic. But as ever, what the hell did I know?

HEARTS had found themselves at the epicentre of Scotland's reaction to coronavirus from the off. On Tuesday March 3, before their derby match at Easter Road, their players and those of Hibs were the first to be banned from taking part in the traditional pre-match handshakes. It seemed a very sensible precaution; you know, as long as they got through the next 90 minutes making sure they never touched each other, coughed or sneezed on each other and as long as the 20,197 spectators didn't touch, cough or sneeze on each other and/or come in contact with a carrier on their way to and from the game. In short, it was a gesture as ridiculous as Boris Johnson's pronouncement that same week that the way to fight off bugs was to 'wash our hands for the length of time it takes to sing Happy Birthday To You twice'.

(At that point, the virus threat was at Moderate, though it was understood that should it be elevated to Serious the advice would be to carrying on soaping for the full five minutes 54 seconds of Bohemian Rhapsody, then to all eight verses of The Eton Boat Song once it became Critical.)

We should have know there and then that Scottish football simply wasn't prepared for what lay ahead. This lack of planning, of joined-up thinking, would soon bring us to a situation where its clubs would sooner have shaken each other by the throat than the hand.

The first fixture-free weekend had been weird, no question. After all, even if your own team isn't playing on a Saturday these days, there's always a live match to watch, a fixed odds coupon to check, a results show to sit glued to. But now, for the first time ever during a season, there was nothing — no previews, no updates, no post-match interviews, no rolling repeats of goals and controversies from every game, no late-night highlights packages.

So, sure, it was a long old couple of days, one not shortened either by the knee still not being strong enough to get myself out on the bike. Time dragged. As Saturday sludged into Sunday, I felt more and more edgy and nothing Sonia said or did could get me out of the funk. But hey, maybe that was it — maybe these apparent withdrawal symptoms from the armchair stuff suggested it wasn't football itself I was falling out of love with, just the excitement of writing about it. Maybe all I needed to bring the hunger back was a break.

Yet by the following weekend, it was actually pretty nice not to be planning everything around what games were on the box, especially when chances were most would fall miles short of the build-up that made you watch them in the first place.

It was nice not thinking that Sonia was having to put up with football because it was my job, for one of us not to have to disappear into the spare room so we could both have our choice of viewing.

It was nice to listen to music instead, to go for a walk at times when I'd normally have been stuck to a chair for hours, nice just to sit and talk.

In short, the more ham-fisted and selfish the response to lockdown became from those running the game, the happier I felt to watch it all from an extremely social distance. And no club was more selfish than Hearts.

By the first Monday without football, March 16, they were warning the game's governing bodies that they would sue if their relegation was confirmed without being able to complete all fixtures. By the Wednesday, their owner Ann Budge was claiming the shutdown had already cost them £1 million through the loss of their remaining home league games and their share of taking from a Scottish Cup semi-final against Hibs at Hampden.

Come the Thursday, as the Scottish Football Association

divided £1.5million in emergency payments between its 42 senior clubs, Budge was demanding all players and staff took a 50 per cent pay cut or risk losing their jobs. Manager Daniel Stendel - by now back home in his native Germany - almost immediately offered to work for free, but admitted 'others clubs are worse off than us'.

Meanwhile, at clubs up and down the four divisions of the Scottish Professional Football League, what was happening at Hearts was setting alarm bells ringing, with owners preparing to take up the Westminster government's furlough scheme — where the state would pay 80 per cent of the wages of any workers laid off — and players contacting their union to demand support if clubs stopped paying them altogether.

Celtic chief executive Peter Lawwell came out swinging over Budge's threat of court action should her club be relegated by making it clear that *his* club wouldn't stand for the season being declared void. The clubs at the top of the three lower divisions - Dundee United, Raith Rovers and Cove Rangers - started making noises about what would happen if *they* were denied promotion, while the clubs just behind them were crying foul over the unfairness of missing out on the play-offs that could potential have taken *them* up to the next level.

Like the first halfwit loading a supermarket trolley with toilet rolls, Ann Budge's panic-stations reaction to football being stopped had sparked a feeding frenzy that was very quickly ridding the Scottish game of what little shred of good sense it ever had.

Just as Vladimir Lenin once warned that society is only ever three missed meals away from anarchy, it seemed for all the world that Hearts had only ever one postponed home match away from Armageddon. All they'd lost so far was one visit from Ross County, a match when 90 per cent of the crowd would have been season ticket holders whose money was already safely in club funds. Yet this was all it took to turn Ann Budge into football's equivalent of the dope with the garage full of Andrex and dried pasta. To be fair, I don't know the nitty-gritty about Tynecastle's finances. The fact that it looked from the outside like they'd spent way too much on too many players who'd contributed way too little is irrelevant.

All I know is that, just when clear heads and careful words were needed, Budge's reaction to the crisis made the way Boris Johnson was dealing with the nation's £90billion hospitality industry appear Churchillian. On Monday, the PM had caused all sort of confusion and anger after urging us to stay away from bars and restaurants while refusing to shut them down. Yet had he kept his counsel for even 48 more hours until a multi-billion-pound Treasury package to cover wages was ready to roll, armies of owners and workers might have been spared a whole load of needless stress and tears.

In the same way, had Budge not steamed into such a public panic over what coronavirus had done to her club, an awful lot of people who were on their side over relegation might still care what league they'll playing in when all this is over.

In this, I include myself, because whereas a week before I'd have gone to the barricades to defend their right to stay in the top flight, once she opened her mouth and let her stomach rumble they were on your own and. All she had to do — as with BoJo and the nation's locals — was keep the powder dry, have a think, get the staff onside and make the best of a rotten situation. Foot on the ball, the coaches call it, foot on the ball.

Had she called the players in, explained how perilous the cash flow situation was, gently guilted them about how their own wage demands had played a large part in this and encouraged them to take what would hopefully be a temporary wage cut to ensure lower-paid staff didn't go short, *then* she could have told the world where they stood and I've no doubt she'd have got a more sympathetic hearing. She'd have looked proactive, the squad would have looked like heroes, the office staff and cooks and cleaners and the rest could have gone home knowing their bills were covered and the fans would have felt proud of how their club was dealing with adversity.

Instead, though? She's on telly one day vowing legal action against anyone who tries to declare the league done and dusted, then the next she's admitting she doesn't have the money to pay the wages — and that if anyone doesn't like it, they're free to rip up their contracts. For me, that was dreadful leadership, not to mention an admission of just how terribly Hearts had managed their affairs. After all, what if the same three home games had fallen to a freak cold snap rather than coronavirus? What if they didn't have that Scottish Cup semi-final windfall to count on, because they'd lost to Rangers in the previous round three weeks before lockdown? Stands to reason they'd *still* be £1 million down, they'd still be unable to fulfil their financial obligations and the dominoes would still be wobbling, which made it more than a little disingenuous to start threatening writs over relegation when the whole campaign had been built on a lie. Theirs was a situation thrown into the sharpest of relief by the way things were being handled over at second-bottom Hamilton, where owner Ronnie McDonald was calling his players in to reassure them that, whatever happened next, their contracts would be honoured.

Honesty and decency on that scale deserves to be rewarded — and I'm certain that, once this is over, McDonald and manager Brian Rice will get that reward in the shape of everyone in that dressing room going an extra yard for the shirt.

See, whatever our walk of life, honesty and trust is everything. It drives work rate on the shop floor and it builds reputations in the outside world. Unfortunately, as Scottish football began to unravel, Hearts looked to have been anything but honest in the way they'd stockpiled a squad using money they didn't have.

STILL, at least one corner of the national sport had proven itself capable of making a decision everyone could agree on, even if not celebrate.

The Highland League - one level below the senior grade of Scottish football and part of the Pyramid System that feeds into it — had taken the decision to end their season here and now and award the championship to leaders Brora Rangers.

They were 13 points clear at the top of the table with two games in hands and an overwhelming goal difference, yet they could conceivably still have been caught and it would have been easy for their nearest rivals to hide behind that catch-all buzz-phrase of "sporting integrity" as an excuse to deny them. So big, big credit to all concerned for seeing the bigger picture and seeing beyond petty grievances.

You hoped against hope it was an attitude that would spread as quickly as the virus itself — and, to be fair, there were plenty in the football community doing their best to help others rather than hinder them for the hell of it. Rangers and Manchester City were among the club who'd offered their stadiums to the NHS if needed. Portuguese superstar Cristiano Ronaldo and Sky Sports pundit Gary Neville had opened up their hotels to health workers unable to stay at home with their families for fear of infection. Entire dressing rooms were filling their time off from training to deliver shopping to those stuck at home. Fans were refusing season ticket refunds to try and keep their clubs afloat.

And then there was Chris Silvestro's medal.

A tiny disc that meant everything to a journeyman footballer who rarely made headlines and never came close to making fortunes. The reward not just for the best season of his career, but for that career itself — yet one he'd decided to sell for the sake of the club where he won it.

Silvestro was a no-nonsense midfielder with the Raith Rovers crew of 2008-2009 who dragged a whole town with them to the top of the Second Division just four years after financial catastrophe had almost shut the doors for good at their tumbledown Starks Park home. To say the success meant the world to individual players and the club alike would be like saying coronavirus had given Earth the sniffles.

Needs must, though. Desperate times call for desperate measures. And more than decade on, with Rovers tantalisingly close to the League One title but with every penny once more a prisoner thanks to lockdown, Silvestro offered to put the one and only medal in his sideboard up for auction.

He did so for the same, simple reason that stadiums and hotels were being offered to the NHS, the same reason players are delivering food parcels when they'd normally be training, the same reason the guy in Row G Seat 64 doesn't want his money back for games that aren't being played.

He was doing it because he could. Because it might make a difference. Because some things are bigger than possessions. On April 6, Silvestro's medal went under the hammer for £1,200.99, every last penny of which went into a Crowdfunding pot set up to keep the wolf from the door during these times of never-ending uncertainty. The fund had been set up on March 25 with a target of £25,000. Within another 72 hours, the response had been such that they raised the bar to £50,000. Chris Silvestro's sacrifice helped take the total beyond £40,520.62.

On the last Sunday in March, the Rovers should have been in Perth to play Caley Thistle in the final of the Tunnock's Caramel Wafer Cup. So many of those who'd planned to be there chose not to save the money they'd have spent on tickets, on petrol, on beer and pies and Bovril to the fighting fund. In terms of where we were all at right then, those fivers and tenners meant as much as all Ronaldo's free hotel rooms and all the wages deferred by the megastar and his Juve compadres. It meant as much as the 30,000 protective masks Barcelona had donated to their country's hospitals.

As for Chris Silvestro? He'd given what he has for the cause and no one can do more. At a time when none of us had a clue where this whole, horrible caper was going, all any of us could do was our best, our kindest.

As March morphed into April, this thought kept me going

and even started to rekindle my old hunger for the game. I had optimistic visions of the shutters coming up and fans turning the way they had after the two World Wars, visions of soaring gates and swelling excitement.

I wrote of those big crowds rediscovering their innocent love of the game, of them losing the anger and the bile while retaining their losing passion for our heroes, of players rejecting the win-at-all-costs mentality and playing the way they dreamed they would as kid.

It felt the perfect time to regroup and re-set, to realise how much energy we'd wasted in hurling abuse and diving around, the perfect time to bury grudges and realise that, in the big scheme of things, it really is just about kicking a ball into a net. It really would be the best thing ever if this game of ours once more became about nothing more than goals and glory.

And yet, I knew it wouldn't take much to knock that optimism right back out of me, because every minute of every day, the whole world was going back on what it believed to be true a minute before, while reserving the right to back-flip again as new information emerged. Twenty-three hours a day stuck at home allows a lot of time for thinking, which in turn leads to a lot of over-thinking, which in turn again can make the mind go a bit flippedy-floppedy — and not just about football, either, but about every aspect of our lives, because even after a couple of weeks locked down, the physical and emotional toll was there for all to see.

The person who's happily lived alone for years can find themselves yearning for company, while the couple who longed for more time together might be in separate rooms after a fortnight of nothing else. The office worker who'd have cut their arm off for a break from the rat-race now wants nothing more than to be back on the wheel. Kids who tells mum and dad they hate school long to be back there with their pals. As for football itself, it's a bit like family; as in, we can and often do give our own a hard time, but we love them really — and woe betide anyone on the outside who dares says a wrong word about them.

So while I'm about to launch six studs at the shins of Liverpool, Tottenham, Newcastle and Bournemouth, the mega-budget English Premier League clubs who've had the brass-neck to take advantage of a Government's furlough scheme allowing them to lay staff off and claim 80 per cent of their wages from the taxpayer, I'll happily follow through into the groin of BoJo's health secretary Matt Hancock for trying to guilt individual players into taking a pay cut.

FOR any business as cash-sodden as those in the self-styled Greatest League In The World — the team finishing bottom of the table is guaranteed £100million in TV money — to plead poverty when their own fans are wondering when the next wage packet might arrive is beyond crass.

So when news broke on April 4 that Liverpool were among the clubs putting workers on furlough, I wondered what their legendary manager Bill Shankly, a product of the Ayrshire mines and a lifelong socialist who was winning league titles while living in a humble end terrace on the same street as punters, would have made of it all. Best guess, he'd have reminded the Anfield board of what the word 'need' actually means. He'd have told them straight just how obscene their financial decision-making was, for all that it was also totally legal and above board. He'd have asked how they could accept handouts when any one of their star players earns as much in a week as 200 fans on the UK average of £585 — if, that is, those fans still even *have* a job. Shankly would have earned the right to have his say on how football sees itself and the world would have hung on his every word.

But Hancock? When he took to the podium on April 2 and chucked in his two bob's worth on the issue, it was the political equivalent of an own goal from the halfway line. He said: "Given the sacrifices many are making, including some of my colleagues in the NHS who made the ultimate sacrifice...the first thing Premier League footballers can do is make a contribution, take a pay cut and play their part."

Now, no one could deny the players in question were technically able to take this cut in their stride; of the 20 teams in the division, Sheffield United's average weekly wage is the lowest at £17,500. But even ignoring the fact that Hancock is in no position to know what outgoings, debts and whatever other responsibilities every player in every dressing room has, why pick on this one category of high earners in the first place?

Why not actors, comedians, rock bands? Why not City traders or hedge fund managers or bank executives? Why not the people who run Google or Amazon or Tesco? Why not MPs with second or third incomes?

The Premier League and the Professional Footballers' Association - the players' union — were already working on a plan for a 30 per cent pay cut across the board, while the top 20 clubs were preparing to donate £125m to help support those in the three leagues below them and a further £20m to NHS charities. Besides this, plenty players were setting up their own funds to support the vulnerable. Yet a leading Cabinet figure was choosing to slap the brush in a bucket of tar and coat the lot of them from head to foot.

Anyway, maybe the ghost of Shankly visited his old club in the night, because on come Monday April 7, Liverpool — champions of Europe and the world's seventh-richest club with a £42m profit last year — reversed their decision and took employees off the furlough scheme.

In a letter to their fans, chief executive Peter Moore said: *"We believe we came to the wrong conclusion last week and are truly sorry for that. Our intentions were and still are to ensure the entire workforce is given as much protection as possible from redundancy and/or loss of earnings during this unprecedented period. We are therefore committed to finding alternative ways to operate while no matches are being played."*

Just another example of what had become ever clearer from the off; that no one, no matter their qualifications or their business acumen or their status, knows anything at a time like this. Prime Ministers, Presidents, chief executives, chief medical officers, me, you, dogs in the street; we're all just throwing ideas at the wall like spaghetti and hoping the odd one sticks, all trying to tie our shoelaces while running at top speed. Little wonder we keep falling flat on our faces. And little wonder, too, that barely into Week Three of lockdown, public confidence in those in charge was already beginning to unravel.

Thursday April 9
·100 days since the first world's recorded case.
·Global case past 1.4 m, death toll 82,100.
·Boris Johnson spends second night in intensive care.

THE show opens without its usual theme tune and dizzying graphics. Just a shot of a blonde-bobbed woman in a short-sleeved red dress sitting behind a desk, looking down at her notes. She raises her gaze to look down the lens and, without so much as a *Good Evening*, launches into an introduction that does precisely what all good journalism should. It says what so many of us in the audience are thinking but which most lack the eloquence to express.

Inside the opening 90 seconds of tonight's edition of the BBC's flagship *Newsnight*, presenter Emily Maitlis took apart the rhetoric currently being repeated by Westminster and much of the mainstream media alike that PM Boris Johnson being struck down by coronavirus proved we were all in it together, that his fight to get back to health epitomised the good old Bulldog spirit that would see us through.

I don't judge those who peddled this line. The London end of my own paper is among those using Johnson's fate as a rallying call to the rest of us to dig in, stay home and stay safe. Matlis's own BBC colleagues are amongst those camped 24/7 outside St Thomas' Hospital in South London, turning the story into a vigil. And it *is* a huge story, the PM first being diagnosed with the bug, trying to soldier on before relapsing and dialling

999.

He was taken in on Sunday night, moved to intensive care on Monday and today he's still pretty poorly. No matter what you or I might think of Johnson, it's one of *the* great sub-plots of the entire crisis. But that's all it was, a sub-plot. No matter how important Johnson is, he was merely part of the story, not the story itself — and tonight, Emily Maitlis had the guts to say so. She takes a beat to settle herself. And then she begins:

> *"They tell us Coronavirus is a great leveller. It's not. It's much, much harder if you're poor. How do we stop it making social inequality even greater..?"*

The theme tunes plays. She wishes us a good evening. Then:

> *"The language around Covid-19 has sometimes felt trite and misleading. You do not survive the illness through fortitude and strength of character, whatever the Prime Minister's colleagues tell us — and the disease is not a great leveller, the consequences of which everyone, rich or poor, suffers the same. This is a myth which needs debunking. Those on the frontline — bus drivers and shelf-stackers, nurses, care home workers, hospital staff and shopkeepers are disproportionately the lower-paid members of our workforce. They are more likely to catch the disease because they are more exposed. Those who live in tower blocks and small flats will find the lockdown tougher. Those in manual jobs will be unable to work from home. This is a health issue with huge ramifications for social welfare and it's a welfare issue with huge ramifications for health.Tonight, as France goes into recession and the World Trade Organisation warns the pandemic could provoke the deepest economic downtime of our lifetimes, we ask what kind of social settlement might be needed to stop the inequality becoming even more stark..."*

Then, once the studio guests and the filmed inserts had come and gone, she led into the closing credits with another passionate statement:

"One of the hardest things about dealing in graphs and numbers, in statistics, in flattening and rising curves is the propensity to forget the names and lives behind the death toll. Tonight, we want to remember some of those who died doing their job. They were not soldiers, they didn't sign up to a career in which they pledged to give their lives. They would not see themselves as heroes, but as ordinary members of the public, going to work at a time that demanded immense courage and kindness..."

Then she's faded out, replaced by a black screen and a slideshow of faces who never imagined that one day they wouldn't make it home from work...

Pooja Sharma, pharmacist. Kenneth Yeboah, bus driver. Kate Fox, teacher. Rebecca Mack, nurse.

As the faces come and go, as funereal strings waft, we cut to a clip from The Queen's address to the last Sunday, thanking those on the frontline for everything they're putting themselves through. Then, fade to black once more...

John Alagos, nurse. Dr Adil El Taya, transplant specialist. Donald Suelto, nurse. Julie Mott, school principal. Alice Kit Tak Ong, nurse. Alfa Sa'adu, doctor.

As the credits roll, it's hard not to fear for all those we know who are out there every day, exposing themselves to danger because we can't do without them. For me, as the last image fades, it begins to feel like my idea that our leaders aren't complicit in this crisis might be naive in the extreme.

NOT that Maitlis had been the first BBC presenter to take an on-air stand over an issue that was getting under her skin.

Three days earlier, Victoria Derbyshire had gone an entire broadcast with the phone number of domestic abuse helpline Refuge written on the back of her hand after the charity revealed a 25 per cent increase in calls and online requests since lockdown began. Refuge say visits to its website are up by 150 per cent, as forced isolation makes life worse than ever for those at risk of physical and mental abuse from partners.

Derbyshire addressed this subject on air, urging those in need to help to call the number any time, night or day. Later, she commented:

> "Two women a week were killed by a partner or ex before coronavirus, a fact that is shocking enough. Now, though, some people will be trapped with a violent perpetrator in self-isolation or partial lockdown and it's even more vital to get the helpline number out there. I'd written the number on my hand to tweet at 7am this morning and left it on my skin deliberately in case it could help any of the millions watching the show."

Again, as with the *Newsnight* intro that would follow, it was a clever way to take an issue beyond the confines of the show's audience and out into the wider world for discussion.

Both were shared globally on social media and made headlines in almost every newspaper. Plus, both were perfect examples of how increasing unwilling even key figures within a State-run organisation like the Beeb were to accept the narrative about how we were All In It Together™ at a time when millions of workers and their bosses were struggling to find out how, when or even *if* they'd be able to claim funds to tide them over — and while Westminster MPs were being given £10,000 each to help them and their staff work from home.

Before lockdown, an MP's annual budget for office costs was £25,910, or £28,800 for those in London constituencies. Now, it had leapt to £35,910 and £38,800 respectively. On top of this, the limit on their company credit cards had been increased to £10,000, though Culture Secretary Oliver Dowden was quick to point it 'isn't going into my pocket', but would simply be available to help with a 'vast increase in people contacting me about coronavirus'.

Well, call me an economic nincompoop, but quite how this increase could be quantified in financial terms is hard to fathom, as thanks to today's all-you-can-eat phone and internet packages it costs the same to send and receive 1,000 emails or calls as it does one. I'm also doubtful that many office staff working for our politicians are paid extra the more voters they're in contact with. Plus, you'd have thought an MP's costs would actually have gone *down*, since they and their staff won't be travelling for the duration.

News of this bonus for our elected representatives went down like a carton of cold vomit at a time when 1.2millon claims for Universal Credit have been made in three weeks and when hordes of the self-employed have learned they'll have to wait until June for a sniff of bailout cash.

As Sir Alistair Graham, a former chairman of the Committee on Standards in Public Life, told *The Times*: "*It seems a very crude approach. The public may be slightly puzzled as to why what looks like a generous payment has been made to MPs without a bit more research into the actual costs.*"

Or as the comedian Frankie Boyle put it with a touch less less diplomacy: "*You have to wonder if the virus is so very different from extractive capitalism. It commandeers the manufacturing elements of its hosts, gets them to make stuff for it; kills a fair few, but not enough to stop it spreading. There is no normal for us to go back to. People sleeping in the streets wasn't normal. Children living in poverty wasn't normal. Neither was our taxes helping to bomb the people of Yemen. Using other people's lives to pile up objects wasn't normal. Governments pour money into propping up existing inequalities and bailing out businesses that have made shareholders rich. The world's worst people think everybody is going to come out of this and go willingly back into numbing servitude. Surely it's time to start imagining something better...*"

REMEMBER back in late March, when Spain's leaders were under fire for not reacting quickly enough to the virus and I asked hypothetically what their critics would have done had they been faced with the same decisions?

Well, today we find this flipped on its head in Sweden, where initial feelings of pride that their Government had resisted imposing lockdown have been replaced by a ground-swell of discontent at the virus being left free to spread unhindered.

While first China, then Italy, then Spain, then Germany and Britain and even their Danish neighbours pulled the shutters down on business and education, the Swedes let life go on as near to normally as possible. Yet as of yesterday, 793 of the 9,141 confirmed with the disease had died; a rate of 7.68 per cent, as opposed to 1.46 per cent and 3.85 per cent in Norway and Denmark respectively. Even the USA's fatality rate was comparatively low at 3.21 per cent. It was as clear a case of *damned if they do, damned as they don't* as it's possible to imagine.

Swedes speak of 'a total and utter absence of panic', saying 'the streets are as busy as they would have been last spring'. Children walk to school, adults meet for dinner at their favourite local restaurant. Gatherings larger than 500 were banned from March 11, a figure reduced to 50 by the end of the month, but this was a rare concession to the pandemic, with the government's chief epidemiologist preaching a herd immunity that let the virus spread through the population until it blew itself out.

It was an approach Boris Johnson had favourited before being convinced otherwise on the basis that the fallout was still likely to overwhelm the NHS - and other Swedish experts in epidemiology had warned from the off that it made no sense because 'we don't know whether you can become immune'.

By the end of March, 2,300 doctors, scientists and academics wrote to the Government calling for stricter measures. Microbial pathogenesist Cecilia Söderberg-Nauclér said the strategy was 'not based on evidence'.

Others argued that Sweden was unique in not having many inter-generational households — as opposed to the likes of China and Italy, where elderly relatives often live with their children and grandchildren — making freedom of movement less risky. Yet even though 40 per cent of Swedish households are single-person or without children, it also has Europe's second lowest number of critical care beds, with only five for every 100,000 inhabitants, leaving hospitals vulnerable should a severe outbreak occur.

It all comes down this, though. In Sweden, the approach has always been to make suggestions and let the public decide. Governments offer suggestions, nothing is enforced. But to Söderberg-Nauclér, this was one occasion when the authorities should taken control, saying: "If you put people's lives at risk in democratic society and then you do not help them... I don't want to live in that society. But you know what? If they are right and we are wrong, I will open a bottle of champagne..."

IN Paris, meanwhile, outdoor exercise was banned between 10am and 7pm as of last night in an attempt to stem a rising tide of deaths. France has now lost more than 10,000 to coronavirus, 16 per cent up since Monday and the fourth-highest total after Italy, Spain and the US. The toll — not counting care homes — was 607 in the past 24 hours. Mayor Anne Hidalgo said the new jogging rules would make people exercise 'when streets are generally quietest', the move following a sunny weekend marked by large groups running and walking despite police having powers to hand out fines for violating lockdown.

Let's pray to all the Gods that the same decision isn't taken here.

Because right now, the very thought not getting outside to walk or cycle is my worst nightmare.

SIXTEEN days into lockdown and you're considering installing swing door on the fridge. You cut your finger with a bread-knife making a sandwich the other night and gravy came out.

The further you're removed from a long-established day-time routine, the harder it becomes to maintain a proper sleep pattern. The less you sleep, the more you wake up tired, groggy, with a head full of cotton wool.

And so begins the cycle of losing daytime motivation, of drinking too much caffeine and eating too much sugar to perk yourself up, of suffering the inevitable crash, of confusing the dehydration that follows with hunger and opening that swing door yet again. It's tough, no question. The deeper we get into this crisis, the more we all feel it. The easy option is to reach for another snack, open another bottle, to lie on the couch and binge-watch movies that morph into one big *Love Bohemian Rocketman Actually Teenage Ninja Rhapsody* blur.

Except that this 'easy' option only ever makes things harder in the long run, which is why it feels like time to start thinking beyond self-isolation and start picturing our new normal: Do we want to go back out into the world with headaches from all the coffee and the sleepless nights, to feel overweight and under-enthused and ready for a kip by 11 in the morning? Or do we want to train for it, as of right now?

For me, it's a no-brainer; as opposed to floundering about feeling sorry for ourselves, which is a dead-brainer.

See, this nightmare doesn't just suddenly end the minute lockdown does. We can't expect businesses and schools to re-open as if they'd never been closed. We can't expect sports stars and actors to come out of cold storage and entertain us like nothing's happened.

We might use the phrase that our world's been put on Pause, but it just isn't as simple as pressing a button to get things moving again. Fact is, the more out of shape we are in body and mind when the shutters come up, the longer it'll take Britain to crank itself into action and the more jobs will be at risk.

So we owe it to ourselves to give this country the best possible chance of getting back to somewhere near its best as quickly as possible — and the only way we can do it is by keeping ourselves as physically and mentally sharp as possible while we wait for the call. But even if you don't want to do it for the economy, do it for your sanity.

Right now, everyone's struggling to some extent. Those living alone feel isolated, those with families around them 23 hours a day can feel trapped. Everyone's fearing for the future, whether they let those fears out or keep them pushed down inside. In our house, we'd be chucking saucepans at each other without the chance to stay fit. Like so many couples, we've gone from ships passing in the night - Sonia running her hairdressing salon all day, me out at football and dinners and whatever else once she's home — to spending 154 hours a week in each other's company.

So every morning, she FaceTimes our pal Cheryl for an online gym session, while I either go out on the bike or for a walk. Last night she linked in with another good friend, David Smith, for his virtual pilates class. Twice a week, I teach those indoor cycling sessions via the Zoom video app. It offers us all a little bit of headspace, a little contact with the outside world, burns calories and keeps our heads more active than watching endless boxsets. There's no reason why all of who *can* do the same *shouldn't* be.

And remember, this doesn't just apply to lockdown. If you're reading this six months, a year, a decade on, it works just the same — the more we put in to keeping out bodies and mind in shape, the more benefits we'll reap in the long run.

Next time you think you need an extra biscuit, have a glass of water instead. Go decaf, or try herbal teas — and how about, if you're a smoker, trying to wean yourself off? You'll thank yourself later, both in terms of your health and the wads of extra money in your pocket.

In short, we have no choice during this crisis but to accept that most of it is beyond our control, so it's hugely important to focus on the parts we *can* influence — and our physical fitness, so intrinsically linked as it is to our mental health, is right up there as the most crucial.

Goodness knows we moaned often enough before all this that we never had the time. So now that time is all we have, we'd be stupid to waste it.

EASY for me to advice everyone to hit the fresh air, though, when I'm not the one trying to keep entire cities safe, like those trying to police the kind of halfwits we can't help breeding.

Take the scenes right now in Greater Manchester, where cops have so far broken up 660 illegal parties during the pandemic. In all, there were 1,132 coronavirus-related breaches reported in the area between 25 March and 7 April. These included 494 house parties — some with DJs, fireworks and bouncy castles — and 166 street parties, not to mention the dispersal of 122 different groups gathering to play sports, 173 more massing in parks and 112 incidents of anti-social behaviour and public disorder.

And what about this from Derbyshire, where police who broke up an 18th birthday party after a noise complaint said a guest "did not believe" in coronavirus? That's the very base level the breakdown of the connection between the public and those running the show is reaching, even just 16 days in. From TV presenters debunking stories of the Prime Minister's bravery, to the Swedes sticking their finger in their ears and going là-là-là-là- to it all, through Paris making daytime jogging a criminal offence to party animals claiming coronavirus doesn't exist, the noises aren't good.

Tonight, it feels like whatever had been holding the globe together was beginning to unravel very, very quickly.

But never fear. The repair kit would be delivered the following morning in the shape of a wonderful man with a heart the size of a planet and an ego smaller than a pea.

10: TOMORROW WILL
BE A GOOD DAY

"He didn't do it for attention. He still says thanks to every-one who gives him any. He's the best of us. When we needed a focus, someone to look up to, when we needed someone to bring us all together, along he came. Not one of us hasn't been inspired by Captain Tom Moore..."

MICHAEL BALL, BBC BREAKFAST, SATURDAY APRIL 18

Friday April 11

SONIA'S watching the Beeb when I come through to make breakfast and start writing a column. The morning news show offers the usual loop of statistics and tragedies and warnings, the kind of coverage we can normally take in little rations of ten minutes at time.

But then, they throw to a man and a story that not only could we both have sat glued to all day, but which would have the same effect on millions of us from that morning on.

A man and a story that couldn't possibly be drip-dripped through the chapters in the diary style promised from Page One; a man and a story that deserve a book all to themselves and which by the time you read this will no doubt have several been battered out at ramming speed, alongside a movie, a documentary and a prime-time TV mini-series.

The story of Captain Tom Moore really should be told over and over again, repeated down the decades and remembered forever for exactly what it was — an instant, cleansing antidote to the misery and frustration the world was mired in thanks to coronavirus.

It started with a 99-year-old retired Army officer telling his daughter he'd like to do his bit to help the NHS in its hour of need. It became an effort to walk 100 lengths of his Bedford-shire garden. - Zimmer frame and all — before his 100th birth-day on the last day of the month. Within hours of him being interviewing by video on telly today, his target of £1,000 was looking like loose change.

By the start of the week, his JustGiving page had adjusted that target to £500,000. By the time a guard of honour from the 1st Battalion Yorkshire Regiment formed a guard of honour for his final four lengths on April 16, the total was at £12million. As I write this, just before 4pm on April 28, a staggering 1,371,458 donors have taken the fund to £29,291,795.25 — and it's still climbing by £200 every single minute.

He's also sitting at No1 in the UK Singles Chart, duetting with opera star Michael Ball on a cover of *You'll Never Walk Alone* which has sold 82,000 copies to date and which leap-frogged *Blinding Lights* by The Weekend after the Canadian singer urged his Twitter followers to make it happen.

Captain Tom's been around for 31 years and a couple of longer than the previous oldest No1 artist, Tom Jones. He's made the Guinness Book of Records for this and also for being the most successful fundraiser from a solo walk. He's received so many birthday cards — more than 100,000 at the last count — that the local school his grandson Benjie attends has been opened to put them all on display. He has inspired dozens of copy-cat charity events, his image is on murals all walls across Britain, his name has been given to a police dog in the West Midlands and a bus in his home town of Keighley in Yorkshire. A petition for him to be knighted has gathered more than 800,000 signatures. He is, in short, a phenomenon.

Near the end of that first BBC interview, that first Friday morning when few outside his own household had even heard of him, Captain Moore was asked what message he'd have for the nation in its time of need.

He nodded, smiled and said: "*My message is that tomorrow*

will be a better day, even if today was all right."

THAT Sunday, I wrote of Captain Tom: *"What an attitude. What a man. If he isn't knighted in the next honour's list, there's no justice."*

Come early afternoon on Wednesday, in my column for the following day's paper, I then wrote that a tap on the shoulder no longer seemed nearly enough and that we should make him our Honorary King.

In the 20 minutes it took to write that second article on his achievements, the fundraising total rose from £6.26m to £6.31m to £6.35m. By the time the presses rolled, it was at £9.33m and by the following morning, when he was completing his walk, it was at £12m and *still* counting.

Right then, the Captain's grip on Britain was the only thing gaining more pace than coronavirus itself. Yet it was typical that his first thought was to shrug that 'the NHS deserve more than we can possibly give them'. His second thought? That was to announce that he planned to keep on walking right up until his birthday. No wonder so many people of all ages had taken to lapping their own gardens or public parks to raise money in honour of this amazing man, many of them dressed up in makeshift Army uniforms. No wonder Michael Ball sat watching the coverage that day and was struck by the thought of helping NHS charities the best way he knew how.

He decided he wanted to duet with the nation's hero.

A flurry of calls to record company, producer and agent later, Ball was putting the idea to Captain Tom himself — and their version of the song written for the musical *Carousel* but made world-famous by football fans took shape.

Ball recorded his vocals at home. Captain Tom spoke his part into his phone from his favourite armchair. In homes across the land, members of the NHS choir Voices Of Care sang backing vocals, all filming themselves in action. And so, within 18 hours, emerged a tune that was never, ever going anywhere but No1. Come the Saturday morning, Ball - unshaven, hair in full burst-couch lockdown mode — went on the same BBC Breakfast show that had made Captain Tom an icon and wept openly as he watched the finished video for the first time. In a Glasgow living room, Sonia and I bubbled too as, no doubt, did legions more watching over their tea and toast. On a neon billboard in Piccadilly Circus, the message blazed:

Congratulations Captain Tom Moore.
A National Treasure.
A National Hero.

But for me, Ball summed it all up quite beautifully in that quote at the top of the chapter: "*When we needed a focus, when we needed someone to look up to, someone to bring us all together when the nation was falling apart, along came Captain Tom...*"

"I WAS always a very practical boy. The sort of toys I liked would be a piece of wood, some nails and hammer — that would keep me happy — and I learnt very quickly that if you hit your fingers, you didn't do it again."

Very Yorkshire. Very matter of fact. Very Captain Tom. He offered that little insight into his childhood self in one of a welter if interviews as his fundraising effort began to hit epic proportions. It spoke volumes for the man he would become over the thick end of the following century.

Tom was born in Keighley on April 30 1920, his mum a head teacher and his dad in the building trade, went to the local Grammar School then completed an apprenticeship as a civil engineer before the Second World War changed everything. He was conscripted at 19 to the Duke of Wellington's Regiment Eighth Battalion under Lieutenant Lord George Saville, training a few miles from home at Otley before being moved to Cornwall to prepare for a prospect of a German invasion.

By the time he turned 21 he'd already been selected for officer training and, in October 1941, was posted with his new unit — the 146th Royal Armoured Corp - to Bombay, a six-week sea journey followed by three weeks by land to Calcutta a few months later, right at the heart of monsoon season. From there, he fought in Burma and Indonesia to push back Japanese forces and by the time it was over he'd earned the 1939-1945 Star, the Burma Star and the War Medal 1939-1945, all three of which shone proudly on his blazer every step of his fund-raising walk.

"It's important to wear them," he told one radio station. "It shows that I was part of a very important and super army at the time who were all battling for our country, which we're all so proud of."

Post-war, he became an instructor at the Armoured Fighting Vehicle School in Dorset and stayed in the Army until the 1960s, when he returned to Yorkshire as a sales manager with a roofing company and dabbled in Spanish property before finally retiring at the age of 72.

Throughout it all, he retained a passion for motorbikes, buying his first for half a crown — 12.5p — when he was just 12, teaching riding courses for his battalion in India, then dismantling and rebuilding engines as a hobby in later life. His other passion? That was his beloved wife Pamela, the woman he met when at a time when, in his own words, 'I'd given up on love'. She was 15 years his junior and office manager with a firm in Gravesend, Kent when in walked this dashing, ex-Army captain turned salesman and fell for her. He told the *Daily Mail*: "She looked terrific to me, like a model — so I had to do various trips and, shall we say, the attraction with the office manager became stronger and I eventually married her."

The couple had two daughters, Lucy and Hannah, but around 20 years ago Pamela's health began to fail and Tom began as much a carer as he was a husband. Eventually, she needed the medical attention only a care home could provide, but Tom was still visited her every single day, fed her and sat with her for hours on end.

Pamela passed way in 2004 and those days when she was ill remain the root reason why he chose to take on the challenge he did to mark his 100th birthday; this and the memory of how they nursed back to health when he was diagnosed with skin cancer and again after a fall at home left him needing a hip operation.

As he said right back at the start of his incredible adventure: "Every penny that we get, the NHS deserve. They're wonderful. Amazing. They've seen me through and they cared for Pamela. I just wanted to thank them."

IN 2008, Tom moved in with his daughter Hannah, her husband Clive and their two children at the Bedfordshire house whose garden he has now made world-famous. It was there, on the final day of April 2020 and the 38th of lockdown, that he celebrated 100 years on this earth.

A Spitfire and a Hurricane flew overhead in his honour, yet more sackfuls of cards arrived at the local school, yet more names were added to that petition demanding he be knighted. Somehow, a telegram from The Queen seemed a little mundane when placed beside all this — and it seems she even thought so herself, because come the day she also announced that his rank would be elevated to that of Honorary Colonel in honour of all he'd done these past few, amazing weeks.

Boris Johnson recorded a video describing Tom as 'a point of light'. Princes William and Harry sent letters of congratulations and thanks. Former England cricket captain Michael Vaughan sent an official team cap and declared him 'the heartbeat of the nation'.

Yet when BBC Breakfast crossed to the man of the moment, sitting in his garden the chilly morning sun and asked how he felt, his answer was typical: "It doesn't feel any different to yesterday. How are you meant to feel when you get to 100? I've never been 100 before, so I don't know how different today will be from yesterday or tomorrow. All I know is how awesome it is to have so many people wishing me happy birthday. To get a message from the Prime Minister is something special — and well done to him and Carrie for bringing another little boy into the world. I've received letters from the Royal Family, which I never, ever anticipated and I thank all of them."

And then, of course, came Michael Ball - hair and beard respectfully combed and done up for the occasion in suit, white shirt and smart tie — to lead the watching nation in a chorus of *Happy Birthday To You*.

"Tom," the singer smiled, "you have given us the most beautiful story at the bleakest of times. You're also the only person who could get me to dress like this during lockdown — this should be our look when we sing together on our Arena tour!"

His chart-topping partner smiled and laughed: "That's right — we will!"

You wouldn't bet against it happening, either.

Still Friday April 10, but in a parallel universe to Captain Tom's
·EU agrees €500billion rescue package for hardest-hit members
·Global death tool a few hundred short of 100,000
·New York begins digging mass graves for its victims

RIGHT now, Scottish football also needs a role model, someone to look up to, someone to bring it together and lead it through a crisis. It needs its very own Captain Tom. Because today is a day that, without exaggeration, could signal the demise of some of its most famous clubs.

We're talking the clubs down at the bottom of the food chain, the ones who don't get live TV coverage or mammoth sponsorship deals and whose crowds as small enough that they could have ducked under Nicola Sturgeon's ban on gatherings larger than 500.

Their plight is as perilous as it is simple — lockdown has left them in a situation where they cannot afford to sit and wait for season 2019-20 to restart. They need fellow members of the Scottish Professional Football League to agree to a proposal that would end the season today and see prize money paid out.

For some, that money could be the difference between survival and oblivion. Trouble is, though, while others around the virtual table might well have sympathy for these shoestring clubs, many also have their own reasons for trying to hang on and see the campaign out officially. These are the ones chasing titles, fighting to get into play-off places, scrapping to avoid relegation. Then there are the ones who'd be saved if the ones below then were relegated. And then there are those who — whether they'll admit it publicly or not — just can't bear to see their rivals either being rewarded or protected without having 'earned it'.

As a fan of the game, all I want to see is a new season arrive with every club still able to take part — and in an era when a 50,000 crowd at Hampden can bring in receipts of £2million and Celtic and Rangers can pay stars upwards of £20,000 a week, the amount we're talking about to make that happen isn't huge. As a fan of St Mirren, currently sitting six points clear of relegation, I'd be relieved if the season was to end and we knew we were safe. But, as already stated, I'd be dismayed if we were bottom and voted against the proposal simply to save our own skins.

For me, it's crucial that when all 42 clubs in all four divisions email their ballot papers for today's 5pm deadline, they find a way — individually and collectively — to do the right thing for each other.

But what *is* the right thing?

From day one of lockdown, I've begged football to give itself every chance of playing this season to a finish. No kneejerk decisions. Sit out the pandemic, get back to business, see out the final fixtures — and let the next campaign take care of itself. I'm not toiling to pay the bills at Albion Rovers, though, I'm not fretting over where the next wage run's coming from at Elgin City or putting off paying the Vatman at Raith Rovers.

At these and every other club existing hand-to-mouth, the option to wait and see simply isn't there any more. Some even swear their end-of-term share of SPFL cash could mean the difference between opening the gates again or not. That's why it feels like it's time to bite the bullet and declare 2019-20 done and dusted. Time to congratulate the title-winners, to console the relegated and live to fight another day. Had I been able to address every club voting today on the SPFL's proposal that this is how it should be, I'd have asked them this one question:

> What is it you're actually voting for? Your own short-term interests? Or the long-term good of the game?

The simple truth is that we can't have both. If we end the season and let the results stand, some will feel hard done by at missing out on play-offs, others more gutted still by relegation they swear they could have avoided. They'll get over it, though. They'll bounce back. Maybe one day, they'll even find the perspective to realise that there was more to life during Coronavirus than kicking a ball.

But if we *don't* end it? The bottom line is that more than one long-standing, historic institution, more than one hub of a community which doesn't have much more to look forward to than Saturday at 3pm, might *never* get over it. For them, the next bounce might just send them plummeting straight into oblivion. So, I ask again: Is your play-off place worth it? Is what division you play in whenever next season comes around really that important in the grand scheme of things?

In a simple footballing context, of course it is. In terms of a global crisis which has claimed more than 90,000 lives? No, no and no again. After all, the latest Government advice on social distancing means we won't kick a ball again until at least June 10. Medical advice dictates it will be six weeks from then before competitive fixtures are allowed. That takes us to July 22 at the earliest, with 2020-21 scheduled to kick off on August 1.

So, play-offs? WHAT play-offs? When do we fit them in — seriously, how do Inverness Caledonian Thistle and Dundee, both reported to be set against the SPFL's compromise plan, suggest they play what would amount to 14 fixtures in nine days to try and make it to the top flight?

Face it. Unless we're going to do a sponsorship deal with the Acme Tardis Company between now and then, there's no conceivable way we still hope to finish this season as hoped.

So, do we put that deal at risk for the sake of individual, short-term interests? As well as risking the lives of fellow clubs? If so, we might as well close the shutters for good.

Listen, in an ideal world we *would* hold steady, we *would* put next season off until this one was properly done. We *wouldn't* send Hearts or Partick Thistle or Stranraer down without a fight. We *would* let the top halves of the Championship and League One battle it out for play-off spots.

Then again, in an ideal world, nearly as many souls around the world as watch Scottish football on an average weekend wouldn't have been killed by this damned bug. In an ideal world, a 13-year-old South London kid's family wouldn't have been banned from his funeral because some of them had Covid symptoms. But it's not an ideal world, it's the real world.

I haven't hidden my dismay at seeing so many within what's supposed to be The Football Family™ sucked into a moral vacuum by this crisis, but it feels like today is their chance to restore some faith. Today, all 42 senior Scottish clubs have a chance to look after each other, to care for the weakest of the herd.

EXCEPT, of course, it wasn't that simple. It wasn't a case of a straight *Yes* or a *No*. In Scottish football, it very rarely is. And so, come the 5pm deadline, the proposal to give the League powers to end the season was one vote short of going through.

Correction: One *missing* vote.

Dundee, from the second tier Championship, claimed to have emailed it in time. The SPFL claimed it hadn't arrived. Hours before the ballot, word had been that Dundee were dead set against the SPFL's plan. Now, the rumour mill was roaring about them having had a rethink/been nobbled/delete where applicable. Their chairman, John Nelms, was said to be asking for more time, which most of us thought there was none us; until, that is, we were informed that by 'deadline', the SPFL had actually meant that 5pm Friday meant there were still 28 days until a final decision had to be made.

Meanwhile, just to complicate things a little more, Rangers weighed in with allegations of 'bullying and coercion' against the SPFL and calling for the suspension of its chief executive Neil Doncaster as well as house lawyer Rod McKenzie. On Thursday, the Ibrox club had tabled a counter-proposal that would have released prize money immediately without a decision having to be made on ending the season and claim contact was made regarding this suggestion at 1.43pm. The SPFL insist they heard nothing until 10.18pm and therefore couldn't put it to the other 41 clubs until this morning, but that in any case they had rejected it as 'legally ineffective'.

As a wise man once said, it's shite being Scottish.

Saturday April 11
•980 people died in the UK in 24 hours — the worst day anywhere in Europe since the outbreak began.
•All 50 US states are under disaster declarations for the first time in history.
•Pope Francis urged people 'not to yield to fear' as he led an Easter mass at an empty St Peter's Basilica.

STILL, it could have been a whole lot worse. The SPFL could have had Priti Patel counting the votes.

Today, the Home Secretary was given the job of delivering Westminster's daily briefing, her first public sighting since the beginning of March, when she'd been accused of bullying her staff. After this performance, though, the next time she's wheeled out might be the week after Prince William's daughter Charlotte becomes Queen Mother.

First, Ms Patel addressed the issue of frontline protective equipment by admitted she was sorry 'if NHS staff feel there has been a failure to provide kit for those treating coronavirus patients'.

Not, you'll note, sorry that those treating said coronavirus patients didn't have enough protective equipment to ensure their safety, just sorry if they *felt* they didn't have enough. It was one of the great non-apology-apologies.

But wait, there was more — because soon, she was moving onto the question of testing — or, more accurately, the fact that this, too, was still sadly lacking — by stating:

> "I can report through the Government's monitoring and testing programme that as of 9am today there have been three hundred thousand and thirty-four, nine hundred and seventy-four thousand tests carried out across the UK excluding Northern Ireland."

I repeat: Three hundred thousand and thirty-four, nine hundred and seventy-four thousand tests.

Or, to express the amount in figures:

300,034,974,000.

We shouldn't laugh when the subject's this grim. But as I wrote before, it's in our national DNA to rip the piss out of ridiculous people who do and say ridiculous things — and Patel's performance today was at least fiveteen trilby, three trumpet and slevery-eight percent ridiculous.

THS morning, I'd been out for a head-clearing scoot on the bike, 15 miles to Ingliston Country Club - where Sonia and I married on a wonderful Friday in May 2016 - and back again.

The weather was glorious, the roads all but deserted, the sense of freedom absolute. Thank goodness for that one break from the man-made madness of the day, because without the chance to exorcise through exercise the combination of Priti Vacant's number-wanging and the bollocks emerging from the 42-club pile-up that is Scottish football I'd have gone tonto.

For the two-teen and a quangly hours before the Home Secretary took to the podium, Radio Scotland's airwaves had thrummed to the fallout from last night's abortive vote on ending what's become known as Scottish Football Season Covid19-20. I won't bore you with what we in the trade call every cough, spit and fart; it's all way too internecine to be of interest to anyone who doesn't have a dog in the fight.

So we'll keep it to this:

•Turns out Dundee *did* tick the No box on their voting slip, but that after apparently sending it to the SPFL's email address and it not arriving, they got in touch to say they'd rather it wasn't considering even it *did* arrive.

•Their chairman, John Nelms, had gone to ground ever since, but his former chief executive Scot Gardiner, now filling the same role at their Championship rivals Inverness Caledonian Thistle, went on radio to reveal that their two clubs, plus Partick Thistle, had formed a WhatsApp group to discuss their common desire to vote against the League's proposal.

•Once Gardiner went off air to walk his dog — true story — Rangers chairman Douglas Park immediately issued a statement reiterating their demands for SPFL top brass to be suspended, claiming there had been a 'lack of fair play' and insisted they would 'not be bullied into silence'. Park claimed to have been 'given evidence by a whistleblower'.

•SPFL chairman Murdoch MacLennan told Park to put up or shut up, though not quite so bluntly: "I will be writing asking him to urgently communicate any and all information he possesses."

What a hopeless bloody shower they are.

In fact, you know what? Come three o'clock next Saturday, we should all throw open our windows and give thanks to Scottish football's elite for all their wonderful work at this time of unprecedented crisis.

They'd hear the silence all the way to Wuhan. Two minutes of tumbleweed for a clueless, classless bunch who've become a virus in their own right.

I'm not just talking here about that slow-moving and slower-thinking target we call the Blazers, the office-bearers at the SPFL and SFA who I've cemented so often down the years the words Sack The Board are programmed in as F7 on my laptop. In fact, believe it or not, I actually feel a teeny bit sorry for both bodies after the pandemic of pathetic posturing we've seen from too many of our clubs past few days. After all, when it comes down to it their main reason to exist us to carry out the wishes of the 42 clubs who employ them, so what chance do they have when those 42 appear to be splintered into about 49 different factions?

Let's be honest, though, what chance would Churchill himself have had of rallying the rabble we've become into some sort of war Cabinet?

The half-chewed cigar would have fallen from this jowls in disbelief as he watched Friday night's mirthless farce unfold, with its 5pm deadline that wasn't and its mystery vote lost in cyberspace. He'd have tuned into to the mud-slinging panto of BBC Scotland's *Sportsound* on Saturday afternoon and reckoned taking on the Third Reich was a picnic in comparison.

Then he'd have put on his most serious voice to tell the nation: "They will fight each other on the pitches...they have nothing to offer but duds, threats and jeers...bugger this for a game of soldiers."

So let's just thank all the Gods in all the heavens that it's only football we're talking about here, because if this parade of incompetents were in charge of tackling this global health crisis, we'd all have cholera and mumps as well as coronavirus. As old Winston himself almost once said, never in the field of human conflict was so much cocked up by so few.

Sunday April 12
•Ecuador's president and cabinet members take 50 per cent pay cut.
•Senior US health officials unite against President Trump's call to reopen the country.

GOD, I miss my salon, she said. My clients are freaking out about their hair, she said. If only there was a way to help them, she said.

OK, I said, why don't we make a video showing them how to look after it at home? Great idea, she said, I knew there was a reason we got married.

So half an hour later, I'm gowned up, the camera's running — and she's just started clippering the back of my head when she blithely announces: "And after this, Bill will be cutting mine!"

She might as well have told the world that after the break, her husband would be sharing his homemade recipe for a COVID-19 antidote.

Now, I'm all for learning new stuff; but generally the kind of stuff where you can afford to learn from your mistakes. Making a rhubarb crumble from scratch, teaching yourself Russian, that sort of caper. But taking scissors to your professional stylist wife's hair? Hacking at her pride and joy, her calling card? In front of literally several viewers? You don't get a second chance at *that* if you've sliced away like a drunk attacking a loaf with the wrong side of the breadknife.

Watching the video back now, I remember trying to stay focussed while she was trimming and chatting, but realising now that my face kept lapsing into the haunted expression of a gambler who doesn't have the cash to pay the heavies who'll be booting his door down ten minutes from now.

And then, all too soon, it was time.

She puts the gown on, sits down and tells the world that Bill 'only' has to separate her hair into sections like a hot cross bun, bring one strip down the middle of her back, lift the strip on each side and clip it on top, comb the central strip out while keeping it at zero elevation to her back, use his free hand to create a guideline, cut an inch — no more, mind — in a perfectly straight line, then bring the other strips down in turn, level them up against the central piece and repeat the process so you could use the ends as a spirit level. All while using right-handed scissors in his left hand.

Dear reader, the next 15 minutes were the longest 17 hours of my life and very probably of Sonia's too, because as reality bit and blades hovered, she tensed up so tight we ended up with ten fingernail-shaped holes in the fawn leather footstool her backside was glued to in lieu of a salon chair.

Snip. The first lock hit the floor.

"Well," said her icy smile, *"I think that's a tad more than an inch..."*

Snip. Section two done.

"Yesssss...definitely more than an inch again..."

So, what, do we leave the last bit longer? Call it the Phil Oakey Cut?

"No, carry on, you're doing great," is what I think she replied, *though it was hard to hear by now above the grinding of her teeth.*

Snip. Section three done. As her face freezes once more, I draw the comb down one last time. It's even. *Ish.* Few little stray strands, snip, snip. Oh, hold on, this little bit here's slightly off-line, snip-snip. At which, there was only one more snip she wanted to make; the same one you give a puppy who's trying to mount the furniture.

"Well, folks, thanks so much to Bill," she said, rhyming my name *with pandemic, "and thanks for watching."*

"And remember," I added cheerily, "if I can do this, anyone can!"

My self-isolation in the spare room is due for review roughly when C-list celebs start pretending to remember coronavirus on *I Heart The 2020s.*

SO all in all, it's been a strange old Sunday.

There was the fun of doing each other's hair. Then there was the sadness at news that former Chelsea and England goalkeeper Peter Bonetti, legendary racing driver Stirling Moss, comedian Tim Brooke-Taylor and Scottish sportswriting doyen Martin Frizzell had all passed away.

And then, there was anger, not so much from the pair of us stuck at home as from a groundswell of the nation as a collective, the ire aimed at the Prime Minister - or, more accurately, at those around him in Westminster and in the media who were portraying his time in hospital as somehow epitomising the bulldog spirit they were trying to instil in an entire nation. More and more were growling that Johnson, rather than the pandemic itself, had become the story — and more so, that the narrative of this story was one of survival being more down to his innate courage rather than the care and skill of the NHS.

In truth, though, today's front pages don't back up this anger, because those which lead on Johnson go with his gratitude to staff at St Thomas's who, he says, saved his life. Others go big instead on the shortage of frontline PPE, how we were running out drugs for our sickest patients, how demands were growing for Parliament to be recalled. Yet more and more often as sources of our opinion-forming change, a scroll through social media shows the perception to be very one of people deciding it's 'all about Boris', with plenty deciding The Media™ were in it with No10 to deflect a failure to deal with the virus.

It was the first real warning sign since the introduction of lockdown that we were drifting towards a Them and Us situation, that our leaders had used up all their allotted benefit of the doubt — and what didn't help, in the wake of Scottish medical guru Cathy Calderwood's demise after sneaking off to her second home, was news that Westminster cabinet minister Robert Jenrick had done something similar.

At first, I personally didn't see much wrong in him having driven 40 miles to deliver food and medicine to his parents, especially when he even stuck to social distancing guidelines by leaving the parcel on the doorstep then stepping back to speak to them from six feet away. But then it turned out the bit he'd chosen not to share was that before this 40-mile drive, he'd travelled 150 more from London to his own second home in Herefordshire.

The growls swelled up through the pavements, growing louder by teatime, when Matt Hancock delivered the sombre news that Britain had followed Italy, Spain, the USA and France in passing 10,000 deaths.

He mitigated the figures by reporting that the increase in cases was slowing, but this simply wasn't a day when anyone was swallowing the sugar-coating — not when Sir Jeremy Farrar, a member of the government's Scientific Advisory Group for Emergencies (SAGE), had warned that the UK was likely to be 'one of the worst, if not the worst affected country in Europe', that in comparison Germany had kept hospital admissions far lower than ours and that 'undoubtedly there are lessons to learn from that'.

Hancock responded: "The future of this virus is depends on the behaviour of the great British public."

At which the Great British Public hissed "Oh, so now it's *our* fault..."

Monday April 13
•More than 30 acts of vandalism to UK phone masts lined to conspiracy theories over 5G broadband causing Coronavirus.
•Global cases reach 1.85 million, with 114,000 deaths.
•Spain reports overnight reduction in deaths from 619 to 517.

TODAY, as Britain simmers with resentment for its leaders and the United States braces itself for peak infection, Russia is finally admitting for the first time it has a problem.

Two and a half weeks ago, while all around were panicking, the message from the Kremlin had been that 'there is *de facto* no epidemic here'. Even when lockdown was then imposed in Moscow, it was done with a shrug that suggested they'd only done it because everyone else was.

It's a different message now, though, with Vladimir Putin conceding that the situation is changing rapidly 'and not for the better' as his nation records its largest daily increase in cases; the official figure jumping by 2,558 to a total of 18,328, with 148 deaths.

Compared with other countries, these numbers are relatively low, but senior officials warn they are only in the 'foothills' of an epidemic. In Moscow, there are already signs that the health-care system is under strain. Last weekend on the edge of the city, dozens of ambulances were seen queuing to drop patients off at a hospital handling Covid-19 cases.

Today, President Putin ordered officials to make contingency plans for the 'most difficult and extraordinary scenarios' and ordered Russia to draw upon the experience of its armed forces, which have been sent to help Italy and Serbia tackle the pandemic. He added: "All the capabilities of the Russian defence ministry can and should be used here."

In Spain and Italy, meanwhile, lockdown measures are finally being eased, with manufacturing and construction among the sectors being allowed to reopen under strict safety guidelines. After close on 17,500 deaths, Spain's crisis is slowly easing, though most of its population must still remain at home. The daily number of deaths dipped on Monday, with 517 reported compared with 619 on Sunday. New infections continue to drop, 3,477 confirmed cases making the total 169,496.

"We are still far from victory, from the moment we recover normality," Prime Minister Pedro Sánchez warned over the weekend. "We are all keen to go back out on the streets, but our desire is even greater to win this war and to prevent a relapse."

However, the head of the regional administration in Catalonia, Quim Torra, said he would not back any easing of lockdown for non-essential workers, warning that 'the risk of a new outbreak is enormous'.

In Italy, 19,900 have died — the highest tally in Europe to date — but they too will allow 'a narrow range' of firms to resume operations from tomorrow, while France is expected to extend its lockdown until May 10 at least after an Easter weekend when dozens attended a secret mass. Police confirmed one priest was fined and worshippers were issued with warnings.

Easter Sunday in New York State brought 671 new deaths, taking the total to 10,056. Governor Andrew Cuomo reported that 24-hour fatalities were falling, but were 'still too high' and that their current curve was 'basically flat at a horrific level of pain and grief and sorrow'.

In the US as a whole, though, reports today suggest the peak *is* approaching, paving the way for the economy to re-open 'step by step', according to Robert Redfield, director of the Centres for Disease Control and Prevention. The United States has recorded 557,663 cases and 116,052 deaths linked to Covid-19, the highest number on both counts in the world.

It felt like the perfect time for a troubled nation's leader to step up to the plate with an address that eased fears and brought one and all together.

Unfortunately, this troubled nation's leader is Donald Trump. Over now for this report from CNN on tonight's White House press conference...

PRESIDENT Donald Trump lashed out at criticism of his handling of the coronavirus crisis during a grievance-fuelled appearance that featured a propaganda-like video he said was produced by his aides.

The appearance only affirmed the impression that some of Trump's chief concerns amid the global public health disaster are how his performance is viewed in the media and whether he's being fairly judged.

He clearly did not believe that was the case Monday. He stepped to the podium armed with a video meant to frame his response in a positive light after his initial handling of the crisis has come under increasing scrutiny. After it aired, Trump grew increasingly irate as reporters probed his response, claiming the criticism wasn't fair.

"Everything we did was right," Trump insisted after an extended tirade against negative coverage. Pressed later about his authority to reopen parts of the country, Trump delivered an eyebrow-raising statement asserting absolute control over the country: "When somebody is president of the United States, your authority is total."

He later added that he would issue reports backing up his claim, which legal experts say isn't supported by the Constitution. Before the President's extended defence of himself, Dr Anthony Fauci stepped to the podium to clarify comments he'd made a day earlier about the administration's handling of the global coronavirus pandemic, a striking show of reconciliation following a day of searching questions about his future on the White House task force.

Fauci said he was responding to a hypothetical question during an appearance on CNN's *State of the Union* program on Sunday when he said more could have been done to save American lives. He claimed his response 'was taken as a way that maybe somehow something was at fault here' and said his remark about 'pushback' inside the administration to some of his recommendations was a poor choice of words.

The episode capped a stretch where Fauci's position in the administration seemed tenuous. On Sunday evening, Trump, retweeted a message critical of comments had made on CNN along with the hashtag *#FireFauci*.

Trump shrugged off the retweet on Monday, but many media allies have fuelled calls for Fauci's departure, painting him as overly focused on the health aspects of the crisis and not attuned to America's economic suffering. Fauci, the nation's top infectious disease expert, conceded to CNN's Jake Tapper that earlier mitigation could have saved more lives and again called for a cautious reopening of the nation, despite Trump's calls to quickly restart the economy.

"You could logically say that if you had a process that was ongoing and you started mitigation earlier, you could have saved lives," Fauci said. But a day later, he sought to characterise that comment as hypothetical and not about any specific actions that could or should have been taken before Trump announced social distancing recommendations last month.

Fauci said that there were discussions among the 'medical people' about the pros and cons of strong mitigation efforts, but when he and Dr Deborah Birx, the White House's Coronavirus response co-ordinator, ultimately recommended mitigation efforts to the President for the first time last month, Trump listened. Fauci added that when he and Birx realised the initial 15-day guidelines would need to be extended, Trump listened to that recommendation as well. Fauci said: "The second time that I went with Dr. Birx into the President and said 15 days are not enough, we need to go 30 days, obviously there were people who had a problem with that, because of the potential secondary effects, nonetheless, at that time the President went with the health recommendations, and we extended it another 30 days."

Fauci's attempts to clarify his earlier comments reflected an attempt to quell speculation he was on shaky terms with the President, who has come under pressure to reopen parts of the economy quickly by some wealthy friends and economic advisers.

Trump spent part of the Easter weekend calling allies and associates complaining about recent media coverage of his handling of the pandemic, people familiar with the conversations said.

"He's been fretting about Fauci for a while," one source said. "His anxiety comes down to: 'Why isn't Fauci being nice about me?'"

IF ever a man appeared on the brink of publicly cracking up, it was surely Trump during this hour-long White House ordeal.

The crux was his insistence that, no matter what measures individual states were taking to deal with coronavirus or how and when individual Governors planned to relax lockdown, he was in total charge. His was the final say and this was simply not up for debate. Pressed by CNN's chief White House correspondent Jim Acosta, the President said: "My authority is total. It's total. It's total. The authority of the President of the United States on the subject we're talking about is total."

A female journalist went further than Acosta, saying: "You claim the authority of the President is total. That is not true."

Trump replied: "You know what we're gonna do? We're gonna write papers up on this, but it's not going to be necessary, because the Governors need us one way or the other."

With a cheery 'yup' he turned away from his questioner and pointed to someone else in the socially distanced press pack. But the lady wasn't for giving up and butted back in: "Mr President, has any Governor agreed that you have the authority to decide when their State opens back up?"

"I haven't asked anybody," smirked Trump, his self-satisfied expression at odds with the sight of his teeny-tiny knuckles visibly whitening around the podium's edge: "Because you know why? Because I don't have to."

Again, he turned away, forced a smile and pointed to another raised hand, but again, she came back at him: "But who told you the President has total authority...?"

At which he looked her in the eye for the first time, raised a teeny-tiny index finger and hissed: "Enough..."

BACK in the studio, Acosta called all over the above 'the biggest meltdown I have ever seen from a President of the United States' and went on:

> *"No reasonable person could watch what we just watched over the last hour and conclude that the President is in control.*

He appears out of control. He was ranting and raving. He was claiming to have authority that he does not have — the constitution does not give the President total authority. The President is realising that the walls are closing in regarding his handling of this crisis. He ignored its severity for a couple of months and is now trying to seize control as Governors form their own plans. One of the most trusted people in America right now, Dr Anthony Fauci, is currently talking to all those Governors, helping them formulate plans — he is working around the President for precisely the reasons we just saw unfold; on multiple levels, Trump doesn't sound like he's in control."

Tuesday, April 14

PRESIDENT Donald Trump today announced state Governors are in charge of reviewing if and when to relax and end lockdown. Trump said: "The governors are responsible, they have to take charge and do a great job. I will be speaking to all 50 and I will then authorise each individual Governor to implement a very powerful reopening plan of their state at a time and in a manner as most appropriate."

Hang on. Didn't he say last night that...ah, let's not overthink the lunatic. Instead, let's meet a gentleman called Nate White, who took to question-and-answer website Quora to reply to a post from a puzzled American who had asked: *"Why do some British people not like Donald Trump?"*

Why? Nate put it as succinctly as anyone ever could:

"Because if being a twat was a TV show, Trump would be the boxed set."

Bless you, sir.
Please accept ownership of the internet as your reward.

11: WHEN THE FINGERS POINT

Wed 15 April
·President Trump stops USA's $400m World Health Organisation payment.
·More than 70 million relief cheques to Americans delayed by several days after Trump demands to put his name on them.
·New Zealand PM Jacinda Ardern and Cabinet take 20 per cent pay cut.

FIRST the public. Now the press. Call it patience running out, call it the benefit of the doubt being past its sell-by date, call it wool being tugged away from eyes — but whatever the reason, we appear to have reached the point in lockdown where Britain has begun to ask serious questions of its leaders.

There's no doubt media outlets have been stung by last weekend's outrage at how so many people perceived coverage of Boris Johnson's stay in hospital. Maybe this has something to do with the way the editorial switch has been switched from 'onside' to 'off' in next to no time.

From left to right to centre and back again, newspapers have taken on a new and darker tone these past 24 hours. Out with the Bulldog Spirit of Boris's battle with the bug, in with the grim reality that those running the show in London and Edinburgh had underestimated the severity of the virus heading our way and overestimated our ability to cope once it got here. We shouldn't be surprised at this, of course. The clue's in the title of the book. We stumble through life, take stabs at important decisions, we bullshit, bluster, bungle and blahdy blahdy blah. The cleverest of the tribe are simply the ones who react the sharpest to the bungling and put it right the quickest. Only question is, who will these sharp ones turn out to be? Which of them will prove they've learned from their mistakes rather than compounding them?

Who'll have the minerals to admit they've got things very badly wrong, but that it's made them more capable leaders?

Because make no mistake — the deeper we descend into lockdown, the more glaring errors of judgement emerge. Today's *Guardian*, for instance, claims Britain missed three previous chances to join an EU scheme to bulk-buy masks, gowns and gloves and 'has been absent from key talks about future purchases'.

A survey by Doctors' Association UK found only 52 per cent of clinicians carrying out the highest-risk procedures said they had access to the correct gowns, while the *Guardian* says it 'understands a consignment of at least 100,000 gowns from China had to be rejected when it was found to be sub-standard', while 'other consignments were mis-labelled as gowns'.

Only yesterday did Foreign Secretary Dominic Raab, deputising for the sick-bedded Boris Johnson, acknowledge for the first time that Britain has a shortage of PPE itself rather than mere distribution issues, but insisted they were 'straining every sinew to roll them out even further and faster'.

Westminster had previously denied receiving an invitation to join the EU's procurement schemes, but it now appears three rounds of meetings had taken place before the Whitehall-based Joint Procurement Agreement Steering Committee realised the invite had in fact gone to an old email address. Even then, though, British officials were missing from a meeting on March 25 - our second full day in lockdown — where participants were invited to spell out requirements for future purchases within 24 hours. The *Guardian* reports that the UK has 'chosen not to be involved in joint procurement of laboratory equipment' and is 'yet to state its position on involvement' in a pan-EU plan on coronavirus therapies.

One district nurse in London told the paper she had being issued with three disposable masks to last a week, while a care home nurse in Devon claimed her employer only allowed staff drinks every four hours to limit changes of masks and gloves. The Royal College of Nursing has advised members they should refuse to treat patients with Covid-19 'as a last resort'.

Today's *Scottish Sun*, meanwhile, points the finger at Nicola Sturgeon's government for frontline hospital staff being forced to work without masks and gowns 'despite experts highlighting in 2006 and 2015 the need for protective equipment'. It alleges 1.5 million out-of-date masks were released to plug the gaps and that her response to the crisis 'has changed almost daily', backing this up with a timeline of the lead-up to lockdown which highlighted Sturgeon's desire to maintain a level of calm as the virus swept towards us from the Far East.

There's a part of me which genuinely respects her for the perspective she put on her public pronouncements as January became February and February became March and the pandemic became unavoidable. Throughout a frightening situation, she's offered a homespun take that plays so much better with the nation than Johnson's pretend mateyness.

And yet, I keep coming back to the Strange Affair of the Nike Conference and wondering just how hard it might come back one day and bite her on the backside.

SHERLOCK HOLMES loved nothing better than what he called 'reasoning backwards'; in other words, being shown a result and asked to work out the steps that led to it.

This Nike business would have had him in his element.

Had he been strolling along Glasgow's bustling Buchanan Street with his ever-faithful Watson on the afternoon of Thursday March 5, his eager eye would no doubt have fixed upon a sign taped to the door of the sportswear giant's store informing shoppers that it had been 'closed for cleaning and will re-open soon'.

What a chain of events the master detective would have set about uncovering from this one scrap of paper.

•The fact that, two days earlier, Nike's flagship London HQ

had also been shut down for deep cleaning after and 150 employees told to stay home in the wake of a colleague's return from an overseas trip.

•The fact that, at the same time, the company's offices in Sunderland were being shut down and scrubbed to within an inch of its life.

•The fact that, on March 1, Nike's base in the Dutch town of Hilversum had been declared off-limits after an employee tested positive for the new disease called COVID-19.

•The fact, most crucially, that this employee had attended a conference on February 25 and 26 at the Hilton Hotel on Edinburgh's North Bridge, an event which would turn out to be Ground Zero for coronavirus in Scotland, yet whose importance in our preparations for dealing with the pandemic was kept away from the public.

Holmes would have visited the hotel and learned that some Nike staff clustered together to perform a rugby-style Haka in the hotel lobby and that others were split into groups for walking tours of the Scottish capital's cramped backstreets. He would have found his way to the premises of the Edinburgh kiltmaker who kitted out ten conference delegates, but who was not warned those delegates had been exposed to the bug.

The closure of that Sunderland office would have led him to the North-East of England, where it would transpire that the area's first reported coronavirus sufferer had been at the conference and had passed on the infection at a child's birthday party. Then he would have stopped in his tracks and asked Watson a question to which he himself already knew the answer: Why *wasn't* all this made public and why *didn't* it bring forward Nicola Sturgeon's plans to halt the spread of the virus?

The answer being that the First Minister was — probably, in her own mind at least, for all the best reasons — determined to keep it all on the down-low, to minimise panic, to allow life to carry on as near to normal as possible while she and her medical and scientific advisers worked on a battleplan.

But by now, Holmes would already have moved on from musing over a politician's reasons for suppressing information and would have been meeting with the BBC team who were already in the process of putting together a documentary which would lay bare the damage done by not informing those on the fringes of the conference — that kiltmaker, a marketing company who'd been at the venue, employees of the Lloyds Banking Group who shared hotel facilities with Nike — that as many as 25 delegates had fallen ill.

This same documentary, fronted by award-winning investigative reporter Mark Daly, would also produce a report prepared by Edinburgh University epidemiologists claiming that by waiting until March 15 before banning public gathering of more than 500, Sturgeon vastly increased the chances of fatalities — possibly by as much as 400 per cent.

As ever, we don't know for sure. We *can't* know for sure. All we can do is guess and my best guess is no matter how homespun and decent a politician may be, there will always be occasions when they believe that there are some things the public don't need to know.

Maybe they're right, too. Maybe there are things going on every day of our lives that, if governments were to be open about them, would leave us terrified of our own shadows. Maybe, for all we scream for our leaders to be more honest, there are some things it really *is* better for us not to know.

But this Nike business?

This didn't feel like one of them.

As a killer virus crept closer with every passing day, as every bulletin told how neighbourhoods, cities and entire countries across the globe were being quarantined as death followed death followed death, it felt like the more we knew about the spread of infection, the better.

By deciding otherwise, Nicola Sturgeon not only took a very obvious risk with public health — after all, if the kiltmaker didn't know the Nike people they were measuring up could have been infected, how was the next customer to be made aware? — but jeopardised the very trust that homespun manner of her was designed to build, a trust then eroded that little bit more when her Chief Medical Officer was forced to resign for flouting her own travel rules.

Which kind of brings us back to where this chapter came in; the difference between the mass of politicians who continually misread the room and the rare breed who don't make the same mistake twice. Nicola Sturgeon not only got it wrong when she kept the Nike outbreak quiet, but failed to learn from this midjudgement by backing Cathy Calderwood just long enough for public opinion to force her hand on the issue.

HAVING said all of which, this is probably as opportune a moment as any to address the fact that the same accusations being levelled at our leaders — namely that haven't been tuned into what's going on at this tortuous moment in history — might just as easily apply to our newspapers. Because it would be an arrogant — no, a *deluded* — journalist who tried to argue that we, individually and collectively, will come out the other side of this crisis satisfied with everything we've written and said along the way.

If we're honest, we'll look back at very least with disappointment and, in some cases, shame at some of the judgements made in the heat of deadline as every story, from page one splash to back page lead, snowballed into one and quite simply overwhelmed us.

We — and by 'we' I mean the industry — have scaremongered at times, we've over-reacted at times and we've under-reacted at times. We haven't always chosen the right tone, the right headline, we've sometimes gone for the scary front page when maybe the uplifting one would have done our readers more of a service. But in this, we're no different to those politicians — or, for that matter, any keyboard warrior who two months ago became an instant mental health guru after TV star Caroline Flack took her own life but has now qualified as a top virologist via the University of Facebook.

We all have first-class degrees in hindsight.

Mind you, although I'm referring to my industry as an entity, it does get to me when one paper publishes something someone doesn't like and it's portrayed as The Papers™ or The Media™, like we all turn up for work every morning on one big Dr Evil-style island where some eye-patched tycoon decides the day's agenda and we write what we're told at gunpoint.

Example: Early on in all of this, a pal went on Facebook to moan about a story he'd read somewhere that he thought was a disgrace and which he blamed on The Papers™. I replied that it wasn't down to The Papers™, it was *one* journalist on *one* paper and that, while I happened to agree with him on the story in question, the fact was that — as in any job — there were good journalists and crap journalists out there. What popped up next really pulled me up sharp. A guy who knew my pal but who I didn't know personally replied with genuine outrage at the thought that not every journalist was a genius. How, he demanded to know, could this be allowed to happen? How could newspapers allow anyone to work for them who got things wrong?

I genuinely didn't know what to say to him — it had never dawned on me that anyone might regard those doing my job as being any less fallible as anyone in any office, on any factory floor or building site, as any teacher or bus driver or anyone else right up to Prime Ministers and Presidents. But after hovering over the keys for ages, it struck me that to try and explain this might make the guy's head explode, so I went and made a cup of tea.

I've never been one for trying to defend whatever paper I've worked for against criticism — and the one I've been with on and off these past 32 years gets more of it than most. I'll try and debate complaints with anyone who has the capacity to debate, while deleting anything that crosses the line from criticism into nastiness; though generally not before being stupid enough to read it and letting it get under my skin.

If there is, however, one breed of critic who pisses me off more than the angry, inarticulate and threatening kind who at least has had the courtesy to read the paper before wishing you grievous bodily harm, it's the self-satisfied, sanctimonious kind who wouldn't waste eye energy scanning anything that doesn't fit into their postage-stamp-sized world view, but who still wants that world to know how much more clued in than the rest of us they are on...well, on *everything*, really.

You know the ones. Always calling for others to boycott papers they themselves don't buy. Always posting someone else's sanctimonious guff as if it's their own then order us to SHARE THE HELL OUT OF IT BEFORE FACEBOOK TAKES IT DOWN! like they're some kind of truth vigilantes. They're crawling out of every skirting board right now, with their rants about how The Tories want us to clap the NHS while wilfully dismantling the system behind our backs. The ones posting and re-posting and re-re-posting the meme about how Boris and his self-serving Eton mafia CHEERED when they voted down a wage rise for OUR NURSES!!

They're right, of course. They couldn't be more right. Britain's inability to deal effectively with this pandemic is due in very large part — as already pointed out in these pages — to successive Governments stripping the health service back to its bare bones. But by Christ, I just can't bring myself to side with them. They're exactly what the Hide Post button was invented for.

As for the ones who give them the oxygen of shares and retweets? They're even worse, because they didn't even have the wit to steal someone else's self-satisfied mince and pass it off as their own; no, they're the ones admitting to being in intellectual awe of someone they don't know who's stolen a third/fourth/seventeenth party's lazy swing at The Right-Wing Media™, but who still crave some sort of credit by force-feeding the rest of us with it.

They might as well take a photo of some graffiti on a railway bridge and hand out copies in the street.

Yet even this lot exist in a wider circle of hell than the ones who don't even read the stupid, dangerous fakery they're sharing. They ones who warn us that, as of tomorrow, Facebook can legally take all your pictures and photoshop silly glasses and beards on and that it said on Channel 13 that the only way to avoid this breach of our freedom was to dance naked around a bowl of coyote blood while watching *Michael McIntyre Live & Disguising A Lack of Comic Talent By Being Manic.*

The same ones who, back in the days when lockdown was something that happened to other peoples in lads far, far away were telling us that they knew for sure that tanks were already on the streets of (insert name here of town at the other end of Britain from where you live) — and that to prove it, here was a picture from The Media™ that turned out to be East German troops on manoeuvres in 1984.

Whatever drives any of the above groups — the smug ones, the mischievous ones, the gullible ones and the plain thick-as-a-rhino-sandwich ones - I wish they could all have read this very, very real message posted by my pal Mark Hutton back on March 29, a week into what wasn't your common or garden self-isolation, but *total* isolation forced on him by Crohn's Disease and Hypertension. That day, he wrote on Facebook:

> *"Hello. My only contact with my wife and kids is either through the door, or on the phone. Due to my medication, I'm in the high risk category and need to shield for a minimum 12 weeks. It's heartbreaking knowing I'm so close to them but so far. Because of this, social media is my outlet, it's what is keeping me sane. So I'm asking everyone on FB/Twitter to stop posting shit and untruths as it's not helping people like me. I know how serious this thing is. Please only post or share something if you can 100 per cent verify its truth. The last couple of days I've also seen so much racist shit too. If groups of people in Govanhill or anywhere else decide not to follow the rules, it's literally their funeral, I don't need to read about 'filthy*

foreign scum' and 'send the dirty c***s back'. If it's you, and that's your thing, that's up to you, but please unfriend me, I don't need this shit right now. I don't want to shut my social media down as it's what is getting me through the day. Please look out for one another and stay cool! See you on the other side, cheers."

MARK'S one of the bravest guys I know.

We met at Glasgow Airport in the autumn of 2012, en route to a fundraising trek across the Great Wall of China in aid of Marie Curie Cancer Care, where the organisers had put us together as tent-mates and when we hit it off from the start. Mark was funny, honest and absolutely down to earth, the perfect partner for a week and a bit of grafting hard, sleeping in a field and pooing in a hole in the ground.

He also turned out to be dealing with the health issues mentioned in that post, as well as a jaw-droppingly unfair catalogue of early deaths among members of both his and wife Marie's families. On the very day we were flying out, his brother-in-law was being laid to rest after passing away from cancer. He decided to have the names of all those taken too young printed on a t-shirt, then realised there were so many he'd need to get two.

So when he wrote those words early on in lockdown, he wasn't looking for attention, he wasn't making it All About Me - he was genuinely appealing for those of us outside the bubble of his bedroom to stop and think before they shared bigotry and fallacies.

Not for us to keep their opinions to ourselves, not to spare him from the reality of the situation, just to do something that seemed to be proving very difficult for an awful lot of people at this hugely troubling time.

To think.

Wonder if it'll ever catch on?

12: GUESSING GAMES

Thursday April 16
·UK Foreign Secretary Dominic Raab announces lockdown will continue at least until May 6.
·EU Commission President Ursula von der Leyen admits 'too many were not there on time' when Italy 'needed a helping hand'.
·German schools will reopen from May 4, along with shops under 800 square metres.

WHEN the groundhog pokes a wary head from its hibernation burrow and sees a shadow, it's said to signal six more weeks of winter. When the Foreign Secretary popped up on TV at teatime today wearing his most serious face, it told the nation to prepare for three more weeks in lockdown.

And that's his best guess, because the truth is that — guess what? — guessing's all anyone has to offer right now. Britain's attempts to get itself moving again socially and economically are about as scientific as our American cousins using a stubby rodent as a weather forecaster.

In the 24 days since we first woke to the prospect of the world as we know it being closed for the duration, the UK's confirmed cases of coronavirus have risen from 8,077 to 109,769 and its death toll from 422 to 14,607.

No one seems able to tell us if this rate is better or worse than our Governments in London and Edinburgh planned for, because the deeper we sink into this crisis, the less it appears they planned for any of it. Day by day, we've waited for our cynicism to be proved ill-founded and for our leaders to show us they've got it sussed and that it just took them a while to get all their ducks in a row. But day after day, all they do is confirm all our worst fears; that they don't have much more idea about how to deal with a pandemic as you or I would in their shoes.

•Today, Dominic Raab, still deputising for the sick-bedded PM, pencilled us in for three more weeks in self-isolation.

•Today, Chancellor of the Exchequer Rishi Sunak extended furlough by a further month to take it into June, but it might as well have been the 12th of Never for all he knows.

•Today, Business Secretary Alok Sharma announced the setting up of a task force charged with the 'colossal undertaking' of finding a coronavirus vaccine, which would take 'many months with no guarantee of success'.

I don't doubt all three are doing their best, just as Boris Johnson is and Scottish First Minister Nicola Sturgeon is and all *her* Cabinet ministers are. But that's a bit like saying that if someone asked me to build a time machine, I'd do *my* best. Because I really would; it just wouldn't be near good enough.

And neither, sadly, is theirs proving to be — because three and a half weeks in, the unfortunate truth is they're struggling to get through the days in one piece, never mind finding the energy to form an actual, cohesive plan that gets us through the other side in as close to one piece as possible.

Could things have been easier on the NHS frontline had successive Westminster administrations — both Labour and Tory - not pared the system down so close to the bone that it didn't have as much as a pair of gloves spare when emergency struck? Course they could, because from Thatcher to Johnson via Major, Blair and Brown, they've all sucked the life out of our hospitals and sapped the spirit of those who work in them.

But please don't come at me with all the sanctimonious guff about those despicable swines letting us down by all of a sudden ruining a service that was the envy of the world, because we've all sat back and watched it happen for decades, yet we've kept on electing one or the other to do their worst. It was only in December that whole swathes of what used to be England's diehard socialist heartlands helped turn Johnson's minority Government into one with a majority of 80, so there's no point those same swathes now moaning that they can't get tested for the bug, because they all played their part in getting us here.

Until that changes, until we're prepared to withhold our votes from both monoliths and let someone else have a go, we as voters remain as much a part of the problem as the politicians themselves. Though there is another way...

EIGHTY years ago, MPs threw away their party rosettes for the sake of the country's future. It's time to make it happen again. Time to climb out of their bunkers, to tell the Whips to take a hike — and to start using the brains and talents that elevated them above the herd in the first place.

The 21 Tories who, back last September, rebelled to defy Boris Johnson's plans to shut down Parliament so he could shove Brexit through without dissent. Their colleagues who decided at that point they'd had enough and changed allegiance altogether, joining the LibDems or going independent.

The Labour diehards who couldn't stomach Jeremy Corbyn's cabal and who don't see new leader Kier Starmer doing enough to restore the values which made them sign up in the first place. The LibDems who still curse their leadership for being wasting the shot at glory they were handed via their coalition with the Tories back in 2010.

This is their moment to come together and form a party of unity that takes on Britain's problems Left, Right and Centre.

Sure, we might not be at war the way our grandparents were when Westminster was last run by a coalition of all ideals. But we *are* clamped in the jaws of the biggest crisis since then, one that threatens jobs and homes and even lives, a crisis that can't possibly be seen off while politicians and voters alike are huddled behind the kind of diametrically opposed viewpoints that turned Brexit into such a sorry stand-off.

Yet when push comes to shove, these diametric opposites remain our only feasible choices to lead Britain. Is that good enough? Is that *really* democracy?

Not for me.

I've long since had enough of polarised play-fight politics, enough of being Yes or No, Leave or Remain, Catholic or Protestant, of wedges driven between friends, families, communities, countries. All we seem to do these days is stagger from one unwinnable argument to the next, enabling the self-entitlement of clowns like Jacob Rees-Mogg, sprawling his lanky legs across the green benches during a crucial Brexit debate as if he owned the place, an insult not just to the chamber itself but to every single voter who, unlike multi-millionaires like him, fears losing everything if quitting Europe goes badly wrong.

He and Johnson and Gove and more keep on drawling that Brexit *has* to happen. They just haven't told us *why*. And, at the time of writing — more than four years on from the vote itself — they still haven't *made* it happen. The reason for this appears for all the world pretty much the same reason why they're not handling the pandemic very well; they're in way, way over their heads. They're all slogans and rhetoric, but very little substance. Like too many in charge around the world, they govern by soundbite.

And meanwhile, back in the real and divided world, I watch these daily televised briefings and wonder how bad things need to get before those in charge in London and Edinburgh swallow their pride and ask for some help. Apart from anything else, the fact that we only ever see Tories at the podium in Whitehall and Nats in Holyrood means that when this is finally all over, they'll be the ones who take the heat for whatever went wrong, rather than being able to say they formed that War Cabinet of all persuasions but still couldn't get everything right.

Though then again, there's every chance the opposition is quite happy to see the ones in charge out front and sweating in the spotlight.

After all, there's always another election soon...

13: THE DREAM FACTORY

COUPLE of nights ago, the former Liverpool and England footballer Neil Ruddock jumped out from a suit carrier hanging in a hotel room, tried to strangle me and forced me to kill him with a car key through the jugular.

Why a car key? Simple - they were still in my hand after I'd hammered down the M8 in lashing rain at rush-hour while unable to open my eyes.

Welcome to the fascinating world of lockdown dreams.

More vivid than ever, more frightening than ever — and the deeper we dive into this new kind of normal, happening to more of us more often than ever. Too much time spent glued to the relentlessly grim loop of bad news on telly, too much thinking time stuck inside four walls, too much of the wrong food, too much coffee, too much booze.

Maybe even too much sleep.

All of the above and way more besides — financial worries, missing our loved ones, you name it — tie our heads in knots all day, leaving the brain with the thankless task of untangling the mess at dead of night. Quite how it all manifested itself in the murder of a retired centre-back and Celebrity Masterchef contestant is way beyond me, because not only hadn't I seen Ruddock's face on telly for yonks, I can't even remember the last time I read his name.

Yet it was definitely him, all dressed in black as the zip came down on the suit-bag hanging from the wardrobe door and he lunged at me with clawing hands the size of small dogs. I can still feel the force it took to press the blunt end of the car key into his neck until the vein burst and claret sprayed and I woke up, freaked the fuck out. Thing is, I don't even *have* an old-style car key any more. My car doesn't have anywhere to stick one, just a button you press. So what car had I been driving? And why wouldn't my eyes open at *that* speed, in *that* traffic and in *that* weather?

These and a thousand questions like them are being asked right now by countless sweating, panting souls as they're spooked into clammy consciousness by the horror movies playing in their heads.

Dreams, it seems, are emerging as a major side-effect of lockdown, so much so that people who know about these things are adopting them as the subject for theses and people like me who know nothing about them are wondering what the hell's making us have them on such an industrial scale.

Over in Arizona, for instance, there's a specialist in sleep and dreams called Professor Rubin Naiman, who says the process we go through while we sleep isn't much different to what goes on with the food we eat; the guts have to work out what to digest and what to reject and so does the mind.

As a practical example, Harvard psychologist Deirdre Leigh Barrett draws a parallel between evidence gathered in an on-going survey she's involved in and dreams British soldiers reported having while in Nazi prisoner-of-war camps. Troops were starved during their waking hours, so when they finally slept their minds conjured up images of more food than they could eat. Now, in the same way, many of those she's studying appear to dream of things they're not allowed to do or have during lockdown.

Many of her subjects say they're being visited in their sleep by living, creeping bugs, which you don't need a PhD to realise represent the invisible, creeping one we call COVID-19. Others experience being engulfed by tidal waves or facing lethal injections from gigantic needles, which again are both understandable in the circumstances.

Professor Barrett's suggestion of how to deal with like this is to either turn it into art the following day or write it down in a journal. She herself recreated a recent dream in a painting called *Help, I Can't Wake Up*; a crow in a hat and black cloak uses a selfie stick while coronavirus organisms float around her like bubbles.

Why a crow? Why a selfie stick? Who knows — all I know is I love it and it fascinates me even more than it freaks me out, which is maybe why I'm currently ploughing through the 17 hour 47 minute audiobook of *The Interpretation Of Dreams* by Sigmund Freud. Trouble is, the narrator's voice is so hypnotic I can't get ten minutes into Chapter One before conking out.

Of course, one of the biggest problems with trying to journal our dreams is that they tend to erase themselves from the hard drive the second our eyes open. Prof. Naiman has a solution to this: Don't wake up all in one go.

"The first step to recalling a dream is to linger in grogginess," he says. "Upon waking, keep your eyes closed and wait for memories of the dream to resurface. Then, write down your recollections of the dream, dictate them into your phone — or draw, if that feels more natural.

"Recognise that the waking world and the dream world are inevitably connected. Bridge whatever memory you may have of the dream into the waking world. Discussing your dreams with a trusted loved one can also go hand in hand with this. It's a great time to talk about dreams."

UNLESS, of course, it turns you're not having dreams in the first place, because you can't get to sleep.

You may be walking about all day like a half-shut knife, you might get to bedtime barely able to keep your eyes open. But once your head hits the pillow, it's welcome to The Wide Awake Club.

This, as I don't need to remind an awful lot of you, is a big enough issue in peacetime, but during this period of internal and external conflict it's...well, it's a nightmare. Lockdown's messing with our heads as much during our waking hours as it is with our dreams and it's about as much fun as having a bad cough and a torn groin muscle at the same time.

Ever since the shutters came down on the outside world, most of us have had to quickly acclimatise to spending more time than ever indoors. Some have had to become accustomed to working from home every day, others have been unable to work at all, but whatever the circumstances our lives have been transformed in a major way.

One of the biggest factors in this is that millions no longer have to wake up at a certain time to get to our job or to school — and the result is that word Professor Naiman used: Grogginess. You see it all the time on social media, posts asking if anyone else is constantly groggy and sluggish, if it's just the poster whose sleep cycle has been ruined. Many say that even if they *do* sleep, they wake up still tired.

The medical term for this grogginess is *sleep inertia*, a phase in between sleep and wakefulness which leaves us with difficulty thinking clearly, disorientated and clumsy. It's no fun.

Matthew Walker, professor of neuroscience and psychology at the University of California and author of *Why We Sleep*, compares the way in which a brain wakes up to an old car engine, saying: "You can't just switch it on and then drive very fast. It needs time to warm up."

Professor Walker says reasons for this inertia include sleeping at a time that doesn't suit your chronotype — night owl or early bird — not sleeping long enough, not enough good-quality sleep or an underlying issue such as sleep apnea, a breathing disorder that commonly results in snoring.

While these reasons may indicate why a person is experiencing grogginess on an occasional or even a regular basis, it's not as clear why so many feel so groggy during lockdown —- though Colin Espie, Professor of Sleep Medicine at the University of Oxford, points to two key reasons:

"The constant influx of news regarding Covid-19 is probably

*putting many people in a state of high alert and feeling a
sense of helplessness, which may be energy-sapping. Good
sleepers don't even think about it when they go to bed, so don't
force it, just accept it; you're struggling with sleep tonight,
so get out of bed, go to a different room, read a book in dim
light or listen to a podcast and only return to bed when you're
sleepy. This isn't the time or place to figure stuff out. This is
the place to get respite from the day and get your recovery
sleep so you're ready for the next day. Then there's the fact
that daylight is the main biological signal to alertness, so lack
of exposure to ambient, or outdoor, daylight makes us feel
less alert. As we approach the sleep period, we get a spike in
the hormone melatonin which is expressed during sleep, just
prior to sleep and during sleep. Melatonin then reduces its
expression towards the morning and is switched off by light,
so if people are not actually getting exposure to light in the
mornings as they normally do when they go to school or they go
to work, there's a likelihood that they will be more sleepy come
the mid-morning. External light is hundreds of thousands of
lux, but even bright light indoors is probably only a few hundred. Our eyes adjust so we don't necessarily realise how dark
it is compared to outside. I think that's a major part of it."*

Yet there we are. Even such an expert in his field only thinks
he knows, rather than knowing for sure.

As for Dr Natasha Bijlani, a consultant psychiatrist at a Pri-
ory Hospital in London, she believes the stress of lockdown is
the other big player in all of this, saying:

*"We find ourselves in unprecedented uncertainty as we
process the implications of all aspects of our lives. Most of us
will be feeling a degree of anxiety, even if it is at a low-grade
background level and it is likely to affect the quality and duration of our sleep. We know that when people are anxious, the
depth of their deep sleep isn't as deep anymore, so when you
are anxious the day before, it usually leads to worse quality of
sleep that night and unfortunately it's a vicious cycle."*

◆ ◆ ◆

SO back to the dream factory, where I've been having a couple of recurring belters since long before coronavirus starting messing with our melons; one where I'm covering a really big midweek football match but my fingers can't work the keyboard or dial the gaffer's phone number, the other where I'm on a holiday with pals that seems to go on forever, only for me to realise when it's time to pack that I've brought absolutely everything from home. The reason for the first one seems pretty obvious, giving my history of anxiety harnessed to the relationship issues (see Chapter 2, there'll be a quiz later) I've been having with football, but the bit I don't get is why it still keeps happening at a time when there's no football to go to.

The dream goes like this...

> I'M in the press box of a huge, packed stadium. I don't know who's playing or who's around me, everything's just shapes. All I know is that there's just been a last-gasp goal that means rewriting the match report in five minutes and I just can't do it. My fingers are sausages, the laptop keys smaller than a baby's fingernails. I try and phone the office to beg for more time, but can't dial. Then the gaffer phones me, shouting about how I'm holding up the presses, but I can't seem to answer him. And on this goes, me not able to type or dial, them phoning and yelling, me unable to speak. The fans have all gone home, the shapes around me have sent their reports and. Are packing up and going home and I'm trying to ask them for help, but they're all ignoring me...

Sometimes, it comes with a different Director's Cut...

> I TURN up at the stadium, get to my seat in the press box, plug all my gear in, then go for a cup of tea only to find myself back outside in the street. Next thing, the floodlights are miles away in the distance and I'm trying to get a taxi to take me back, but the driver can't find his way. Again, I try to phone but can't dial. Again, the gaffer phones and yells...

So, sure, either of these are easier to compute than the footballer, the car key and the spurting jugular. But the other one I've been having for years now is totally beyond me...

> IT'S some kind of holiday island. We have to take a ferry to
> get to it, then a bus. Or sometimes jeeps. I'm there with loads
> of pals from different parts of my life, staying sometimes in
> rooms, sometimes in beach huts. There's a main strip of bars
> and restaurants and nightclubs that sometimes I recognise
> from real life, sometimes not. But the constant is that the
> holiday lasts an inordinately long time and, while all the
> others are having an absolute ball, I'm constantly miserable,
> constantly trying to get their attention to tell them I want
> to come home, but forever arriving where they're meant to
> be only to find they've gone. Then, finally, it's the last night
> and I decide to go out and have some fun, but everyone else
> has stayed in to pack. By the time I get in, there's hardly any
> time before the bus/jeep/ferry's leaving and it turns out I've
> furnished my room/hut with every one of my possessions —
> all my books, DVDs, CDs, sofas, tellies. So I'm trying to cram it
> all into one holdall while everyone else is already on the bus/
> jeeps/ferry, joyously oblivious to my blind panic...

Despite none of us going further than the supermarket right now, I'm still having that one. There's no logical explanation to it, or as to why most nights I get vivid images of the house we lived in from when I was ten through until my early 20s. Or to last night's back-to-back feature performances, in which first everyone in the world was shouting so damn loud to get their theories on the virus heard that the sky turned blood red and engulfed us in a nuclear explosion and then Australian cricket legend Shane Warne had a sex change and came onto me at a party while Sonia went room-to-room asking where I was.

Never a professor of psychology around when you need one, is there? However, there *are* always plenty of friends going through the same weird night-time experiences and who were happy to share them.

This is their contribution to lockdown history...

Rikeera Kaur, children's worker*:*

"I'm responsible for 40-50 tiny kids, in a house full of hazards like no bannister on the staircase. I went kayaking on the canal at Maryhill, the water was clear and turquoise. Lockdown was lifted and normal life just resumed, except that I was walking with my arms out wide, shouting at people not to stand so close to me on the London underground. Usually I forget dreams quickly, but during these times they've been way more vivid in terms of the emotions I feel within them. In one, I went on a Spin retreat with loads of other women. We shared a dorm, maybe 15 of us, but I was coughing in my sleep, everyone else freaked out and said I had coronavirus and chucked me out. I had to stand outside on the street on my own, waiting for someone to come test me. I was protesting that there was nothing wrong with me, whilst drenched in sweat and coughing and grudgingly phoning work to tell them I wouldn't be in, so they also fell out with me."

Marie Clark, adult learning tutor and children's storyteller:

"Most of mine have been based on my flat being broken into. I've had it nearly every night, always with the same pattern. Having looked it up, it seems to dream your house is broken into suggests that you are feeling violated and may refer to a particular relationship or current situation in your life; I suppose the current situation violates my freedom. Separate from dreams, I've also taken to eating things I remember from

childhood — like salad cream. I've not bought it for years, but now I have it on a roll with ham and tomato. My granny, who died when I was 13, used to make me that. Maybe I find it comforting."

Susan Batchelor, lecturer and indoor cycling instructor:

"My most memorable one was inspired by a clip from Pasolini's retelling of The Canterbury Tales, which I saw on Mark Kermode's Secrets of Cinema. All I am prepared to say is the original clip involves Satan's ass and some friars..."

Jocelynne Togher, personal trainer and beauty technician:

"My 11yr old daughter had a dream that we all had to be shrunk in boiling water and packed in vacuum bags to beat Coronavirus. She could sell that to Trump..."

Paul Murphy, personal training company owner:

"I was running in the woods and a guy with a face mask on kept catching up with me and jogging alongside me. This was right at the start of the lockdown. I stopped watching the news before bed after that..."

Ruth Burns, international philanthropist:

"I woke up with hubby lying next to me in a bad mood, because he'd a dream where we were at the beach, I disappeared and he was surrounded by families. He moved in case I couldn't see him, but when he finally got back to where he'd been he found me watching two guys doing magic — when I told them I'd see them later, he shouted: 'Will you f...!' Hence the grumpy face..."

Sonia De Rosa, hairdresser and my amazing wife:

"I dreamed that Jesus came to me and he had the crown of thorns on his head, he looked very serene, not hurt. I also had one with two cockroaches in it. They didn't do me any harm - I think maybe they appeared because just before going to sleep we'd been watching a show where one of the characters was talking about having cockroaches in his apartment. My favourite one is about flying — it starts with me walking, then running and then I go up into the air. The weather's lovely and I can see everything below so clearly, nothing bothers or fazes me. It's such a wonderful feeling."

Renata Szilagyi, lash extension specialist:

"In on dream, my mother was trying to make me feel bad about something I did regarding my children. She was being bossy, we had a big fall out and she started to explain she was the nearest person to God and had the right to control everything. She's very religious and can't accept that I am not. I woke up feeling very angry. Another dream, I think, has to do with the fear of not being able to protect my children, which is weird as in real life I'm not the worrying type. We were sitting in the living room when I saw a lorry and I realised it was going to overturn and crash through our window. I tried to move my oldest, who was sitting next to me, but couldn't reach her in time and next I saw her lying under the truck. I was scared but lifted it up and got her out. Her face was smashed in, but then it turned back to normal. The night after I went out on my bike and fell off, then dreamed I had a big cut on my thigh. I tried to fix it with transparent plasters, because I didn't want it to be sewn up and ugly. My mother started to sew it, but I was worried because I knew it wouldn't look nice if she did it. Then when I looked, it was almost invisible."

Allan Preston, broadcaster and ex-professional footballer

"I was in a packed pub in Leith called Wilkie's watching England v Italy on TV with some Fife lads but there was a group of casuals in who I knew wanted to fight them, so I sneaked them out just as Paul Walsh — why Paul Walsh?? - scored for England. The Fife lads gave me a lift home in a VW camper van and my neighbour was in my garden, swinging in a hammock. Lockdown dreams have been been weird, crazy and sometimes frightening — I've had that mad one a few times where you fall off a bridge and wake up shouting."

Karen Roberts, hairdresser, basketball player and coach, single mum of four:

"I had a really vivid dream about a massive tiger who talked to me. It was like a cross between Dumbo and Tiger King - I'd only seen posts on Facebook about the show, so I'm guessing the comments planted something in my mind. Plus, I did have a cheese toastie that night, which may have made the dream stronger. The tiger kept on teasing people and giggling and they had no idea what he was saying or what he could easily do, but all I could do was laugh."

Sheena Armour, accountant and indoor cycling Master Trainer:

"I have a recurring dream about a spider that's living in my throat, then bites me and I wake up bolt upright, struggling to breathe."

Elaine McDonald, Health and Social Care Worker:

"I was at home with my family. We couldn't open the doors or windows. We didn't have any keys and I never figured out where they were or who locked the doors and how. There was what seemed like a cat flap but we didn't have pets. A van *would come round someone would put food through the flap in takeaway containers. When we finished, we put the container back through the flap. The weirdest thing was that in the dream it didn't feel like I was living in the present, but in the future."*

David Winnie, sports business lawyer and ex-footballer:

"I'm a sniper in a dusty hillside wasteland and I've got my sights set on a bus full of people winding it's way around the mountainous road. Feels seriously weird. It's really clear, too. It's like I'm in some dusty Afghan hole and I can see the bus winding it's way round the hillside. Maybe it's trying to get rid of fears/enemies/issues from a safe distance."

Georgia Leckie, biology student and world's No1 daughter:

"I'm at a funeral and someone kills themselves. I'm being attacked at the supermarket where I work part-time, or I'm coming home only to realise I'm meant to be still there, or that young kids are outside my flats, making fun of my uniform. There's also a lot about loss, about death and destruction. I find all this Covid-y stuff really interesting."

Jim Rankine, recruitment consultancy owner:

"My wife Lorna was shaking in her sleep and shouting no, no, get away...then shouted for me to call the police. She went back to sleep, then five mins later shouted 'that's because you were talking s***e about everybody' followed by more shaking and cries of 'no, no, no'. Later, she said her dream was about work — she's just been laid off because of lockdown as a cabin attendant with EasyJet — and a male passenger tried to attack her. Brave boy..."

Collette Neill, singer and vocal coach:

"I'd gone into a school, maybe to collect my niece. While I was waiting I found a lost wee boy. Matt Smith from The Crown and Dr Who was the teacher. Somehow the school became some kind of lab facility you'd see in Resident Evil. I'm presuming some crazy disease got loose, because people started changing, zombies-looking folk started appearing and I was having to run and hide with the wee boy and try and find a weapon whilst protecting him. Then Matt Smith appeared again, but like a crazy navy seal all in black and gave me a gun. Then I became a crazy action hero. I watched a bad scientist guy get eaten or infected and that was horrific, then had to try and find a way out and shoot all the infected zombie people. Was glad to wake up…

14: IT ONLY HURTS WHEN I LAUGH

Saturday April 18-Tuesday April 21
•Spanish death toll passes 20,000, UK hospitals deaths at 15,000.
•New Zealand PM Jacinda Ardern promises to re-open country after one more week of lockdown.
•Vaccine trials to begin on Thursday at Oxford University.

SOMEWHERE deep in the heart of what we might chuck a blanket over and describe as Redneck America, there's a dude driving round in a pick-up truck adorned with the Star-Spangled Banner, a Confederate flag and the hand-painted legend:

NO YOU'RE RIGHT'S.

It's been cruising in Barfbucket, Louisiana or Spitoon, Texas or wherever its owner's trailer is parked for the moment, a quite outstanding totem for the anti-lockdown protests spreading across USA in the wake of President Trump's latest tweet hobby horse, howls of *"Liberate Michigan!"* and *"Liberate Minnesota!"* after citizens of both took to the streets to demonstrate against ongoing self-isolation regulations; tweets he then followed these up with one roaring *"Liberate Virginia"*, though this was more about its governor demanding stricter gun controls, snowflake, peacenik, flag-burner that he is.

Trump's intervention — which I like to think, as with all his social media outbursts, was made while parked for hours on a White House loo, straining to evacuate several kilos of compacted Bacon Cheese McWhoppers — was the catalyst for numbers to grow on the streets of Michigan and Minnesota, as well as for fresh demos in Texas, Maryland and Ohio.

Many of those involved wore masks, but the way football hooligans wear them to avoid identification and/or tear gas.

They carried placards with felt-penned messages such as THIS IS AMERICA, NOT NAZI GERMANY, though shots of a group brandishing swastikas and nooses as they tried to storm the state capitol in Lansing, Michigan kind of blurred those lines.

Right-wing trappings aside, though, most of those involved seemed genuinely scared of what lockdown was doing to the economy, both local and national. In the past week, 5.2 million Americans have registered as unemployed, taking the total since mid-March to 22 million. The £349 billion set aside to help small businesses has evaporated already. Two-thirds of Americans are said to be worried that the Government will lift restrictions too soon and be responsible for a second wave of infection; but it stands to reason that anyone who believes this is unlikely to take to the cobbles to make themselves heard.

So, in a country where conspiracy theories are more of a way of life than anywhere else on earth, it was left to a small but loud and seemingly bright-as-a-blackout minority to express the opinion that the decision to keep them stuck at home and their workplaces closed isn't for their own protection, but through some sort of oppression: You know, like somehow the people who run their cities and states want the economy to tank and for them to go back to the Great Depression days of eating dust and living in shacks made from possum pelts.

This minority harbour a simmering denial of scientific and medical advice on how to cope with the virus, with plenty doubting it even exists — witness the crowds outside the Texas state capitol, faces uncovered and flaunting social distancing as they demanded the immediate firing of White House chief medical officer Dr Anthony Fauci, as if this was all *his* fault for drawing attention to the fictional virus in the first place.

Trump's mixed messages — there's nothing to worry about but it's an emergency, my authority is absolute but states are in charge of their own affairs, stay home but get out and fight for freedom — certainly don't help. When Michigan governor Gretchen Whitmer described some of those milling outside her HQ yesterday as embodying 'some of the worst racism' in the nation's history, for instance, the President tweeted that they were 'very good people'.

Amidst calls from protestors to 'lock her up', Whitmer, a Democrat whose policies during a crisis which has claimed 1,900 lives in the state have 71 per cent support, said: "We know people are not all happy about having to stay home — and I'm not either. But we must listen to the experts. These demonstrations are how how Covid-19 spreads."

Tell that to the crowds in Columbus, Ohio, who gathered on the town hall steps to express their individuality by chanting 'We Are Not Sheep!'

More to the point, tell it to Johnny Pick-Up Truck as he cruises round town, his Confederate emblem blowing in the wind. Because there's a man who *really* No's Hims Right's.

NORMALLY, I'd laugh at the awesome lack of intelligence and self-awareness that not only allows anyone to publicly flaunt such a dumb-as-dogshit message, but also prevents those around him from being able to point out that he'd mis-spelled the only three words the world would remember him for.

But today, it hurts too much. Because today, I came off my bike; cruising at 22mph one split-second, into a pothole the size of a council swimming pool the next, up and over the handlebars and whumping onto the tarmac. Thank goodness for helmets that can take this kind of impact flinching — not to mention for roads being pretty much traffic-free right now — or this might be quite literally being ghostwritten. Call it one of those moments that reminds us how quickly life can change, from happy as Larry to as dazed and confused as Davy and Carol the next.

As I write this, it's the evening following an afternoon when

Sonia had driven the ten miles from Glasgow to Kirkintilloch to pick up me and my tangled wheels and give me Coca-Cola and sweets to deal with the shock that I didn't even realise had kicked in yet. An afternoon when I'd winced at the sting of a hot bath laced with Dettol, when I'd had a bacon sandwich — four out of five doctors recommend nothing else for cuts and bruises — then gone for a sleep punctuated with flashbacks to the crash, except that each time my mind had a car speeding up behind me and everything going black.

My right knee has a decent gash across the site of February's op, the shin already starting to turn a pleasant shade of lilac. Both elbows are skinned raw and my tights, top and gloves are shredded and in the bin. Yet it could have been a whole lot worse, those flashbacks might have been the real thing.

I was still trying to peel myself off the road a woman in a hired van who stopped and asked if I needed her to phone an ambulance. When I said no thanks, she said she'd have offered to get out and help me up, but...at this, she made a sign as if to say: "I would if I could, but this situation..."

Soon after, my pal Stuart McGregor - who lives a couple of hundred yards along the road - pulled up opposite and asked if I needed to go to hospital. When I said no, he said he'd have taken me back to his house to clean up, but...

I tried to get an Uber, but none were open for business. I rang Sonia to come and get me, only to realise with sinking heart that she'd need to bring my car as hers is a two-seater, but that my keys were in my pocket because I'd needed something out of the car that morning and couldn't be bothered going back up to the flat to drop them off again. So now we were trying to remember where the spare set was and...

Actually, hold up. It's just hit me — not quite as hard as the tarmac did, but firmly enough — that I'm maybe going into quite a lot of forensic detail here about what was, after all, just a guy falling off a bike.

But I do so because, right now, this is what matters most in my life — and because all over my city, this country, the whole world, there are people for whom little things that mean nothing to anyone else are all that matters to *them*. Maybe their sink's blocked, their baby's teething, they can't find their car keys, they've forgotten the most important thing they went to the shops for or any one of a thousand other annoyances; all these kitchen sink drama irrelevant in terms of the over-riding problem facing the planet, but all of them, in this moment, still the only thing their brain can focus on.

This isn't something any of us should be ashamed to admit to. It doesn't make us cold or unfeeling if, now and again, coronavirus isn't uppermost in our minds. Particularly if we happen to be suffering from any illness apart from it. For instance, while I refused that nice lady's offer of calling an ambulance, a check-up at A&E is probably advisable. But two things stop me — the thought that hospitals are already over-run without twonks coming in with self-inflicted wounds and the fear of picking up the bug in there and passing it on to Sonia.

And I'm wondering now how many others who've tripped and fallen on the pavement, taken a tumble down the stairs, sliced their finger making the dinner, sprained an ankle jogging or who simply feel crap are also putting off a visit to the doc or the emergency room. Worse, I'm wondering how many people with more serious health problems are scared to reach out for fear of being a burden on the NHS in its toughest hour. Already, more than three million non-emergency operations have been cancelled to free up beds for the expected peak of Covid-19 cases.

In logistic terms, this makes perfect sense.

In economic terms, it's estimated that it could cost £3billion in surgical and nursing cover to catch up with the backlog once this is all over.

In human terms, it's causing untold psychological pain as well as physical pain.

As the president of the Royal College of Surgeons in England, Professor Derek Alderson, put it:

"The consequences are really serious. There are patients who have cancers that are usually slow-growing, but this may impact on long-term survival. A patient's condition may deteriorate so they are no longer fit for the operation. Someone may be waiting for a hip replacement, not be able to exercise and become even less fit for surgery. They may become addicted to opiates to manage their pain. And this is only the physical side. There are still mental health consequences to consider."

This brings to mind my spin buddy Ewan, whose treatment for the blood cancer Myeloma including a major procedure at the turn of the year which was meant to see him return to Glasgow's flagship hospital, the Queen Elizabeth, every day for the following few months.

But now, the risks of him catching a bug are through the roof, so all he can do it sit at home and hope for the best. He's allowed out for his hour a day, but in his case social distancing means being more like 20 feet from strangers than six.

Even in the relatively minor case of my knee getting cleaned out, the consultant's had to cancel all follow-up appointments and the same goes for the fortnightly physio sessions that had been pencilled in. This hasn't been a hassle, because everything's healed double-quick and — up until that pesky pothole reared its sneaky wee head — the leg's never felt better.

But it might easily have been a whole lot different. And it *is* different for so many around the world whose ailments have been relegated to side-issues because of the virus, even though many are suffering far more than most who've caught it.

It will be the blackest of ironies if they're left to suffer while oceans of emergency beds in makeshift coronavirus hospitals lie empty.

Sunday

TODAY'S *Sunday Times* will have made Boris Johnson's break-fast eggy soldiers stick in his throat. They've given him and his government a right pasting, its front page and two inside accusing them of 'losing five weeks in the fight to tackle Coronavirus' after 'ignoring warnings from scientists'.

They quote anonymous whistleblowers — one from within No10 itself — as well as scientists and emergency planners as calling the Government 'complacent', of failing for years to prepare for a potential pandemic and of allowing stockpiles of personal protective equipment to run out of date.

And at the core of all this, the paper claims, is the Prime Minister's half-hearted attitude to the threat.

Before the end of January, scientific advisers were warning that the virus had a comparable infection rate to the 1918 Spanish flu that killed 50 million people. By late February, they were estimating that the UK could suffer 380,000 deaths without urgent intervention and recommended a lockdown to stop the disease spreading. Yet it was almost a month before ministers acted, allowing it to embed itself in the population. It quoted a senior Department of Health insider who attended preparation meetings in February as saying: "I assumed we weren't worried, because we did nothing. We just watched."

The report claims that in January and February, the PM failed to attend any of the five virus summits at COBRA - the Bond villain-sounding body that's actually an acronym for Committee Briefing Room A - and also spent 12 days out of the public eye on what he described as 'a working holiday' at a grace-and-favour mansion in Kent, leaving Health Secretary Matt Hancock to take his place.

This weekend, Hancock is under severe pressure after NHS Providers, a group representing England's healthcare trusts, warned that stocks of medical gowns and lab coats would run out within 48 hours. The Sunday Times *reports that the government failed to make 'meaningful contact' with British PPE manufacturers.*

The British Healthcare Trades Association, an umbrella of almost 500 companies, said it had been ready to supply PPE for the past two months, but it wasn't until April 1 that its offer to help the NHS was accepted. Meanwhile, British suppliers had been sending PPE overseas to make ends meet and, by late February, the Government itself had answered a request from China for 266,000 items, including 37,500 gowns.

The Downing Street adviser who spoke to *The Sunday Times* said PPE stockpiles had been allowed to deteriorate during the years of Tory-led austerity, that planners had been diverted to prepare for a no-deal Brexit and that Johnson's lack of leadership in the early weeks of the pandemic was there for all to see.

"There's no way you're at war if your PM isn't there," the adviser said. "Boris didn't chair any meetings. He liked his country breaks. He didn't work weekends. It was like working for the chief executive of a local authority 20 years ago."

The body representing 110 UK diagnostic test companies claimed the Government failed to seek help with coronavirus testing until April 1, the night before Hancock announced a target of 100,000 tests a day by the end of this month.

As the paper went to print, a No.10 spokesman said: "The Prime Minister has been at the helm of the response, providing leadership during this hugely challenging period for the whole nation."

AT lunchtime on January 24, Matt Hancock emerged from chairing a meeting to tell reporters the risk to the UK public was 'low'; this despite a study in *The Lancet* that same day in which Chinese doctors suggested for the first time that the virus was comparable to the Spanish flu pandemic which had killed up to 50million in two waves 102 years before.

Five days later, the first coronavirus cases on British soil were found when two Chinese nationals from the same family fell ill at a hotel in York. The day after that, the Government raised the threat level from low to moderate. The PM had been missing from that Friday lunchtime meeting, yet he found time later that day to join in a Lunar New Year ritual as part of Downing Street's reception for the Chinese community, led by that country's ambassador. It was, as the report reminded us, a big day for Johnson because the withdrawal treaty from the European Union was finally being signed in the late afternoon. That afternoon, his spokesman reassured the nation that we were 'well prepared for any new diseases'.

On December 31, when China first alerted the World Health Organisation to several cases of 'an unusual pneumonia' in the 11m-population city of Wuhan, the PM had been in Mustique with his pregnant fiancée Carrie Symonds.

In the time it took to hold those first five COBRA meetings as the UK slowly came to terms with the threat, he had dealt with flooding across the UK, reshuffled his cabinet and gone away to a country retreat with Symonds. By then time he finally took his place around the table, on March 2, the virus had already wormed its way deep into Britain's infrastructure.

On January 31, two days after those first UK cases were reported, Johnson made a rousing 11pm speech to make our official withdrawal from the European Union, calling it 'the dawn of a new era, unleashing the British people to grow in confidence month by month'.

Those with their eye on the ball thought differently, not least the World Health Organisation, who had the day before declared coronavirus a global emergency. Then there were Westminster's teams of contingency planners, who reminded No10 that its last rehearsal for a pandemic — a 2016 exercise codenamed Cygnus - had predicted the NHS would collapse and highlighted a long list of shortcomings, including a lack of PPE and intensive care ventilators.

According to the *Sunday Times*, a list of recommendations to address these deficiencies was never implemented and preparations for a no-deal Brexit then 'sucked all the blood out of pandemic planning'. During 2019, Government pandemic planning meetings were repeatedly 'bumped' to make way for discussions about issues such as the beds crisis in the NHS.

Members of the advisory group on pandemics are said to have joked among themselves that there had better never be one, as 'there wasn't a single area of practice being nurtured in order to meet basic requirements, never mind cope well'.

The paper's Downing Street source claimed: "Almost every plan we had failed to be activated in February. Almost every government department has failed to properly implement their own pandemic plans. There was, for example, a failure to give firms early warning that there might be a lockdown so they could start contingency planning. There was a duty to get them to start thinking about cashflow and their business continuity arrangements."

WHEN Steve Walsh, a 53-year-old businessman from Hove in East Sussex, was identified as the source of the second UK outbreak on February 6, all his contacts were followed up with tests. Walsh, who'd returned from Singapore, is believed to have passed the virus to five others in the UK plus six overseas.

This, scientific advisers said, should have been the model from then on; when one person is infected, check everyone they've been in contact with — and, from there, restrict mass public contact as much as possible to slow the spread.

Trouble was, the Government was still working on the principles used to deal with the country's annual flu outbreak, where once the virus invades the population, it's allowed to take its course until the onset of 'herd immunity' — that is, once we've all had it, the danger's seen to have passed.

This, to be fair, is pretty much what I'd thought in the early weeks of the year, when this was all someone else's problem.

I'd been one of those convinced that flu was flu and, as with every wintertime, we'd either be lucky and avoid it or unlucky and catch it. But I'd like to think that if I'd had a team of scientific whizzes looking over my shoulder while I was writing that the delete key might have taken a battering.

Devastatingly, it seems despite having this expert support at its fingertips, Downing Street chose to clatter on regardless. As one senior politician told the *Sunday Times*: "Conversations at the end of January were absolutely focused on herd immunity. With flu, this is the right response if you don't have a vaccine and all of our planning was for pandemic flu.

"There's basically been a divide between scientists in Asia who saw this as a horrible, deadly disease requiring immediate lockdown and those in the West, particularly the US and UK, who saw this as flu."

Doris-Ann Williams, chief executive of the British InVitro Diagnostics Association, representing 110 companies that make up most of the UK's testing sector, told the paper they didn't receive a 'meaningful approach' from the Government until April 1 - to repeat, the night before Hancock announced his target of 100,000 tests a day by the end of this month.

The NHS could have contacted UK-based suppliers. The British Healthcare Trades Association (BHTA) was ready to help supply PPE in February but, again, it was only on April 1 that its offer of help was accepted, its chief executive Dr Simon Festing saying: "Orders undoubtedly went overseas instead of to the NHS."

On February 24 — five days before NHS chiefs warned a lack of PPE left the health service facing a 'nightmare' — Downing Street admitted the UK government had supplied 1,800 pairs of goggles and 43,000 disposable gloves, 194,000 sanitising wipes, 37,500 medical gowns and 2,500 face masks to China.

A senior Department of Health insider described the sense of drift witnessed during those crucial weeks in February: "We missed the boat on testing and PPE. I remember being called into some of the meetings n February and thinking, 'Well, it's a good thing this isn't the big one...' "

Martin Hibberd, a professor of emerging infectious diseases at the London School of Hygiene and Tropical Medicine, had advised on his speciality in Singapore and said: "As soon as Wuhan reported cases, Singapore knew it was going to turn up there, so they prepared for that. I looked at the UK and I can see a different strategy and approach. The interesting thing is, Singapore basically they copied the UK pandemic prepared-ness plan. The difference is, they actually implemented it."

◆ ◆ ◆

MEANWHILE, by the second week of February, our Prime Min-ister was — in the words of the *Sunday Times* - 'demob happy'.

After sacking five cabinet ministers and saying everyone 'should be confident and calm' about Britain's response to the virus, Johnson vacated Downing Street after the half-term re-cess began on February 13 and headed to the country for what he called 'a working holiday' with Symonds and would be out of the public eye for 12 days. His aides, said the paper, were thankful for the rest, as they had been working flat out since the summer to try and Get Brexit Done. They were warned to 'keep their briefing papers short' and to 'cut the number of memos' if they wanted them to be read.

The retreat, it turned out, was to prepare his family for the news that Symonds, then not quite 32, was pregnant and they'd been secretly engaged for some time. Relations with his children had already been strained since his separation from wife Marina Wheeler, who was diagnosed with cancer in 2019. Midway through the 'working holiday', the High Court announced the couple had reached a settlement that left Wheeler free to divorce him.

Back in London, meanwhile, some ministers were said to be frustrated by their boss's failure to take the lead on a loom-ing public health crisis. By now, there was mounting unease among scientists about the exceptional nature of the threat.

Sir Jeremy Farrar, an infectious disease specialist and key government adviser, told the BBC: "From early February, if not late January, it was obvious this infection was going to be very serious and it was going to affect more than just the region of Asia. It was very clear that this was going to be an unprecedented event."

By February 21, the virus had already infected 76,000 worldwide, had caused 2,300 deaths in China and was taking a foothold in Europe with Italy recording 51 cases and its first two fatalities. Yet here, key Government advisory committees decided to keep the threat level at 'moderate' — although this may not have been the case but for a failure in technology.

According to the *Sunday Times*, leading infectious disease modeller John Edmunds wanted the level raised to 'high', but the link went down as he tried to make his point. Edmunds later emailed making his view clear, minutes of the meeting confirming:

> *"JE believes the risk to the UK population should be high. There is evidence of ongoing transmission in Korea, Japan, Singapore and China."*

Peter Openshaw, a professor of experimental medicine at Imperial College, would have backed up Edmunds, but he was in America at the time of the meeting. Three days earlier, he had given an address in which he estimated that 60 per cent of the world's population would probably be infected if no action was taken with 400,000 dying in the UK.

By February 26, four weeks before lockdown and with 13 known UK cases, Edmunds warned ministers of the latest 'worst scenario' that 27 million people could be infected and 220,000 intensive care beds needed if no action were taken to reduce infection rates. The predicted death toll was 380,000.

Nick Davies, who led the research as part of Edmunds' team, modelled the effects of a 12-week closure of businesses and schools, of shielding the elderly, of social distancing and self-isolation. While delaying the pandemic's impact, he said even this might not prevent 280,000 deaths over the year.

ON Monday February 24, the PM had returned to London for glitzy Conservative fundraiser The Winter Party, at which one donor pledged £60,000 to play him at tennis. Next day in the Commons, Labour leader Jeremy Corbyn labelled him a 'part-time Prime Minister'.

By the Friday, with UK cases rising to 19 and stock markets plunging, Johnson summoned a TV reporter to Downing Street to declare that 'coronavirus is now our top priority', after which it was announced he'd finally be attending a meeting of COBRA - once he'd had a weekend at Chequers with Symonds to publicly announce their engagement and baby.

But back to that Winter Ball, its centrepiece not so much an auction as an intervention for the terminally under-endowed, who bid for the chance to fly in a Lancaster Bomber with transport secretary Grant Shapps, lunch in a prison canteen with justice secretary Robert Buckland, go whisky-tasting with trade secretary Liz Truss, watch cricket in a box at Lord's with chancellor Rishi Sunak, put on an all-over plastic bib for dinner at a Mayfair club with wet-lipped freak Michael Gove and even deliberately lose a game of tennis to Boris himself.

Today's Tory cabinet wasn't just up for sale, it had been bought and paid for by tycoons with more money than sense and way more than morals.

On that Tuesday night in south London, 700 of the best-heeled faithful paid £15,000 a table to dine on red mullet and artichoke; God help the poor soul sat opposite Gove. Among 11 organisers listed were mobile phone magnate David Ross, who'd sorted a free Caribbean holiday at New Year for BoJo and Carrie, as well Jay Rutland, banned from City trading in 2012 for "a lack of honesty and integrity".

One donor is reported to have shelled out £60,000 on gold and silver versions of the Brexit Day commemorative coin and a signed copy of the withdrawal agreement, after which it was time to pimp out the Cabinet in a money-grubbing mechanism that made payday loans seem palatable.

Is that really what their gig's about when the country's lurching from crisis to crisis amidst Brexit and coronavirus, a wonky economy, the future of the Union and goodness knows what else? Whoring themselves out to the highest bidder?

Seems it is, right from the top down.

◆ ◆ ◆

Monday and Tuesday

AND now, dear reader, an admission. I am unable to bring you either of these days as they happened, because I spent them in a drug-fuelled haze. All legal, you understand, all prescribed. But heavy-duty enough all the same to write off 48 hours.

On Sunday, despite losing that argument with the pothole, I'd felt well enough to write a sports column for the Monday, then teach an indoor cycling class without going on the bike. Worked my way though that *Sunday Times* exposé, had a long chat with my sister on what would have been her late husband Brian's 66th birthday, made some dinner, watched telly.

Then, come late evening, everything down the right side — thumb, wrist, chest, ribs, knee, shin — started to ache and bruising to blossom, so I popped a couple of 500mg cocodamol and drifted into dreams of smashing my napper on the road while wearing a paper helmet. Come morning, the knee was swollen, the thumb wouldn't move and the ribs felt like Sonia had given me a good kicking in the wee small hours. Cue more cocodamol, more weird-dream-filled sleep. Woke up, ate, went for a walk, last about five minutes before feeling faint, came home, more cocodamol, more fitful sleep.

And so it went on into a Tuesday punctuated — as was nearly a lung — by the arrival of my new spin bike, the delivery guy an extremely pleasant type who apologised profusely for not being allowed to bring it any further than the four front steps of the building because of Covid rules. After a certain amount of ham-acting on my part, he relented and helped get it up the steps, but then I was on my own to drag it across the lobby to the lift.

Two floors up, I left it on the landing, chapped a couple of doors and was delighted to find our neighbour Greg was not only in but happy to help humph it into the flat — though even then, taking one end down four little steps, across the stairhead, up four more little steps, through the front door and to rest in the hall left me gasping.

Had a cocodamol toastie for lunch and next thing it was Wednesday...

15: THE LOCKDOWN LOTTERY

Wednesday, April 22
·Global death toll exceeds 180,000.
·Scientists say fatalities among UK ethnic minorities disproportionately high.
·Nobel Prize-winning economist accuses USA of "third world reaction" to pandemic.

THERE are days when it breaks a son's heart to be kept at arm's length from his parents by the virus. And then, there are days when it really isn't an issue. Like the one when he pops round to announce he's just won a £58million lottery jackpot.

To be exact, the amount joiner and dad-of-one Ryan Hoyle has cashed via EuroMillions is £58,366,487. Little wonder, then, that when he learned at crack of dawn on Saturday that he'd scooped the pool, he took in the figures a bit like Priti Patel trying to understand how many Covid tests the Government had carried out.

So he did what any boy does when he needs reassurance — he raced round to see his folks, where, just for once, the rules that kept them six feet apart and conversing through a closed window didn't matter a bit.

Today, Ryan, from Rochdale, Greater Manchester, popped the champagne after picking up the traditional gigantic cheque and said: "When I found out I was shaking and really needed a second opinion, so I jumped in the van and drove round to mum and dad. I always wake up early and one of the first things I did was check my lottery account. I was sat on the edge of my bed but couldn't work out what I was looking at — there was an email linked to my account which looked like a lot of numbers and I thought it might be millions, but

I couldn't make sense of it and really needed to talk to some-one, so I called mum and dad.

"It was 6am, so they assumed that I had locked myself out of the flat somehow as that's happened before! I stuck to the guidelines, kept a safe distance and passed the phone through the window for them to double-check the numbers. And it was real - I'd won fifty-eight million! Mum's a cleaner who's had hip trouble for ages and she shouted out: 'Can I retire now?'

"I just shouted back: 'YES!'"

According to the *Daily Mail*, the windfall makes Ryan 'on a par financially with One Direction's Harry Styles', but he's in no rush to spend, spend, spend. His first plan is to finish a job on his brother's house, then to book trip to Disney World with his 11-year-old daughter, who might 'might get an iPhone 11 too if she behaves'. In between, he wants his factory worker dad to retire and his mum to get her hip fixed.

There's a good lad.

SO it's blue skies all the way for the one family — and the good news is, in one of the few positive side-effects of lockdown and its impact on global trade, that more and more of us around the world are seeing the sun peek through a little brighter with every passing day as smog clears and fumes dissipate and our waters start to return to their natural colour.

World Meteorological Organisation secretary-general Pet-teri Taalas today predicted a six per cent fall in carbon emis-sions for this year, but only described this as 'short-term' good news for the environment, as it still won't be enough to get the world back on track to meet the 2015 Paris Agreement targets, when close on 200 nations agreed the first-ever legally binding pact limiting global warming to well below 2°C and pursuing efforts to limit it to 1.5°C. Taalas said:

"This crisis has had an impact on the emissions of greenhouse gases. We estimate a six per cent drop in carbon emissions this year because of the lack of emissions from transportation, from industry and rom energy production. But whilst Covid-19 has caused a severe international health and economic crisis, failure to tackle climate change may threaten human well-being, ecosystems and economies for centuries. We need to flatten both the pandemic and climate change curves."

Trouble is, the chances of doing both will also flatten those of getting the economy back up and running at a time when bosses and employees alike are baying for some sort of compromise between keeping us safe through social distancing and self-isolation and somehow allowing them to start making a living once more.

In our house, the pain shooting through my ribs is being matched by the constant gripe Sonia feels as she approaches two months without laying scissors on any head apart from mine. As a self-employed stylist, she's one of a huge number of people struggling to fit into any of the Government's financial aid packages as well as being unable to work from home.

We're luckier than many in that I'm working normally and being paid in full. But for those in Sonia's shoes who don't have another income to lean on, it's becoming desperate and she can't hide her feelings each time another loan/grant/furlough door slams in her face. We're looking at setting up an online page where clients can buy a gift voucher towards their next appointment, but while that would provide some cash flow now, it means less somewhere down the line. The simple but unpalatable truth is, she's just one of the hordes who've fallen through the economic cracks during lockdown, the ones who still have bills to pay but no wages to pay them with.

Not that she's been cut completely adrift; no, the Scottish Government have sent her a food parcel. Apparently because of her history of respiratory issues, they have her down as high-risk and so, a box arrived yesterday containing a loaf, pasta and sauce, tinned peas and various other essentials. It was nice of them.

But she was mortified.

She doesn't *want* a bag of pasta and three pounds of potatoes, she wants to be able to pay her way. She's not a charity case, she runs a thriving business that's integral to the community. So she stuck the box in the car, took it to her 74-year-old mum, came back and took her name off Holyrood's list.

What had been a generous enough gesture really only made her feel even more helpless than before. So you can imagine her reaction when she turned on the TV news this morning to see the story of billionaire Richard Branson asking the Government for £500m to see Virgin Airlines through the worst — yep, the same Richard Branson who, never mind what's in the kitty from all his other businesses, has a reputed personal fortune of £4bn and could afford to keep the wolf from the cabin door with the interest from his savings account.

Apparently he's offered his private Caribbean island as collateral — this'll be the island devastated by a fire and a hurricane inside the past ten years, which makes it a bit like you or I putting up a rusty Hillman Imp to guarantee us for the mortgage on Windsor Castle.

In a fair world, the Chancellor wouldn't just tell the cheeky sod to take a hike, he'd been asking him to stick a few million in the pot to help the NHS, since he's forever telling the world what a wonderful philanthropist he is. But it's not a fair world; our memories of the banking crisis tell us that — they use our savings to bankrupt themselves at the investment roulette table, then we give them countless billions to get them out of a mess — so let's not be surprised if Branson gets his bailout.

While the Sonias of the world are left struggling for their bus fare, never mind a flight with Virgin Atlantic.

OVERNIGHT, the number of confirmed UK hospital deaths rose from 17,337 to 18,100, with health secretary Matt Hancock promising we'd 'hit the peak' of the outbreak.

However, today's *Financial Times* suggests the real figures could be *double* what we're told at daily Government briefings, findings based on data from the Office of National Statistics — unlike those Government numbers briefings — include deaths outside hospitals 'updated to reflect recent mortality trends'.

ONS data showed deaths registered in England and Wales in the week ending April 10 were 75 per cent above normal at 18,516, the highest level for more than 20 years and way up on the most recent five-year average of 10,520 for the same week of the year.

Thirty days into lockdown, there have been 1,616 presumed or confirmed deaths from coronavirus in Scotland. Of that number, 537 have lost their lives in care homes.

That's one in three of an entire country's toll.

And the grim news from the First Minister is that it could get worse still.

We'd been warned from the off that the elderly would be among those most vulnerable to infection. We accepted that our parents and grandparents and aunties and uncles would be forced to spend a long time more isolated than most. But no one was prepared for these figures. No one imagined that buildings designed to allow the those parents and grandparents and aunties and uncles to rest in through their later years would become such a fertile breeding ground for Covid-19.

Yet today, the realisation of just how terrible this epidemic within a pandemic has become left Nicola Sturgeon trying to defend her Government's performance on protecting residents — 35,000-plus of them — and staff at more than 1,000 privately and council-owned care homes. Sturgeon was clearly struggling at her daily briefing as she admitted:

"Reporting these numbers is really horrible, the most difficult

experience I have had as First Minister. They are higher than any of us ever want to think about, but this information is very important because it gives us as clear a picture as possible of the effect the virus is having. We know older people in care homes are particularly vulnerable...but that does not mean we consider any of these cases to be inevitable. It all feels very real, raw and personal."

Sturgeon went on to admit the numbers could get worse, with global data suggesting care homes may account for between 40-50 per cent of all coronavirus-related deaths.

The *Daily Record* reported how it had been highlighting since March the lack of PPE in care homes as well as the fears of staff as infections broke out. It said 46 per cent of Scots care homes have now had an outbreak of Covid-19, with 35 per cent - 384 - still dealing with active cases and multiple deaths being reported on an almost daily basis.

It quoted Donald MacAskill, chief executive of care sector body Scottish Care, as saying: "There should not be an immediate assumption that this reflects a failure of care homes to provide high quality support, follow infection control guidance or respond quickly to cases. Unfortunately, the particular impact of this virus on many individuals who are elderly, frail or have existing health conditions fits closely with the needs of our care home residents and makes this population particularly vulnerable. It's why care homes continue to need all the support they can get to keep residents safe."

Gary Smith, secretary of the GMB Scotland union of which many care staff are members, added: "This is a crisis within a crisis and what has been happening was predictable and avoidable. There have been problems with PPE and testing. The care workers on the frontline of this crisis, earning less than £10 an hour, are going through hell. It is a scandal."

THIS week alone, 15 elderly residents have died at a facility in

Dumbarton, 13 in Liberton, Edinburgh and six in Kingswells, Aberdeen, with more in every corner of the land.

The numbers are stark. The heartache for loved ones who didn't even get the chance to say goodbye must be simply horrendous. The pressure on Nicola Sturgeon today is bearing down from all sides. As Brian Sloan, chief executive of charity Age Scotland, put it: "These aren't just statistics. Each one is a mother, father, grandparent, sibling or friend...it must be absolutely terrifying for residents, staff and families."

Yesterday, the FM had denied her strategy, which included putting patients discharged from hospital after displaying Covid symptoms back into care homes, had been 'reckless'.

Reckless or not, though, today's harrowing figures suggest that strategy has failed spectacularly, leaving Sturgeon to promise 'lessons would be learned in the fullness of time'. Trouble is, that time has run out for way too many of our elederly population and more would follow as surely as night follows day. Defending her government's methods, she said:

> "This is not to say for a single second that I don't regret every single loss of life from this virus. But we have to take steps that are properly advised and informed. We adapt that where we think that is appropriate and we've taken several decisions that demonstrate that. I don't accept we were slow to understand the risk in care homes or to act. We have been taking actions around care homes since the start of this epidemic. We continue to learn, to look at what more we can do. Unfortunately a significant proportion of all deaths that are registered will be in care homes because of the nature of the people who are in care homes —frail, elderly people, often nearing the end of their lives. But that doesn't mean we accept the inevitability of this or that we don't do everything we can to prevent cases, prevent outbreaks and prevent deaths."

DEPRESSING stuff. So let's balance it out with better news today about the nation's efforts to help the homeless during the pandemic.

According to *Daily Record* reporter Mark McGivern, rough sleeping in Scotland has been 'virtually eradicated' after hotels in Glasgow and Edinburgh were signed up to get more than 140 souls off the streets during lockdown. The dilemma or homelessness charities is finding a way to make sure that whatever the 'new normal' will be once this is over, they don't simply return to the *old* normal of vulnerable men and women sleeping — and often dying — on pavements and in doorways.

I've never understood why anyone should have to live on the streets, not when we have enough empty buildings in every village, town and city to provide shelter for all who need it. That's why it's been my privilege these last couple of years to get involved with a charity called Social Bite who run cafes which fund projects to get people off the streets, off drink and drugs and into permanent homes and jobs.

For the last three years, they've run mass fundraising Sleep Outs in the dead of winter, starting small in Edinburgh, then at four venues across Scotland the next time, then globally just before Christmas gone by, tens of thousands in total choosing to spend one night living the way the homeless do every night.

Four of us were among those thousands when the event came to Kelvingrove Park in Glasgow in December of 2018. Believe me, we would have happily given Social Bite our bank account details and pin numbers there and then if they guaranteed we'd never have to go through such discomfort again in ours cosseted lives.

A few weeks before lockdown, I then organised a 24-hour indoor cycling event that raised just over £10,000 to help kit out Social Bite's next cafe in Glasgow city centre and the plan for mid-2021 is to roll the same idea out at gyms across the country to help fund a social housing village in Glasgow that matches one already up and running in Edinburgh.

Social Bite's run by Josh Littlejohn, a restaurateur's son who devotes his life to helping the homeless and who, since the pandemic struck, has been chasing donations to help deliver 4,000 food packs a day to those who need them most. I bought into what they do because their attitude to homelessness is the same as mine: That it's easily fixable.

Yes, there will always be people who find themselves lost and alone because of addictions or — more often — family fall-outs, but there's no reason why they should *stay* lost and alone.

Yet only last December, as Britain went to the polls in BoJo's snap General Election, homelessness wasn't high on any party's agenda. And for me, the reason for this was simple: The homeless don't have addresses. Which means they don't get a vote. Which means they're of no use to politicians.

Cynical? Maybe, but sometimes the truth has to hurt. There's no use Boris or Corbyn or Nicola and the rest promising homeless people anything, because there's nothing to be had in return. Two quid for a cup of tea doesn't buy ballot box support from the disenfranchised.

Because in this society of ours that Boris, Jeremy, Nicola and the rest all agree has to be inclusive — they love that word, so all-compassing and yet at the same time so utterly meaningless — whenever the polls loom it reminds us that thousands sleeping rough couldn't feel more excluded.

That for the first time in our lives we were going to those polls in the dead of winter only rammed the message home harder. Or is it only me sees the irony in community centres and school assembly halls being thrown open to everyone apart from those with nowhere to go?

In the past two years, just short of 150 people without permanent accommodation have died on Scotland's streets. Across Britain as a whole, it's more than 1,000, with numbers rising year on year as the crises of addiction, mental illness and poverty swell to Dickensian levels. Their corpses are an inconvenience to Governments. They are a moral burden Governments neither need nor want. The same system that's sharp as a tack when it comes to chasing debt allows the vulnerable to fall through its cracks on a daily basis, many never finding the strength to claw their way back out again.

It's not a simple issue, of course. The reasons for people ending up on the streets are many and varied, the economic pressures behind their struggles hugely complex. Yet at the same time, it's a problem which could have such a simple cure; or, at very least, a first step towards that cure, namely opening the doors of vacant buildings and bringing as many of these frozen souls as humanly possible in off the street.

Shops and offices are closing by the day. Warehouses lie empty. As for churches, if ever there was a sector of society that by definition needed to be doing more for the neediest people on its doorstep, it's religion. We're never done hearing moans from the clergy about how their pews are empty, about how faith doesn't seem to mean anything anymore. So how about they reinvent themselves to be what the holy books portray them as, places of sanctuary for any who need it?

Yes, there are many individual places of worship who have for many years run excellent programmes to feed and clothe the homeless and who offer shelter from the elements as well as the dangers of living rough. What it needs, though, is one huge, concerted effort by Christians, Muslims, Sikhs, Hindus, the lot, for them to club together and actively market themselves as 24/7 places of safety, warmth and support.

Landlords, too, should be doing more to free up commercial properties as shelters. Communities would rally round to volunteer as helpers, I'm sure of that. Doctors, education authorities, JobCentres, re-training companies, they'd all be able to work better to improve more lives if there were more identifiable venues where the lonely and the vulnerable could gather and listen and learn.

As I write this, the question in my head is whether it really could be this easy. And you know what? The answer is *yes, it* could. After all, if we can organise something as complex as a General Election at the drop of a hat, if we can declare war and be ready to carpet-bomb entire countries within days, then why *can't* we co-ordinate a nationwide plan to tackle homelessness? Boris, Nicola and the rest, please tell me why, in this inclusive society of yours where we can find a billion quid to bribe a minority party in order to save a Prime Minister's skin and promise billions more to give every household free broadband or put a car-charging point on every street corner, we can't spend relative peanuts on taking those who sleep outdoors and bringing them indoors? On saving the most precious thing we have, life itself?

Let's leave aside the argument here over who on the streets genuinely has no one and nothing and who's scamming money on behalf of organised gangs. That's a side issue, it's a criminal issue. And let's focus on the thought that what really shames us here is, in this age of plenty, even having ONE person out there through no fault of their own.

If I was standing for Parliament, this would be my ticket. But then, that's why I'd struggle to out-poll the Monster Raving Loonies. Talking of which...

16: DONALD TOILET DUCK

Y OU know when a video clip looks genuine, but then you think *nah, no way* because it's just too ridiculous, so you go and check it out and it turns out to be a really clever spoof right enough?

That was the White House press conference of Thursday, April 23, 2020. The evening when President Donald Trump suggested to his nation that coronavirus might be treated by injecting disinfectant into the body.

As the words came out of a mouth way too small for his head, but just the right size for his teeny-tiny hands, you sat there thinking that this had to be some pretty smart over-dubbing by a pretty brilliant mimic. After all, the daily re-workings of Nicola Sturgeon's briefing by a comedian called Janey Godley have gone, well, *viral.*

So as I watched this, just a couple of hours ago, it felt like, yeah, that must be it. He's being pranked. It had to be the *Saturday Night Live* crew or Rory Bremner sticking it to him — had to be, because not even someone as ferociously stupid as Trump, not even someone with his absolute lack of a filter, could stand in front of the vulnerable, desperate and all-too-gullible millions and suggest they draw off a syringe of Domestos and stick it in their arms to keep them safe from the bug. Except that, yeah, he could.

Now, I'd guess by the time you read this, two things will have happened: This conference will have gone down as one of *the* defining moments of the entire pandemic and some gink in Diddylyboing, Iowa, will have goned and doned what him President sayd and flushed out his system with Toilet Duck.

The first part of that prediction will always be good for yet another laugh at The Donald's expense. But only if it was heard in isolation, rather than in conjunction with the thought that there a pretty good chance of Point Two coming true.

Because let's be honest. It wouldn't be America in the Trump era if someone, somewhere wasn't so lacking in the ability to think logically for themselves if they weren't reaching for the nearest ten-gallon drum of Wal-Mart MegaBleach with one hand and a turkey-baster with the other.

◆ ◆ ◆

IT WENT like this.

As the President waited impatiently to speak — I like to think all he hears when anyone else is on the microphone is a sort of cartoon muted-trumpet blare while he runs through the McDonalds menu in his head — one of his health advisers mentioned that sunlight and disinfectant were known to kill the infection.

US Government research had found, the adviser said, that coronavirus appeared to weaken more quickly when exposed to sunlight and heat and that bleach could kill the virus in saliva or respiratory fluids within five minutes, with isopropyl alcohol acting even quicker.

Now, most of us who heard this would either have enough basic savvy to presume it meant using bleach to kill the virus in saliva *already ejected from the body* — a sneeze, a cough — or would check to make sure.

Trump, however, isn't most of us. So, as the mental muted trumpet parped and he tried to decide between two Big Macs and double fries or 300 McNuggets blended into a nourishing shake, all he heard was that 'light and bleach kill the virus'.

And so, as he took to the podium, he turned to Dr Deborah Birx, the long-suffering White House virus response co-ordinator and mused: "Supposing we hit the body with a tremendous light — whether it's ultraviolet or just very powerful light — and I think you said that hasn't been checked but you're going to test it. And then I said, supposing you brought the light inside of the body, which you can do either through the skin or in some other way. And I think you said you're going to test that too. Sounds interesting."

Now, let's leave aside that there are barely two words of that statement slevered in the right order. Try not to dwell on the thought that the guy doesn't so much express his thoughts as he does hack them up like a toxic furball. And let's instead put ourselves in the shoes of Dr Birx as she sat by the most powerful elected representative on earth, his every syllable filling her with more dread at the prospect of having to answer him.

But wait. As ever with The Donald, there was more.

"And then," he said, "I see the disinfectant where it knocks it out in a minute. One minute. And is there a way we can do something like that, by injection inside or almost a cleaning? So it'd be interesting to check that."

At which he points to his head and nods: "I'm not a doctor. But I'm, like, a person that has a good you-know-what."

Do we? Do we *really* know what he has a good one of? Comb-over? Fake tan? Collection of baby-sized gloves? Record of putting his own failing businesses under so he can write off mounting debts?

No, it really does appear he means that he has a good brain.

Only recently, he'd used that brain to promote a little-known malaria medication, hydroxycloroquine, as a possible treatment for the virus, though even *he* toned his support down after a study of coronavirus patients in a US government-run hospital for military veterans found more deaths among those treated with the drug than given standard care.

You'd maybe think iffy calls like that one might make him a tiny bit more circumspect next time. But if so, you've confused him with the sane Donald Trump from a parallel universe — and to prove we were dealing here with the one from the real world, he turned to Dr Birx again and asked if she had ever heard of using 'the heat and the light' to treat coronavirus.

She took a breath, forced a smile and replied: "Not as a treatment. I mean, certainly, fever is a good thing. It helps your body respond. But I've not seen heat or light…"

"I think it's a great thing to look at," Trump nodded, having heard something completely different to what she'd just said.

As for 'cleaning' our insides with disinfectant? Here's BBC health reporter Rachel Schraer's guide for kiddies everywhere:

> *"It's a very good idea to keep clean the things you touch, using products with anti-microbial properties. But this is only about infected objects and surfaces, not what happens once the virus is inside your body. Not only does consuming or injecting disinfectant risk poisoning and death, it's not even likely to be effective. Equally, by the time the virus has taken hold inside your body, no amount of UV light on your skin is going to make a difference. And since UV radiation damages the skin, using it to kill the virus could be a case of the cure being worse than the disease."*

Pulmonologist Dr Vin Gupta later told NBC News: "This notion of injecting or ingesting any type of cleansing product into the body is irresponsible and dangerous. It's a common method people utilise when they want to kill themselves."

John Balmes, like Dr Gupta a respiratory expert, warned: "Even inhaling chlorine bleach would be absolutely the worst thing for the lungs. The airway and lungs are not made to be exposed to disinfectant. Not even a low dilution of bleach or isopropyl alcohol is safe. It's a totally ridiculous concept."

Perhaps most succinctly of all, though, Kashif Mahmood, a doctor in Charleston, West Virginia, tweeted: "Don't take medical advice from Trump."

YET it seems that, for some, warnings as stark as these had come too late. Because some Americans didn't need their

President to tell them how good a blast of toilet clean would be the idea way to find off the virus.

Believe or not (though what am I talking about, of course you believe it) the US Centres for Disease Control and Prevention was already reporting before Trump's latest moment of undiluted genius that calls to poison centres had 'increased sharply' at the beginning of March for exposures to both cleaners and disinfectants.

The US Food and Drug Administration, meanwhile, was issuing fresh alerts about ingesting disinfectants, citing the upsurge in sales of bogus miracle cures containing bleach:

> "The FDA has received reports of consumers who have suffered from severe vomiting, severe diarrhoea, life-threatening low blood pressure caused by dehydration, and acute liver failure after drinking these products."

Last week, a federal judge secured a temporary injunction against one organisation, The Genesis II Church of Health and Healing, for marketing a product the equivalent of industrial bleach as a remedy for coronavirus.

The church's leader, calling himself Bishop Mark S. Grenon, markets it as MMS - Miracle Mineral Solution - and had written to Trump urging him to 'embrace' it as a cure not only for coronavirus, but also for HIV, cancer and autism.

Please note here and now that there is absolutely no suggestion of a connection between this appeal to the President and his subsequent suggestion that disinfectant might work just as well as a vaccine. Absolutely none. Heaven forfend. Don't be so silly. Who'd think of such a thing? Don't dare insult the intelligence of the Leader of the Free World by even thinking he might be influenced by some two-bit preacher on the make.

Hope that's made things perfectly clear.

Anyway, as you might imagine, The Genesis II Church of Health and Healing did not take this judgement well. And as you'll undoubtedly have predicted, their response came in a wonderful array of RANDOM CAPITAL LETTERS, font sizes, multiple !!!!s and quotes from the scriptures reminding the courts there is a higher power to which we all must answer. This response was signed by the church's Bishop Grenon and I reproduce it here in all its tin-foil-hatted, swivel-eyed glory...

HERE is a letter I sent the US Attorneys who are bringing the case from the FDA to the US Federal Judge. We have NOT agreed to any warnings, orders, summons, injunctions or to their contempt threat.

We are in a time of prayer and have stopped to sending out of our much needed G2Sacraments 'under duress' until CLEAR direction from the Lord of what to do OR sit back and watch Him do it for us!

As the Head Bishop of the G2Church have answered them as a 1st Amendment Church with freedom to worship and practice our Sacraments to fulfil the Holy Scriptures. We believe that the Lord is watching ALL of us and yes including those that oppose Him and Truth. Below in Psalm 94 sums up our frustration of this situation and our belief that the Lord will do to all those that oppose Him and Truth one day. We pray it is soon and He, the Lord, will avenge and be glorified!

NOTE: We pray that all involved in this 'obvious' breaking of the 1st Amendment and the Word of God will 'see the LIGHT' and change from their ways to accept logic, truth and the Word of God!

(Bishop Grenon then quotes 23 verses of Psalm 94 from the King James Version of The Bible. I'll leave you to check it out in your own time.)

*Here is the Letter sent yesterday to those involved in this case except the Genesis II Church! They responded with a signed preliminary injunction on our Sacraments and a Threat to hold us in contempt of court. Are their hearts being 'hardened' as Pharaoh was in the Old Testament? He, that being **often reproved** hardeneth his neck, shall suddenly be destroyed, and without remedy.", Proverbs 29:1 KJV*

(Bishop Grenon then quotes Exodus 8-14 from the King

James Version. Again, in your own time, but its last line leads neatly back to the rant...)

6 And he made ready his chariot, and took his people with him:

> YOU KNOW WHAT HAPPENED
> AFTER THAT! Pharaoh and
> ALL his army were destroyed, and God
> was glorified and this story is as relevant
> today as it was 1,000's of years ago

**My letter to the FDA, FTC, U.S. Attorneys
and the U.S. Judge
May 1st, 2020
Dear Judge Williams, U.S. Attorneys Feeley,
Goldstein and others involved.**

I wrote the following to all of you and to President Trump, Attorney General Barr and Asst. Attorney General Eric Dreiband, Civil Rights Division as well as every Media outlet that wants a statement from us and the American people, our Jury and that is submitted to God, our Judge.

We ask peaceably, logically and in the name of the Lord to DISMISS IMMEDIATELY the CASE against the Genesis II Church of Health and Healing and to COMPLETELY STOP this Unconstitutional harassment of the G2 Church from this day forward. If you continue to pursue this unlawful case, we leave you all to the judgment of the good people of the U.S. and God!

**Bishop Mark S. Grenon, Head Bishop
of the Genesis II Church**

Friday April 24

ANYWAY, back on Planet Sane, I'm scared to show Sonia this morning's papers, whose headlines warn that government ministers fear hairdressers may have to stay shut for another — gulp — six months.

My way better half's still praying that her industry might be belatedly granted key worker status so she can reopen her salon, albeit with a bit more social distancing than she was used to; which was none.

Pop into Bespoke Hair and you'd see one head immersed at the backwash, one having colour applied, another with their already developing, one in mid-cut, a client being gowned up and another two reading magazines on the sofa by the big picture window while they wait. Coffee, cakes and Prosecco are being served, music's playing, dryers roaring, laughter and chat flying. For Sonia and her fellow stylist Barry, it's pretty much that way from eight till gone six.

So when, as February drew to a close, it became clear that having ten people in what's basically a big, bay-windowed ground floor flat living room with water particles being blown about the place was a no-no, it was a huge culture shock.

For the last couple of weeks until lockdown, Sonia and Barry worked on a one-in-one-out basis, which drastically reduced the risk of spreading germs but also their takings. Yet today, as the first of Britain's non-essentials businesses begin to ease out of cold storage - do it yourself chain B&Q are reopening 155 branches - Sonia, Barry and legions of fellow stylists would kill for even that trickle of appointments rather than the numbing prospect of, as *The Sun* puts it:

182 Bad Hair Days

That's a hell of a long time to be stuck indoors with a bored woman and a whole toolbag full of scissors.

Saturday, April 25
•Global death toll approaches 200,000, of which the UK has ten per cent.
•Doctors and nurses in Pakistan on hunger strike over lack of PPE.
•UK suppliers say hair clippers have sold out.

MY right leg is now a magnificent melange of purples and yellows from knee to ankle and all the way round the calf.

The right thumb sports the same colour scheme and is pretty much dead, while the left knuckles look like they've been...well, like they've been whacked off tarmac after a heavy fall. All of this had possibly - OK, definitely— been exacerbated by the decision on Thursday morning to hammer out 30 miles on the new spin bike. A stupid idea? Without doubt.

But hey, the most fun ones usually are; that's why we have hangovers, tattoos and babies.

What it has most likely done, however, is knacker my plans to take part in the latest ingenious online scheme to keep us fit and raise money for charity at the same time.

Two days back, ultra-marathon cyclist Mark Beaumont launched World In A Day, where he and 79 pals aim to pedal round the globe from the comfort of their homes each Thursday between now and the end of lockdown. Mark has pledged £1 for every mile to the Who Cares Win campaign run by *The Sun* in aid of NHS workers, with a target of £100,000.

I'd signed up to join in this Thursday, though it's doubtful whether the 240 miles Mark and his crew each clocked up in last week's first session would have been possible even before Saturday's crash. But 100? That was doable. Until now.

Because now, all I want to do is clatter tomorrow's column — it's on a survey claiming half of us won't be comfortable shaking hands post-social distancing — then sprinkle several cocodamol on a bowl of porridge and sleep until my name changes to Rip Van Leckie.

THAT survey on changing attitudes to us being up close and personal might once all this is over fascinated me.

After all, when future pub quizzes ask what symbolic gesture's banning was the first sign of Scotland taking the virus seriously, some anorak will recall that it was the pre-match handshake ritual before Hibs played Hearts on Wednesday March 3. We know now this was as effective as putting up a brolly under Niagara Falls, yet at the time it was a big deal, given that extending our right paw to the person opposite is such a basic part of our body language, our everyday etiquette.

Handshakes have been seen on paintings and pottery since the fifth century BC. They began as a way of warriors proving they weren't holding weapons, extended into a show of trust that sealed deals and have become the most recognised way for men in particular to greet each other.

Yet the questions now is how many of will ever offer one again, the answer being that half of 23,000 Americans asked in the YouGov survey claimed they will *never* shake hands again for fear of infection.

Two-thirds plan to practice some form of social distancing for years to come. Three in five say they'll no longer greet pals with a hug or a kiss and will avoid crowded places. Eighty per cent vowed to keep washing their hands more often than before the outbreak and a fifth intend wearing face masks.

Of course, we say a lot of things under pressure that we mean at the time but which maybe won't stand the test of time - New Year's Resolutions, anyone? Vowing 'never again' as a hangover rips our knitting? — so let's wait and see whether we really *do* become more suspicious of physical contact, or if our brains are so conditioned that muscle memory takes over.

For instance, I'd have bet my last ten bob on hearing the all-clear sound and seeing a curvy little blur as missus hurtled at the nearest stranger and hurled her arms around them. That's her, she's a hugger; I swear half her clients come in as much for a squeeze as for a haircut.

It's the Italian half in her; they don't just love an embrace and a double-cheek-kiss, they get insulted if it isn't reciprocated. In their eyes, our handshakes aren't so much a sign of respect as of repression. Yet when I told her about this survey, even *she* admitted to be unsure about going back to the old normal. That's how completely lockdown has made us think about the smallest, everyday gestures and greeting we've grown up taking for granted. No one ever taught us to hug or to shake hands, we just saw grown-ups doing it and mimicked them to make ourselves seem mature.

I really hope it doesn't come to the point where we see each other as little more than potential carriers, because physical contact — be it a handshake, a hug, a high-five or an Eskimo nose-rub — is as vital to our well-being as eating healthily and exercising regularly.

For me, not being able to hug my kids and my sister during all this hurts like hell. For others, it's not being able to see their parents from closer than the front step. Most heartbreaking of all, though, is the thought of those with family members in hospital whose bedsides they can't even sit by when all they want is to feel the touch of a hand.

We need the warmth of closeness, the reassurance of touch, even if it's only an arm around the shoulder or someone's hand in ours. A post-pandemic world where we're *still* denied that contact feels utterly unimaginable.

◆ ◆ ◆

Sunday, April 26

I BELIEVE the word we're searching for this morning is: Ouch.

With a capital F.

It's not the knee or the shin or the calf, nor the knuckles or the thumb. They're just colourful extras by this stage. No, it's the ribs and the chest that hurt all down my right side like they've been twatted all night with a big length of four by two.

How sore? Not only do I call off from teaching my noon Zoom session, I also turn down Sonia's offer to make me a square sausage sandwich, that's how sore. It's even painful to type out a column for tomorrow's sports pages, though that might be partly down to the subject matter.

Yet more in-fighting between Scotland's football clubs.

All these weeks on, they still can't stop yelling and sniping long enough to decide how and when we finish a season that can't possibly restart. So I'm calling on them to compromise, though with as much hope of success as if I was asking Boris Johnson not to be posh, blond and bumbling.

That done, I catch up on two articles from yesterday's papers, written from opposite ends of the political spectrum but echoing the gathering uncertainty 33 days into lockdown.

The *Daily Mail* champions easing restrictions to let groups of up to ten socialise at home in 'an idea reminiscent of BT's *Friends and Families* scheme', these group drawn from no more than one or two households and with that group barred from mingling with others outside the cluster. It claimed No 10 was 'grappling with how to prevent a free-for-all that could allow the coronavirus epidemic to take hold again'.

Meanwhile, the *Guardian* claims 'the fate of millions' hangs on virus trials being rushed through an Oxford University lab:

> *"The stakes could hardly be higher — the prize still out of reach. It is no exaggeration to say the fate of many millions rests on the discovery of a vaccine for Covid-19; the only sure escape route from the pandemic. Yet the optimism that accompanied the launch of Oxford University's human trials this week has to be put in context — and the hurdles facing the scientists need to be understood."*

Scientists referred to as — Discovery Channel mini-series alert — 'the vaccine hunters' are trying to 'outwit an invisible enemy so small that a million viral particles could fit inside a human cell, but whose biological ingenuity has brought everyday life to a standstill'.

The dilemma within that challenge is that clinical trials have always been approached 'cautiously and slowly; especially when there are no effective treatments for a disease', but that 'slow is not ideal in a pandemic'.

Of 76 applicants to develop a vaccine, 74 have promised a fast-track plan in which the immune system does not need to see the entire virus to generate the ammunition to fight it off.

"If the virus is the warship," says the Guardian, "then, in theory, the immune system needs only to see the enemy flag to form an indelible immune memory. In the case of Covid-19, this flag takes the form of prominent protrusions, known as spike proteins, that form a halo or 'corona' around the virus."

The good news today is that teams around the world have moved at unprecedented pace, going from having the genetic sequence for the spike protein in January to vaccine candidates a matter of weeks later.

The slightly iffier news is that many of these technologies are unproven and success is far from guaranteed; this week, pharmaceutical lab Gilead reported that its drug remdesivir 'failed to speed the improvement of patients with Covid-19 or prevent them from dying'. Yet beyond the question of how and when vaccine becomes available, there's an equally important argument to be had: *Who gets first crack at it?*

A company called Imperial RNA, for instance, believes it can produce tens of millions of doses by the end of this year — but there are 60-odd million of us in Britain alone and more than seven billion on Earth as a whole, so we're looking at hundreds of projects on the same scale to immunise the planet.

It's predicted several vaccines could be ready to go by September and although these still wouldn't be licensed, the World Health Organisation are considering rolling them out to high-risk groups, using a precedent under which more than 200,000 in the Ebola-ravaged Democratic Republic of the Congo were given the Merck vaccine before it was licensed.

Oxford vaccine researcher Sandy Douglas said: "If you're an intensive care nurse or living in an old people's home, the risk/benefit balance may be favourable because you have the most to gain from being vaccinated."

These risks, says Douglas, make it crucial that anyone offered an unlicensed vaccine gives 'transparent informed consent', which means accepting that 'if you're being offered a vaccine in October that didn't exist in April, there will not yet be a long-term safety follow-up'.

In other words, you gets your jab and you takes your chances.

Of course, the WHO, the UN, governments and — of course — the banks could get together and agree that, rather than scores of labs in dozens of countries racing to produce a raft of vaccines, we pool our brainpower and come up with one drug that works for everyone.

Experts predict it would take a global commitments of tens of billions of pounds to do this and then to organise this global distribution according to need.

But maybe it's time to re-think what is and isn't a good investment..

17: BUST RIBS, BORIS AND THE BABY

WOKE up this morning and decided enough was enough with the pain caper, especially now that the cocodamol cupboard is bare. So I ring the doc, whose receptionist tells me to go to hospital and, half an hour later, that's where I am.

The fact that someone who answers the phone in a surgery knew what needed to be done really should have told me how stupid and stubborn I'd been.

Nine days ago, a few hours after going over the handlebars, I'd written about the reluctance most of us have right now to put our hands up to any ailment other than the virus — and there's no disguising the fact that it felt a little bit wrong to be walking through the sliding doors of the nearest accident and emergency unit to our flat.

Stobhill is one level down from the full-scale A&Es at the Queen Elizabeth Hospital and Royal Infirmary, in that nursing staff rather than doctors see you and if they can't sort you, they send you up the food chain.

Just after ten this morning, there are five us in the waiting area, two who've already been seen by a triage nurse who does an initial assessment then takes notes back through to the treatment area. When she reappears, she calls the other three of us over one by one and repeats the process. There's me with my bad ribs and other assorted ouchies, a bloke off a building site who's whapped his hand with a lump hammer and a mum with a wee girl who's stood on something sharp 'because she's aye doin' daft things'.

Nurse Triage's manner is smiling and kind and makes me, for one, feel a little better about taking up valuable NHS time during. The waiting area is certainly quiet enough that we can hear everyone in turn mutter some sort of apology to her for being there.

Just as she disappears with our notes, another mum comes in with a kiddie, this time a boy of about ten whose nose and knee are skinned to the bone from a tumble. Nurse Triage returns a few minutes later, speaks to them and pops off again. While she's away, a woman in pyjamas comes in, looking distressed. I ask her what's wrong, but she's weeping and isn't making much sense. It doesn't take a medical degree to know she's in severe pain.

I go for a wander, find a nurse and ask her to help. She can't get much out of the poor woman either, but luckily what I presume to be the husband comes in after having parked the car and explains that she'd fallen down the stairs and he thought she'd burst some ribs.

Soon after, my name's called and through I go. The first nurse, all masked and gloved up, asks me to change into a gown, then takes my blood pressure and goes over my details. She tells me someone else will be in soon and I'm left in an empty room, feeling as awkward as all of us always are while dressed in a weird hospital-stamped sheet of cotton that ties up the back and exposes our backside.

Within five minutes, Nurse No2 arrives, takes my details a third time, has a feel about, dots a stethoscope here and there on my back and gets me to breathe deeply. She's pretty sure I've cracked a few ribs, that there's heavy bruising coming out on my chest wall and that there's not an awful lot more she can do except hook me up with more of those yummy 500 mg painkillers, plus some not-quite-so-yummy antibiotics for an infection around the knee op site.

In less than an hour, I'm done, dusted and back in the car, well impressed to know that if Stobhill's staff are feeling the strain of the pandemic, they sure aren't showing it. The calm, friendly, professional way they're carrying on dealing with run-of-the-mill aches and pains is exactly what those suffering from them need right now.

I stop by the sliding doors and wish the woman who fell down the stairs all the best. In her pain, it doesn't seem to register. Hope she's ok.

I'M home just in time to sit with Sonia and watch Boris tumble out of No10 like he's been shoved by his mammy, heading for a podium from where he'll tell us all how it feels to be back to work after his dice with death.

He's looking pale, as befits someone who'd been in intensive care with the virus. Like millions around the world during lockdown, his hair — a burst couch at the best of times — appears to have been trimmed with a breadknife.

But he's still Boris; bullish, burbling, way-brighter-than-Trump-but-way-less-like-his-idol-Winston-Chuchill-than-he-longs-to-be Boris, that weird cocktail of Blitz Spirit rhetoric and Boys Own optimism, all grit and guts one moment and cheeky grins the next.

He has moments where he sounds truly passionate, when he's clearly speaking from the heart, but almost in the same breath –– this morning, a faintly wheezy breath — he can come across as a snake-oil salesman, as the second-hand car dealer whose ego convinces him to front his own TV ad. He speaks for eight minutes and 45 seconds peppered with all his usual umms and aahs and attempts not to grin during the serious bits and which I guess will be remembered mostly for two soundbites.

The first is his assertion that 'many people will be looking at our success' in tackling coronavirus, a properly jaw-dropping boast when, in a world where 220,000 of seven billion inhabitants have perished, our population of 66 million has contributed one in ten. Our care homes are being overwhelmed by tragedy, his Health Secretary's promise of

100,000 tests per day by the end of the month is still over-optimistic by half and the NHS still screams for decent levels of PPE.

If this is success, please spare us details of the failures.

Then there was soundbite No2, his analogy that dealing with the virus was, right now, like 'tackling a mugger' and how we although we've wrestled him to the ground, this moment of opportunity was also the moment of maximum risk.

You could only sit there and think that the man's head must still be mush from all those drugs they fed him in hospital. Because the truth is that if coronavirus really is a mugger, our Prime Minister's had us dancing in front of it, waving the wad of cash we've just taken from the hole in the wall.

ANYWAY, maybe I'm just an anorak for this stuff, but one of the most fascinating things of all about the PM's speech this morning was finding out how it appeared on the autocue. I wanted to reproduce it here, word for word, as a record of one of lockdown's pivotal moments, so I looked on www.gov.uk for a transcript and not only was it right there, it was reproduced exactly as he'd seen it, broken up into neat little phrases and devoid of all punctuation. To me, it reads like a very sad, free-verse poem; fitting, this, as free-verse s, like Boris himself, defined by its total lack of rhyme or rhythm…

> I am sorry I have been away from my desk for much
> longer than I would have liked

I am sorry that I have been away from my desk for much longer than I would have liked
and I want to thank everybody who has stepped up
in particular the First Secretary of State Dominic Raab
who has done a terrific job
but once again I want to thank you
the people of this country
for the sheer grit and guts

you have shown and are continuing to show

every day I know that this virus brings new sadness and mourning to households across the land

and it is still true that this is the biggest challenge this country has faced since the war

and I in no way minimise the continuing problems we face

and yet it is also true that we are making progress

with fewer hospital admissions

fewer covid patients in ICU

and real signs now that we are passing through the peak

and thanks to your forbearance, your good sense, your altruism, your spirit of community

thanks to our collective national resolve

we are on the brink of achieving that first clear mission

to prevent our national health service from being overwhelmed

in a way that tragically we have seen elsewhere

and that is how and why we are now beginning to turn the tide

If this virus were a physical assailant

an unexpected and invisible mugger

which I can tell you from personal experience it is

then this is the moment when we have begun together to wrestle it to the floor

and so it follows that this is the moment of opportunity

this is the moment when we can press home our advantage

it is also the moment of maximum risk

because I know that there will be many people looking now at our apparent success

and beginning to wonder whether now is the time to go easy on those social distancing measures

and I know how hard and how stressful it has been to give up

even temporarily

those ancient and basic freedoms

not seeing friends, not seeing loved ones

working from home, managing the kids

worrying about your job and your firm

so let me say directly also to British business

to the shopkeepers, to the entrepreneurs, to the hospitality sector

to everyone on whom our economy depends

I understand your impatience

I share your anxiety

And I know that without our private sector

without the drive and commitment of the wealth creators of this country

there will be no economy to speak of

there will be no cash to pay for our public services

no way of funding our NHS

and yes I can see the long term consequences of lock down as clearly as anyone

and so yes I entirely share your urgency

it's the government's urgency

and yet we must also recognise the risk of a second spike

the risk of losing control of that virus

and letting the reproduction rate go back over one

because that would mean not only a new wave of death and disease but also an economic disaster

and we would be forced once again to slam on the brakes across the whole country

and the whole economy

and reimpose restrictions in such a way as to do more and lasting damage

and so I know it is tough

and I want to get this economy moving as fast as I can

but I refuse to throw away all the effort and the sacrifice of the British people

and to risk a second major outbreak and huge loss of life and the overwhelming of the NHS

and I ask you to contain your impatience because I believe we are coming now to the end of the first phase of this conflict

and in spite of all the suffering we have so nearly succeeded

we defied so many predictions

we did not run out of ventilators or ICU beds

we did not allow our NHS to collapse

and on the contrary we have so far collectively shielded our NHS so that our incredible doctors and nurses and healthcare staff have been able to shield all of us

from an outbreak that would have been far worse

and we collectively flattened the peak

and so when we are sure that this first phase is over

and that we are meeting our five tests

deaths falling

NHS protected

rate of infection down

really sorting out the challenges of testing and PPE

avoiding a second peak

then that will be the time to move on to the second phase

in which we continue to suppress the disease

and keep the reproduction rate, the r rate, down,

but begin gradually to refine the economic and social restrictions

and one by one to fire up the engines of this vast UK economy

and in that process difficult judgments will be made

and we simply cannot spell out how fast or slow or even when those changes will be made

though clearly the government will be saying much more about this in the coming days

and I want to serve notice now that these decisions will be taken with the maximum possible transparency

and I want to share all our working and our thinking, my thinking, with you the British people

and of course, we will be relying as ever on the science to inform us

as we have from the beginning
but we will also be reaching out to build the biggest possible consensus
across business, across industry, across all parts of our United Kingdom
across party lines
bringing in opposition parties as far as we possibly can
because I think that is no less than what the British people would expect
and I can tell you now that preparations are under way
and have been for weeks
to allow us to win phase two of this fight as I believe we are now on track
to prevail in phase one
and so I say finally if you can keep going in the way that you have kept
going so far
if you can help protect our NHS to save lives
and if we as a country can show the same spirit of optimism and energy
shown by Captain Tom Moore
who turns 100 this week
if we can show the same spirit of unity and determination as we have all
shown in the past six weeks
then I have absolutely no doubt that
we will beat it together
we will come through this all the faster
and the United Kingdom
will emerge stronger than ever before.

TIME was when we'd have had to wait until next morning to
find out what the papers thought of it all, but now the reviews
hit the web as quickly as keyboards can be clattered.

So, with the autocue machine barely packed away until the
next address to the nation, Simon Jenkin in the *Guardian* was
already capturing the mood with a withering assessment of
what he described as 'waffle':

> *"The British people are in the dark. The rest of Europe - an
> entity Johnson despises — is already well into the process of
> what he presumably means when he says phase two. Yet his
> speech was empty of specifics. No indication of ending the bias
> against the private care sector, the poor bloody infantry of this
> pandemic. Meanwhile the illogicalities of lockdown grow more
> absurd by the day: the banning of bench-sitting in parks, the
> closure of rural resorts and beaches, permitting supermarkets
> to open but not garden centres or small traders. Covid-19 is
> clearly lethal chiefly to specific sections, yet the one-size-fits-
> all shutdown ignores this. Johnson demands that we honour
> 'past efforts and sacrifices'. This is meaningless against the*

*certainty of the toll he is taking on British lives and livelihoods
for years to come. Britons must listen in agony as leaders in
Berlin, Stockholm, Copenhagen, Brussels and Rome articulate
routes out of this mess. Johnson and his colleagues have articulated nothing."*

HIS rallying call made, the PM chaired his first Covid-19 war
cabinet meeting in three weeks, spin doctors having briefed
the media that he could be ready to ease lockdown before
the next scheduled deadline of May 7. In England yesterday,
deaths in hospitals fell to 413, the lowest number this month
and a 58 per cent drop from the peak, with the hastily built
Birmingham Nightingale Hospital reporting it has not treated
a single patient. The *Daily Telegraph* reported:

> *"An Opinium poll published yesterday showed…more than
> half of people want restaurants, offices, shopping centres and
> schools to reopen as soon as new infections decrease, though a
> majority want sports stadiums to remain closed until there is
> a vaccine. Ministers have discussed whether businesses with
> large premises such as garden centres and car showrooms,
> where social distancing can easily be adhered to, should be al-
> lowed to open. Discussions are also at an advanced stage over
> how and when schools will return."*

Foreign Secretary Dominic Raab, meanwhile, said the PM's
return boosts 'the Government and the country', with a
source adding: "The building has not been the same without
him."

Feel free to take that last line any way you choose.

Tuesday April 28
•Nationwide minute's silence for NHS workers killed by Coronavirus.
•£60,000 compensation for families of those who died at work.
•More than 100 hospital and care staff have perished across Britain.

JANICE GRAHAM was 58, a mother to Craig and a district nurse working out of Inverclyde Royal Hospital in Greenock.

Kirsty Jones was 41, had two kids, had worked for the NHS in Lanarkshire since she was 17 and had just taken up a new role on the frontline of the fight against the pandemic.

The word 'was' tells anyone all they need to know about how the story of that pandemic worked out for both.

Janice and Kirsty are among the ever-growing number of healthcare workers being claimed by their desire to help others stay safe. Everyday people doing vital jobs under horribly trying circumstances that broke their bodies and took their lives.

Today, bosses and colleagues alike were full of praise for them as nurses and as friends. Today, books of remembrance opened in their memory. Today, ministers promised bereaved loved ones would not suffer financially from these tragedies.

But somehow, right now, all of it has such an empty ring; the tributes, the respectful silences, the compensation packages, they're all as ultimately meaningless as they are heartfelt; because all those bereaved loved ones, those colleagues and friends really want is not to have lost Janice and Kirsty and too many more like them.

Both these women, like all the other hospital and care home staff claimed by the virus so far, had gone home plenty times with hearts broken by a patient's death; from the stillborn baby to the pensioner whose organs had nothing left to give, their complete investment in everyone they treated made theirs so much more than a job or even a career.

A dedicated nurse is fulfilling a calling every bit as much as a man or woman of the cloth would claim to be. Our faith in has to be absolute. We might simmer at how long it takes to be seen at A&E or how late our clinic appointment runs, we might lie in a ward infuriated thst we can't someone to bring us that cup of tea we're gasping for, but our frustrations are never — or *should* never be — aimed at staff themselves.

We know, without them having to remind us, that they *do*

their absolute best with what they have. And we know only too well that, even in what might ne called normal circumstances, what they have is not nearly enough. Not numbers, not beds, not equipment and, most certainly, not pay.

I mentioned earlier a post that's been going round social media, reminding us of how Tories cheered last time they turned NHS workers down for a wage rise. In light of this and so many other injustices within the health service, when each Thursday at 8pm we clap and cheer and bang pots and pans in appreciation of those workers, it's hard not to feel that our leaders only show that same appreciation when it suits.

To witness a Johnson, a Gove, a Hunt or a Hancock so desperate to be seen to be just as in awe of the NHS as you or I are is faintly nauseating. Hearing the Prime Minister eulogise about the treatment he received when the virus put his life on the line makes you want to grab him by the lapels and scream:

"THEN GIVE THEM MORE MONEY, YOU TWO-FACED CLOWN! GIVE THEM MORE MASKS AND GOWNS!"

But what makes our NHS truly special is the ability of those drawn to it to separate the personal from the professional, to leave their personal or political feelings in a locker with their handbags and cycle helmets.

These are the people who try with all their might to save the lives of terrorists injured in the unforgivable act of trying to kill as many innocents as possible, who stitch the wounds on the wife beater whose victim has turned the tables with a pair of scissors, who take out the rapist's burst appendix, who pump the stomach of the drug mule whose cargo bursts, who tend to the critically injured drunk driver with as much care as they do the family who were in the car coming the other way.

I've been arguing in print for two decades now that our emergency workers — nurses, firefighters, police, paramedics, ambulance crews — shouldn't have to *demand* better pay and conditions, they should have them as of right. Yet anything anyone writes or says clearly falls on deaf ears, because today, nurses working for the devolved NHS Scotland earn an average of just over £32,000, one per cent below the average salary for all other jobs; not to mention £6,000 less than a Westminster MP can claim in expenses.

How can this be fair when even in 'normal' circumstances they can quite literally have our lives in their hands? How can it possibly be anything less than an insult when, at a time of unprecedented crisis like this, we're asking them to lay their *own* lives on the line every time they go to work?

How can we not feel angry about the state of our National Health Service? How can we not compare the lack of investment in the basics it requires with what we expect it to achieve every hour of every day?

Sure, when NHS staff are dying, Westminster can reach up into the Magic Money Tree and bring down a bag with £60,000 in it for each bereaved family — and I'm sure it's money that will come in handy. But is that what each life was worth? Ten months of an MP's salary? In fact, forget their salaries, back in December several of those MPs collected more than £30,000 compensation after losing their *seats*, never mind their lives.

That's the perspective of how much this country genuinely cares about lost souls such as Janice Graham and Kirsty Jones. That's what we — and I mean *we*, because we're the ones who keep voting in governments who treat NHS workers as slaves — think of Catherine Sweeney, the care home worker believed to have been the first frontline Scot to die from the virus.

It's what we think of Brian Darlington, a 68-year-old porter from Crewe, a husband, a dad and grandad who colleagues say was 'always smiling, always handing out sweets to the team'.

It's how much we care about Charlie Goodwin, a 61-year-old ambulance driver at King's Mill Hospital in Nottinghamshire with 20 years experience whose grieving family say only wanted to 'get out and help people' when the outbreak struck.

It's how much we care about Julie Penfold, a 53-year-old

nurse at Wirral University Teaching Hospital on Merseyside, who had fostered 20 children as well as having two daughters, a son, an adopted daughter, two step-daughters and 11 grand-children — not to mention losing another son and daughter — and who later thi year would have been 25 years married to Nick's words, who called her 'everything I lived for'.

Yet she died, like so many more frontline workers have died, for what amounts to the price of a ministerial Jaguar.

◆ ◆ ◆

Wednesday, April 29

BUT hey, let's dry our tears, forget the pandemic, unfurl the bunting and let church bells ring out across the land. Because today, the Prime Minister has once again become a daddy.

And this, as that true man of the people Jacob Rees-Mogg put it, is a great joy for the whole country; not just for Boris and his fiancée, not just for their circle of close loved ones and friends, not even for the big, extended happy family that is the Conservative Party.

No, says the Right Honourable Dickensian Fruitbat of the House, we should *all* be set free of lockdown'd cares and woes because this is all we've needed to divcert us from the fastest-spreading dose of Covid-19 in Europe; yet more fresh produce from the loins of our philanderer-in-chief.

Don't know about you, but he had me at hello. The NHS can whistle for applause tomorrow night; my hands will instead be turning red raw in gratitude to every sperm Boris ever produced.

A sentence that, on review, is wrong on so many levels.

The PM was, according to a hospital spokesperson, present throughout the birth, a surprise in itself, given that he's only just survived a life-threatening joust with Covid-19 and that maternity units across Britain have been making mums-to-be deliver with their partners locked outside. But hey, maybe Boris's Bulldog Spirit was enough to sterilise the entire area.

By the by, this nugget about the PM being there when Carrie went into Conservative (no way was she having anything as common as Labour pains) is, added to the news that it's a boy, pretty much all we've been told so far, since No 10 won't say what time the wee chap was born, what weight he is or even what hospital it all happened at.

Neither would they confirm if Ms Symonds was admitted as an emergency, one of the first thoughts many had this morning; after all, the couple only announced in February that she was pregnant and had given the due date as 'early summer'.

Weirdest of all, though, No 10 point-blank refused to reveal how many children Boris now has. The smart money says six — four from his second marriage, one from a fling and now today's arrival — but a spokesman refused to confirm or deny this. Even Rees-Mogg, himself a father of six, would only hint that he 'thinks' they now both belong to 'an exclusive club'.

Anyway, tallest to the right, shortest to the left — fall in the Johnson Kids that we're allowed to know about...

LARA LETTICE, 27, is the eldest, conceived ahead of Boris's 1993 wedding to Marina Wheeler, a barrister he met while married to socialite Allegra Moston-Owen. She goes by the surname Johnson-Wheeler and was schooled at £33,000-a-year Bedales before gaining an MA in Latin and Comparative Literature at St Andrews. During her father's stint at Mayor of London, she boasted of a family holiday 'we were fortunate to experience complimentarily'. Described as a writer, editor and broadcaster, she has contributed to *The Spectator* (which her father once edited) and *Evening Standard*.

MILO ARTHUR, 25, went to £27,174-a-year Westminster School where he was said to excel at sports. He graduated in 2014 from London's School of Oriental and African Studies and took up a five-month internship in Dubai at men's magazine *Esquire Middle East*. His LinkedIn profile says he can speak

Arabic, Russian and French. He was pictured helping his mum clear the family home after she decided to leave Boris.

CASSIE PEACHES, 22, studied at £18,000-a-year Highgate School in North London. She too is a writer and during her schooldays was editor of their magazine *Cholmeleian.*

THEODORE APOLLO, 20, is another whose upbringing is deliberately kept more than a little unclear. Which school he went to has never been made public and although it's known that he's currently at Cambridge University, which college and which subject are, again, classified.

And then there's **STEPHANIE**, born in 2009 after the bold Boris dallied with art expert Helen Macintyre when he was Mayor and she was an adviser to his office. He denied paternity, wasn't named on the birth certificate and by 2013 sought — and was denied — an injunction to prevent the tot's existence being reported. Helen then met William Cash, a publisher, son of a Tory MP and ex-husband of both a Bulgari fashion heiress and a Venezuelan model who'd dated Mick Jagger. At 43 and childless, Cash offered to bring the tot up as his own before he knew who the father was. Once he found out, though, he decided he didn't want to fall foul of Boris and demanded Helen tell him of their plans. In his book *Restoration Heart,* he wrote:

> "*Alexander Boris de Pfeffel Johnson was the last rival d'amour you'd want, a heavyweight champion of conquests, a veteran swordsman and super-hack paid £250,000 a year for a newspaper column. I felt as if I'd been pushed into the Circus Maximus to fight a seasoned gladiator.*"

There's never a ravenous lion around when you need one.

Thursday, April 30
•Captain Tom Moore celebrates his 100th birthday by being promoted to Colonel courtesy of The Queen as his fundraising effort pass £30million.
• Russia confirms 7,099 new cases, a record 24-hour rise, and 1,073 deaths

in all.

·Global deaths reach 228,625, though 991,999 have survived the virus.

AND now, once more, we rejoice — for Health Secretary Matt Hancock hit his promised target of 100,000 tests in a day.

Ok, so he only actually hit it today. And, yes, close on 40,000 of the tests included in the total were posted out to people who may or may not have returned them. But as the great Scottish boxer Benny Lynch once yelled after winning a title against the odds: *"Ah said Ah'd dae it an' Ah dun it."*

Today, Matt Hancock has also done what he said he'd do by taking tests from 10,000 less than three weeks ago to 100,000; even though quite what difference reaching the magic mark does in the overall fight against the virus remains unclear..

For me, it feels very much like a stunt cooked up by a man thrust into the spotlight while his gaffer was in hospital, but one which seemed to become more important to him than the job of actually getting the nation safe and healthy again. I'm guessing the thought of the humiliation that would have come with failure didn't bear thinking about.

Or maybe that's just my cynicism creeping back in.

It's been doing that a lot recently.

18: MAYDAY..MAYDAY..

LOCKDOWN has been about sticking to rules that mess with our heads. Don't be lured to the park just because it's sunny, don't hug the old pal you meet in the street, don't sneak a visit to your granny just because she's lonely.

And, as it turns out, writing this book hasn't been a whole lot different, except with a different temptation to avoid; no sifting back through the chapters and making yourself look smarter with the benefit of hindsight.

The nearer it got to the end of April, though, five weeks into self-isolation, the more difficult it became to resist creating an overview of how we've dealt with the pandemic rather than sticking to the plan of documenting it in real time.

This was partly down to the sheer volume of headlines, of comment, of statistics and predictions and reactions flying at us from every direction, day in and day out, growing from those long-gone early days when all we had to grasp was that we were dealing with this thing called coronavirus and to wash our hands while singing *Happy Birthday To You*.

Like the bug itself passing from one victim to two to four to 16 to 256 and on and on, this single story had spawned one more, then two, then ten, until it became a roaring avalanche, gathering volume and pace as it rushes down the mountain to engulf us. Which makes keeping tabs on it all for posterity like trying to catch several thousand tons of snow in a string bag.

This month, I've finally given in. Every day in May, I've noted down my thoughts as usual, trawled the world for key developments as usual, read the best and worst of mainstream and social media as usual. Yet every day in May, I've sat down to put it all together and it just hasn't felt right. There's just... well, there's just too much of it all.

The white noise out there is getting to me way more than being stuck indoors 23 hours a day. The squabbling and the squawking, the latest London government briefing telling us one thing then the latest from Edinburgh recommending the opposite, supporters of each refgme retreating into their trenches to lob grenades full of bile at each other, the never-ending processions of experts one lot chooses to believe and the other decries, neither have a clue who's right or wrong.

This is what we've come to, this is what it's done to us. If the five recognised stages of grief are denial, anger, bargaining, depression and acceptance, then so far the four we've come through in dealing with coronavirus are novelty, frustration, confusion and cynicism. I write this nursing a growing fear that the fifth element will be naked anger.

BACK at the end of March, for all that things felt a little bit dys-topian and scary, there was definitely also something quite new and intriguing about what we were getting into.

There was the thought of how we'd deal with working from home or not working at all, of how we'd handle being around our loved ones 24/7, of how parents would manage as stand-in teachers for the duration and of so much more besides.

It felt like we were part of some huge social experiment, one which after a week or so had plenty chirping optimistic-ally about how we'd come out the other end as better people, as a less materialistic race who'd learned to appreciate what we had in our lives. Then the novelty wore off.

Two, three weeks in we started getting fed up, feeling the first pangs of stir-craziness. We were missing the office, the factory, the cafe, the pub, the freedom of a normality that not so long before we felt certain we'd had enough of. We started finding it harder to watch the news or read the papers, because the never-ending gloom only made our days longer.

Then, ever so gradually, we began to doubt the validity of the bits we *did* watch or read, because it felt like we were being fed the same guff over and over, just so much blah without a hint of a genuine plan to get us out of this.

Marriages were coming under strain, finances too. Families being thrown together 24/7 had led to a huge spike in calls to domestic violence and mental health helplines. Frazzled mums and dads were appreciating more than ever the job real teachers do as they struggled to make kids concentrate on keeping up with their studies. We were eating too much, maybe having a vino too many at night, our sleep patterns went all to pot.

All those plans we'd had at the start of Chapter One —write that best-seller, build that beach body, clean the house top to bottom, learn a language, reconnect with ourselves — were getting harder and harder to commit to with every day that didn't so much pass as drag.

What was the point, what were we doing it all for? What was the end game? The questioning of every aspect had begun; questions, questions, questions from a population confused by how none of this had been our fault yet somehow our leaders were warning that we'd be to blame if it kept getting worse.

Why were they keeping us cooped up? Why hadn't they locked us down earlier so it was all over sooner? Why was our infection rate and the death toll that came with it climbing higher than Italy's or Spain's, since being able to watch them suffer had offered us every opportunity to react quicker and smarter? How come the media weren't holding the feet of our politicians to the fire about it all at those daily briefings?

Why wasn't anyone listening to us? Why wasn't anyone trying to get us out of this mess? What harm would it *really* do to pop in and sit with my mum in that care home, just for half an hour? Questions that, when the answers weren't the ones we wanted to hear, led us into the fourth stage of lockdown — cynicism. Or, as it's known in Scottish: *Aye, right.*

A world-weary turn of phrase which comes complete with a sarcastic expression no one ever taught us but every one of us knows from birth and which defies the mathematical theorem that two positives can't make a negative. Two single-syllable words capable of bringing the most powerful and committed oratory crashing down in a million pieces.

Dr Martin Luther King: "When we allow freedom to ring, let it ring from every village and hamlet, from every state and every city, we will be able to speed up that day when all of God's children, black men and white men, Jews and Gentiles, Protestants and Catholics, will join hands and sing in the words of the old Negro spiritual, Free at last! Free at last! Thank God, we're free at last!"

Passing Scotsman: "Aye, Right..."

THIS is where Britain appeared to be as the May arrived, a place where patience and trust was running out as fast as loo roll and hand sanitiser had in the final week before the shutters came down.

A Britain where if Boris said *Relax*, Nicola said *Be Afraid.* Where every newspaper column and podcast and TV satire seemed to have taken on a new, harder edge. Where an ability to keep smiling had long since morphed into a defensive shield of black humour that was now replaced by a nastiness in our jokes and memes. Even the ritual of Thursday night's doorstep round of applause for the nation's key workers had lost its warmth, its feeling of spontaneous joy now more about who could clap the loudest, whose kiddies could look cutest for the camera as they banged wooden spoons on pots and pans, who could chalk the most ornate NHS rainbow on their driveway.

Not to mention an exercise in judging those *not* throwing heart and soul into it; or, worse still, weren't take part at all.

"See them upstairs? They didn't come out and clap last night."

"Well, I hope if they get ill the ambulance doesn't take them..."

It had begun to echo the uneasy vibe that's grown up around Remembrance Day, an event whose title used to offer a decent clue to how long it was scheduled to last, but which now seems to go on for a month and which has become a who's-got-the-biggest-and-blingiest-poppy contest; and don't get us started on anyone who goes around *without* one pinned to their lapel, printed on a t-shirt or hooked to their car grille. The ungrateful, Britain-hating, terrorist-loving bastards.

To me, this one-upmanship isn't only unhealthy, it ignores what both the Thursday night NHS ovation and Remembrance Day are meant to be about, because once we bully each other into taking part or face running the gauntlet of shame, once the only reason for some of us to clap our hands or wear a poppy is to ensure a quiet life...well, what next?

Does the whole thing flip on its head and people start giving two fingers to the Establishment by refusing to take part at all?

Apart from anything else, it feels right now like it's going to take more than well-meaning acts of symbolism to united a country as seriously fractured as ours has become. From the bank bailout and the decade of austerity that followed, through the spiteful Independence campaign to the whole, horrible Brexit fiasco, politics and economics had already helped isolate families and friends from each other long before the virus made it mandatory. But if God really does love a trier, than He/She/It must adore Boris Johnson, because he spent the entire first week of this manic month hammering home how the 75th anniversary of VE Day would be just the thing to pull us all together in celebration of what puts the Great in Britain - yes, even more so than the birth of his newborn.

As with his bizarre back-to-work speech comparing the struggle to control the pandemic with wrestling a mugger to the ground, he couldn't resist the most tenuous of imagery, this time with World War II. He was all about how beating the virus would take 'the same spirit of national endeavour' that saw off Hitler, though the analogy kind of broke down when he reminded us that the ones we fought back then are now among our closest friends, something you can't see happening with coronavirus.

Unless, of course, he's already planning streets parties on the first anniversary of lockdown being lifted, so we can all try our best to infect each other again and remind ourselves how wonderful it was to beat it first time round.

Then, come VE Day itself? With its blanket media coverage, the lump-in-the-throat tributes to Dame Vera Lynn, the news footage of families done up in 40s gear, houses an explosion of Union Jacks? The patronising interviews with some of the last remaining conscripts who actually went through the hell of it all? Boris's inevitably sub-Churchillian speech?

Sorry, but it all felt so forced.

As with the ones who need to clap and cheer louder than their neighbours each Thursday night or who need to slap a poppy on the day after they come home from their summer holidays, it seemed to be about *showing* everyone how much you respected those who went over the top to defeat the Nazis. It clearly wasn't enough just to *remember* them; no, it all had to be done with as much display as it takes to make a TV researcher double-take your Instagram post and stick you on that night's bulletin—which, miserably, is how way too many stories make it onto our screens or into our papers these days.

(Warning: Tired old newsman in rant mode approaching.)

Once, the job of the junior reporter was to get out, knock doors, go to fêtes and sports days and to turn up news on the basis that everyone has a story to tell. Now, they're trained to interview Facebook or Twitter, to pass off cut-and-paste posts as quotes rather than speaking to people face-to-face. Little surprise, then, that as May drew to a close we'd even learn that Microsoft was to replace hundreds of human journalists (if that isn't a contradiction in terms, before you say it) with bots which would read, analyse and re-post stories from around the world, 24/7.

And why not? Half the political posts we see on social media today are already created via artificial intelligence and aimed at us based on individual analytics of our personal opinions.

The game as we know it, as even older journalistic hands than yours truly have been sighing for many years now, is fucked.

BUT that's a discussion for another day. For now, we're talking about VE Day 75 years on and the way war is still consistently spun as a scrap between our nice troops and their nasty troops.

Governments deny ownership of these wars, making them sound instead like scraps that just kind of happened, rather than being orchestrated by leaders who settle their differences not with words, but with the sacrifice of countless young men and women and a seenmingly bottomless pit of money to buy ever more sinister weapons.

The threat of this recurring insanity — literally, committing the same mistakes while expecting a different outcome — is why I find Brexit all the more bizarre. Yes, the European Union has a thousand faults; it's a bureaucratic maze and it gave Nigel Farage a platform to become famous, to name but two. But everything wrong with it is outweighed by its one, massive positive, which is its route to open trade between France and Germany, the neighbours at the root of more conflict than any other nations in the history of mankind.

While they can do business freely, it's beyond ridiculous to expect them to fight. So it blows my mind that we, still licking the wounds of two world wars, would choose to mess with this accord, this means of maintaining the longest spell of peace Western Europe has ever known.

Unless I fell asleep and missed a crucial debate, it's hard to remember this absolutely pivotal issue being raised during the EU Referendum campaign. Far less complex to paint a blatant lie on the side of a battle bus about how Brussels owed us

£350million a week which we'd pass straight to the NHS.

Far easier, as a far wiser man than I am once put it, to prey on the bigotry of people who want to shut our borders with Europe because they don't like Pakistanis.

Bottom line, I'd be a lot happier if Remembrance Day and VE Day became less of a flag-waving celebration of the Honest Tommy's courage and more of a protest against governments who continue to send troops into conflicts — the Falklands, Kosovo, Iraq, Afghanistan, Syria, Libya and more, all within the past 40 years — where not only are the reasons for their sacrifice less and less clear, but where the more the global landscape changes the less and less we're even aware of who the enemy is. I'd far rather we stopped reconstructing the Blitz as entertainment and instead staged an annual protest against the arrogance that makes our leaders try to bomb democracy into far-off lands.

If this sounds hopelessly naïve, I'm happy to admit the charge, because far better to live by this belief in something better than simply admitting with a shrug that the only way to ends wars is to keep on having them.

I just find it incredible that we've developed in so many ways since the days of colonialism, yet for all our scientific, technological, medical and social advances we still haven't sussed that war genuinely is good for absolutely nothing.

If we had sussed this, then rather than calling on us to celebrate some sort of victory, Johnson would have used this unique occasion — a VE Day that not only fell in the middle of a global pandemic but which might be the last where those who fought the Nazis will still be around to tell the tale — to instead apologise on behalf of his hero Churchill's political generation for condemning so many innocents to death.

In the 1900s alone, wars killed at least 123 million troops and civilians. Not many of them were those who picked the fight in the first place.

◆ ◆ ◆

AT which point, I have to pull myself up sharp and think about a piece of advice I've spent years offering to others and which during this mad month has become more relevant than ever.

Let go of the issues in life we can't control.

A mantra which has had a hugely positive impact on my mental health and which could do the same for so many others as lockdown enters such a fractious stage. Dump the baggage, stop clinging onto stuff that makes us angry, sad or frustrated but which we can't do a thing to change, and you *will* feel lighter, trust me.

But, like sticking to Government guidelines on staying home or to your own rules for writing a book, this is easier said than done; witness the end of the last chapter and the start of this, when I've gone off on one about the PM becoming a dad and how loudly people clap for nurses and how size matters when it comes to poppies. Lapses like these are why it's crucial to keep repeating that mantra.

Let go of the stuff you can't control.

Let go of the stuff you can't control.

Let go of the stuff you can't control.

Come the evening of Monday May 11, off the back of a VE Day that had turned into a long weekend, the mantra was echoing ever louder. As with the avalanche of mainstream news, the noise coming off social media was unbearable. I was concerned for so many normally gentle and intelligent souls who were now lashing out in all directions, so much so that I stuck this on Facebook:

> *"It's obvious a lot of people on here think it'll do them good to unload about who's to blame for whatever during this pandemic. And dogs in the street can see most of what's being posted about the idiots who run the show is pretty much on the mark. But there's no point getting bent out of shape about stuff we can't control. All we can do is look after ourselves and, by doing so, help look after others. So please, focus on that - and do your mental health a favour by letting the other stuff*

go. "

THIS drew an instant and powerful response, one or two even admitting the situation had got to them so much they were feeling physical pain at the thought of going outside.

There's no doubt from their replies, both public and private, that while the virus itself and the constant media barrage about it played a major part in this, they were also genuinely freaked out by some truly thoughtless rants and ramblings on what's supposed to be 'social' media. So, by the following morning and with responses were still coming in, it felt like this throwaway post needed to be expanded into a full-scale column that got out to hundreds of thousands rather just my own circle:

The Scottish Sun, Thursday May 14

NEXT time you're about to hit Send on the latest post making yourself out to be the world's greatest expert on handling coronavirus, do me a quick favour: Stop and read it over a couple of times first.

Ask yourself whether you really, really know what you're talking about or are just spewing pent-up frustration born of seven weeks shut indoors. Think whether what you're about to share is even your own thoughts or if you're simply cutting and pasting someone else's.

If it's the latter, do you know the person whose views they are? Is it a trusted friend who's articulated what you've been thinking, or a stranger whose opinions just happen to kind of dovetail with yours? Again, if it's the latter, think about their motivation for writing it. Click on their name, find out who they are. Ask yourself if you've even read what they've written properly, or whether a few key words were enough to make you claim ownership.

Once you've done all that? Sure, if you're 101 per cent satisfied that you're putting it out there for the right reasons, rather than just to make yourself appear clued-up, by all means punch that button.

But even then, in that final split-second of hovering index finger, please remember one way-too-overlooked fact — that there are people out there spending lockdown terrified. And I mean properly terrified, people who have developed a proper, rational fear of the bug and everything it touches. People who develop physical pain at the thought of going in to a supermarket. People whose worst nightmare right now is the thought of everyone around them being allowed to roam freely and leave nasties behind them everywhere they go.

Think of them before you hit Send on that post. Because if it makes even one person's torture even a tiny bit worse, it'll be your fault.

241

Harsh? Maybe, but no less true for it. Trouble is, of course, that as this crisis enters its most socially divisive stage yet — Ignore Boris, Trust Nicola, blah blah blah — very few of us are thinking before we let rip. Everyone wants to be the prophet of doom, everyone wants the world to know Them Nasty Tories are sentencing innocents to death.

I'm not saying they're wrong. I've already written on the dangers of countries who share a border not also sharing a policy on containing a pandemic that has killed more than 30,000 on this one island. All I'm asking is that we calm down a bit, resist the temptation to launch into the social media equivalent of running around with our hair on fire.

See, right now there are things we can control and things we can't and, for me, there's absolutely no point in getting bent out of shape about the things we can't; why we're stuck with such idiots running the show, why we can't go to the pub or get a hug from our families, why garden centres in Carlisle are open while they shut in Dumfries.

As important as these issues are, all we do when we allow them to take over our thought process is waste mental and physical energy. We make ourselves tense, which makes us more difficult to live with, which makes lockdown even tougher to deal with than it already is.

Yes, Johnson's making it up as he goes along. Yes, you might trust him as far as you could throw a dead rhino up a spiral staircase. Yes, you might in turn believe with all your heart in the Sturgeon Method of staying safe.

But what difference would it make if you thought Boris was right and Nicola was wrong? It wouldn't make one jot, because both leaders would still be guessing as blindly as they have been from the off. Downing Street would still be admitting, as it did yesterday, that it doesn't have a Scooby what effect letting millions off the leash will have on infection rates. Holyrood would still be under fire for a death toll in our care homes far worse than in England's.

In short, the virus would still be the virus and we'd still be the ones ultimately responsible for keeping ourselves healthy and sane until it goes away. And that's the bit we CAN control. Rather than shouting our frustrations at each other across the internet, concentrate on doing things properly within our own households. Keep our hands clean, keep our distance when outdoors, cover our faces in shops.

If everyone does these simple things, all our individual dots will join to form the best possible barrier against coronavirus. Day by day, those poor souls too scared to go our for a pint of milk will begin to conquer their fears. Those who today find watching the TV news or reading a paper too much to cope with and whose only link with the outside world is a social media brimming with anger, recrimination and scaremongering might tomorrow enjoy going online once more.

Put it this way. Would you go up to an elderly neighbour's door and shout through the letterbox that Boris's plans are going to kill us all?

Because if not, don't bawl it online either.

◆ ◆ ◆

THAT Monday, it had been harder than ever to hear yourself think for the howls of confusion and anger that followed the night before's live TV statement by the Prime Minister.

I'm pretty sure that, as he looked down the lens, still relieved at surviving the virus and euphoric at becoming a daddy yet again, was ready to loosen the shackles from around Britain's ankles.

In fact, at the end of a week buzzing with rumour and counter-rumour about just how loose those shackles were to become, I still firmly believe that had a posse of scientists and doctors not talked him off the ledge, he'd have been inviting us all to rush out the front door the second his broadcast ended, grab the nearest passer-by and stick a tongue in their ear to confirm that the worst was over.

As it was, even in watering down the promises he wanted to make to the self-isolating and fed-up masses, he managed to leave Nicola Sturgeon worried enough to issue an immediate statement warning that to ease up on restrictions now would risk a deadly second spike of the virus and she was extending Scotland's lockdown for a further three weeks.

What a mess, eh? What a total lack of joined-up leadership.

If only there had been some way — and stick with me here if this is getting a little too far-fetched — for the PM and FM to get together before we got to this stage, say by some sort of combination of phone call and video link (if such a space-age concept even exists) so they could work out a compromise that didn't leave two neighbouring countries separated by nothing more physical than a road sign dealing with the same deadly problem by using two different sets of rules.

This inability to understand the difference between a non-existent border and a bio-secure Perspex bubble was at the crux of the growing disconnect between Westminster and Holyrood. It made me think of those hazy, faraway days when the partition between the Smoking and No Smoking sections in a restaurant was a sign - because that this was what we were heading back to unless Sturgeon and Johnson could synch over easing up on lockdown.

A country on the side of that sign reading **England** running about mad, having picnics. A country on other side reading **Scotland** simmering with resentment at not being allowed to join in. And in the middle, a virus that gave not a toss about signs, politics or anything apart from doing its worst.

That's why it seemed crazy that as the PM made that live TV statement, he'd either seemed unaware or unconcerned that England was geologically joined at the hip to Scotland and Wales and that one rogue cough in any of the three could spell fresh disaster for an entire island.

All it took for Covid-19 to spread first time was one carrier passing symptoms to three friends who each infected another three and that's all it would take again.

The one saving grace is that people who know better than Johnson - which is just about everyone - had spent the past week reminding him of this after he seemed ready to take as huge a risk with the nation's health as he had back in February, when he was so unmoved by the prospect of a pandemic he missed those first five COBRA meetings on it and was advising anyone who'd listen that shaking hands was still hunky-dory.

I'll always be convinced he all for releasing millions from self-isolation today and hoping for the best, the polar opposite mindset to that of Sturgeon, who'd spent the whole of last week defying suggestions from her gurus that a bit more outdoor time wouldn't do us any harm.

Like it or not, this better-safe-the-sorry policy of hers was validated within hours, when Whitehall's chief statistician Professor Ian Diamond reported that the care home epidemic was driving up the 'R' rate of transmission which determines how close we are to being over the worst. News to reinforce the sense that lifting lockdown, even gradually, isn't a decision that can be made unilaterally.

Just this once, we really *were* all in it together, wherever we lived and whoever we voted for. This wasn't about backing Nicola over Boris, but backing the bloke next door with Crohn's Disease and the hospital staff who'd have to save his life if he caught the bug. Between them, the PM and FM had one job — to find a solution that hung as few of us as possible out to dry.

◆ ◆ ◆

SO back to that Sunday night at seven, when millions had tuned in to see Boris to look us straight in the eye and clear up our concerns on all of the above.

We're still waiting.

Because, for all that his speech announcing the arrival of lockdown 48 days earlier had been clear, concise and powerful, this was one's absence of clarity was summed up in by his revelation that the key message of his guidelines was changing from STAY AT HOME to STAY ALERT.

What did that mean? No one seemed to know, not even the PM himself, judging by a look on his face that suggested he was trying to calculate 113 times 46. Not that much else he said made sense; witness this soundbite on getting people back to work from the following morning:

> *"We said you should work from home if you can and only go to work if you must. We now stress that anyone who can't work from home, for instance those in construction or manufacturing, should be actively encouraged to go to work."*

Once we'd rewound and replayed this nine or 14 times, the reality dawned; thousands of companies had 12 hours flat to galvanise hundreds of thousands of workers into preparing factories and sites, to run health and safety assessments, ordering stock, contacting customers, you name it.

And, as Boris continually reminded them throughout his address, to stay alert while they did it.

> *"It is now almost two months since the people of this country begin to put up with restrictions on freedom — your freedom — of a kind that we have never seen before in peace or war. And you have shown the good sense to support those rules overwhelmingly. You have put up with all the hardships of that programme of social distancing. Because you understand that as things stand, and as the experience of every other country has shown, it's the only way to defeat the coronavirus — the most vicious threat this country has faced in my lifetime. And though the death toll has been tragic and the suffering immense. And though we grieve for all those we have lost, it is a fact that by adopting those measures we prevented this country from being engulfed by...a catastrophe in which the reasonable worst case scenario was half a million fatalities. And thanks to you we have protected our NHS and saved many thousands of lives. And so I know — you know — it would be madness now to throw away that achievement by allowing a second spike. We must stay alert."*

NOW, don't get me wrong, I'm not anti-alertness. If anything, I'm the opposite, a huge fan both in principle and practice.

After all, alertness is what stops us confusing beer with bleach or wearing Speedos to a funeral. Alertness is what keeps us out of potholes when cycling at 20mph. Without alertness, we'd need multi-storey cemeteries to cope with all the excess corpses whose cause of death was entered on the post-mortem certificate as *Not Paying Attention*.

All I'm saying is that to tell an already confused nation that staying alert was now all we had to do to see off coronavirus was, in Nicola Sturgeon's words, 'vague and imprecise'.

And in your author's, an exercise in advanced half wittery.

Sturgeon was already super-miffed that No10 had leaked this new message to tame journalists and hearing it officially hadn't chilled her out one bit as she announced: "Clarity is paramount. We respect the right of other nations to make their decisions, but not to confuse the guidance."

She went on to call Scotland's progress was 'fragile', said it could be 'catastrophic' to drop existing measures at a 'critical time' and added, for the avoidance of doubt: "I don't know what Stay Alert means."

NEXT day, the simplicity of the PM's speech — or, as he called it, 'first sketch of a roadmap for reopening society' — was highlighted in his presentation to the Commons of a 60-page explanatory dossier. Nicola Sturgeon, meanwhile, said on TV:

> "Staying at home now is an expression of love, kindness and solidarity. We are doing it for each other, not just ourselves. It is how we protect each other, protect our NHS, and save lives and it will bring forward a return to normality."

She was way too prim to throw in a *Fuck You, Boris* for good measure. But it was understood.

Already, memes were flying around changing the *Stay Alert, Control The Virus* message to *Ignore Boris, Listen To Nicola*. We'd feared Scotland and England were speeding towards a fork in the road with a different opinion on which direction to take — and now, it was clear one had decided to head for John O'Groats while the other was halfway to Lands End.

What's more, just a few weeks on from Sturgeon claiming that 'politics is the very last thing on my mind', this situation had become 100 per cent political.

It was Yes versus No all over again, North versus South, Leave versus Remain, Nat versus Tory; in other words, Us versus Them. And while plenty seemed to warm to this, to welcome the chance of taking sides and pointing fingers, for me it was a depressing turn of events that brought out the worst in too many, a pettiness that did no one any good.

The one saving grace from a Scottish point of view was that we were still in the Stay-At-Home camp, because given that there's nothing we like better than showing the English up, we seemed hell-bent on being world Staying-At-Home champions while seeing our cousins across the border as so many chimps running riot in a giant warehouse full of bananas and tea.

Had it been the other way around, though? Had the PM been the ones urging caution while the FM was the one allowing us greater freedom?

Trust me, I'm a Scotsman who knows for sure we'd have kicked the arse right out of it.

We'd have been firing up barbecues on top of Hadrian's Wall and blowing the smoke southwards with industrial-sized fans. We'd have been jogging in thousand-strong crowds, not to get ourselves fit, but just to stick it right up our neighbours.

Had it induced mass coronaries, we'd have died laughing.

Friday May 15
•China marks one month with no new coronavirus deaths, Slovenia becomes first European country to proclaim an end to its outbreak.
•Lithuania, Latvia and Estonia reopen borders to each other.
•Former UK chancellor of the exchequer Alistair Darling predicts the cost of lockdown will be greater than that of the 2008 banking crisis.

TODAY, we became the proudest of parents to a beautiful, bouncing puppy.

His name is Sherlock, he's an apricot-coloured, coal-eyed, fleeceball of an Australian Labradoodle and an absolute force of nature. Born six days before lockdown at a farm out in the Dunbartonshire countryside, that old devil called self-isolation dictated we couldn't get to pick him in person. Yet this turned out to matter not a jot, because from the first photo the breeder sent of a dewy-eyed, fortnight-old litter, we knew he was the one. In that snap and all those that followed, he was the only one who looked right into the camera lens.

This fluffy little bundle with dark, sparkling eyes and a yellow ribbon around his neck was so alert he could have taken over Boris's daily briefing and the nation would have got the message in an instant.

When we bumped over a mile of rutted track to pick him up that drizzly Friday morning, he was waiting outside the farmhouse in a little pen, looking up at us without a shred of nerves. A quick barf on the ride home aside, he never missed a beat all day then slept like the baby he was all night. By late on Saturday, he'd got the concept of the toilet-training pad and I'm not ashamed to say that when, just before bedtime, he did his first-ever poo on one, I had a little weep of sheer pride.

Every day since has been an adventure; a mega-panicky scoot to the vet when he had an upset tummy, his discovery that underneath the sofa was a better place to kip than the bed we'd put together for him (complete with pillow, blanket and an alarm clock wrapped in a towel to replicate his mummy's heartbeat), the puncture-marks on our arms from gnashers like little needles as he began to suffer teething pains, taking him for his second set of jags that meant he could go out for walkies a few days later, seeing him make pals with Gracie and Bruno and Flora and Leyla and all the other neighbourhood doggies; all of whose names we found out before we knew those of their owners, for this is the way of the pet-owner.

Most of all, it's been a wonderful adventure seeing him grow so fast he seemed an inch taller and wider each time he wrestled himself out from a hidey-hole that, like a bloke having a mid-life crisis who's determined to pour himself into a muscle-fit shirt, he refused to admit was already way too tight for comfort.

I absolutely loved the couple of weeks before his final jags, when he wasn't allowed out on the lead and I'd pop him into a papoose (possibly the wankiest piece of West End wankery ever invented) and we'd go for walkies with his blond, fuzzily inquisitive little head poking out of the top. The attention he got from those early days out made us wonder about pimping him to single friends as a sure-fire pick-up magnet.

But the best thing of all about Sherlock is the focus he brought to our lives at a time when we both really, really needed it; because by early May, six weeks on since she'd last been allowed to work, Sonia was properly climbing the walls.

Every mention of this country or that country re-opening their hair salons had her clinging to the hope that we'd soon do the same. She'd study every regulation laid down in Denmark or Germany or New Zealand, work out from this how to plan her appointment diary to suit the new normal. She started warning clients they'd have to dry their own hair at home to avoid spreading germs through airborne water particles.

All in all, she was pretty well demented, even if the one upside was that we'd settles her financial worries, her bank agreeing to what the government called a Bounceback Loan, a few-questions-asked advance repayable over six years with the first 12 months free. Off the back of this, we set up an online store selling gift vouchers, which flew off the shelves.

It wasn't ideal; all it meant was that, somewhere down the line, she'd be out of pocket again. But at least for now she wasn't fretting about cashflow.

Whereas I was fretting about everything.

A few days after Sherlock arrived, with Sonia's spirits finally lifted thanks to having something to take care of, to comb and bath and fuss over, I went the other way and took a major anxiety attack that lasted a day and a bit; shaking, weepy, scared, tired, weak. It took until well into the second day before it flashed into my head why it was happening.

Back in the spring of 1984, my mum and dad had got a little golden Labrador pup who, one Saturday morning, dashed out the front door when I was trying to get his lead on for a walk, squeezed through a gap in the hedge, hurtled into the road and went straight under a silver Volvo.

I don't remember anything about the driver — who must have got a horrible fright — yet despite having repressed the incident for 36 years, the make and colour of the car were clear as day. So too the picture of going out with a shovel and a black binbag to lift the pup and clean bits of him o the tarmac, of going to the vet to dispose of the wee soul. Now, more than half a lifetime of repressing the memory later, it all came back and messed me up.

Anyway, we talked some stuff out, I got properly upset and the shaking began to settle. A couple of 20mg fluoxetines, a good long sleep and the fresh air of a bike ride later, life felt like it was easing back to normal; until, early the following week, the shaking returned, bringing with it the feeling of being permanently on the brink of tears, the ton-weight tiredness, the inability to put a finger on the keyboard or to drum up any enthusiasm for what was usually the joy of building my indoor cycling classes. This time, the reason didn't come in a flash of recollection. It was just...*there*, clinging, dragging me down.

Sonia's assessment was that I'd become more isolated over the previous couple of weeks, that I'd seemed increasingly withdrawn, that I'd seem to have the weight of the world on my shoulders. Her solution was an order to get on the phone to my kids and to close pals; not to pour my heart out and plead for sympathy, simply to engage.

All you've done is write for the paper, write your book, work on your classes, she said. Everything's inside your own head, she said. And, as always, she was right, though as always with mental health issues, the theory's far easier than the practice. In other words, had it been *her* having the anxiety attacks I'd have told her exactly the same things she was drumming into me, but putting her advice into action was a different problem.

As ever, getting on the bike was the first step to sweeping away the cobwebs, even if she virtually had to dress me and lift me into the saddle, as right to the very last I was making excuses about the tyres not inflating properly and not finding my favourite sunglasses and goodness knows what else. But I went — and it was the most amazing therapy money can't buy.

Trouble is, you can't cycle all day, every day. You have to work, clean the house, walk the dog, pay the bills, return phone calls, be a husband and a dad and a pal. And when anxiety strikes, all of these mundane tasks that we usually carry out without even thinking become that bit more onerous.

I'm guessing that of the millions of you reading this — hey, a boy can dream — more will recognise yourselves in the above than do not, especially at a time when *We Know Nothing* seemed a title harder than ever to argue with.

As this manic month's avalanche of information overload and ever more mixed messages barrelled down the mountain and took us with it, we suddenly plunged into an echoing chasm of story after story, drama after drama, that made us wondered if the speed of the fall of the crunch of the impact would kill us first.

And if it seems as if I lost control of that metaphor there, what the fuck else do your expect?

ON May 19, the *Daily Mail* went to war with England's teaching unions, blaming them for Westminster's failure to nail down a date when schools could re-open. Evidence from 22 EU states, it claimed, showed a return to the classroom "suggests little or no risk to pupils, teachers or families".

Denmark had reopened primaries and nurseries a month ago and has seen infection rates continue to fall. Norway had taken similar action without a rise, while 1.4 million French pupils went back last week and of around 40,000 schools and nurseries only 70 were closed again following virus cases. Germany has reopened schools for older children and plans to bring younger age groups back later in the summer.

In England, though, a string of local authorities rejected

No10's timetable for reopening schools, while the National Education Union claims it isn't even safe for teachers to mark workbooks.

ON May 20, the world saw its largest daily rise in coronavirus cases yet, 106,000 in 24 hours. World Health Organisation director general, Dr Tedros Adhanom Ghebreyesus, said the virus was spreading in poorer countries just as wealthier nations were emerging from lockdown. Researchers at Johns Hopkins University in Baltimore say at least 4.9 million are known to have become infected and at least 326,000 to have died.

ON May 21, we learned that 1,000 hospital patients had been transferred to care homes in Scotland before mandatory Covid-19 testing kicked in — more than three times as any as health secretary Jeane Freeman had previously admitted to.

In mid-April, Ms Freeman had reported that 'just over 900' elderly patients had been taken out of hospitals but 'primarily' went home, with only around 300 placed in care. Just a couple of days ago, she was still putting this care figure at only 38 per cent of hospital discharges, but last night she admitted it was 921 for March alone, with the total by April 21, when testing was introduced for patients leaving wards, expected to be significantly higher.

To make a difficult day for Holyrood tougher still, it was then revealed they had also missed a promised target on testing within care homes. Three weeks back, Nicola Sturgeon had vowed to check all residents and staff in premises with a Covid-19 outbreak, but by today — despite having spare testing capacity — had only delivered in half of them.

When the First Minister made her pledge, Scottish NHS staff were able to deliver just over 8,350 tests a day. Since then, that has risen to 13,000 and is due to reach 15,000 by the end of this week. But tests have only exceeded 3,000 in a day once this month and have been as low as 1,280.

ON May 22, however, Nicola Sturgeon was back in 'nothing to

see here, please disperse' mode as she announced a four-stage plan to ease lockdown.

Within a week, we'll be able to meet one other household, but only outdoors and within five miles of home. Sunbathing and picnics will be allowed, as will non-contact outdoor sports (golf, tennis, bowls, passive-aggressive marital disputes) while garden centres and recycling facilities will reopen. Come June 18, it's hoped beer gardens and outside restaurant areas can follow, with punters allowed inside by July 9 at the earliest. Sturgeon's plan is for schools to reopen on August 11, but on a part-time basis with parents still expected to oversee some home studies.

Train and bus services will continue to be severely reduced, with passengers wearing face masks. Office workers will operate from home until at least July 9, though the construction industry is preparing to return 'towards the end of this month'.

Football may resume in phase two — if it ever gets its arse in gear enough to decide who's playing in which league — but with matches behind closed doors and even then only if clubs make stadiums 'bio-secure' and players receive the regular testing NHS frontline workers still can't get.

All of which sounds far too straightforward, so it was only right that the FM should then throw in a note of confusion by suggesting that although we're meant to stay outdoors when visiting friends and family, we might be able to pop indoors should we need the loo.

She said: "We want to be more flexible when it comes to maybe visiting your elderly mother who you haven't seen for ages, to sit in the garden. But if we have to travel a very long distance...you might have to go into the house to use the bathroom and risk leaving the virus on surfaces."

AND then, come Saturday May 23, the avalanche caught fire

19: DOMINIC GOES FOR A DRIVE

T O TELL the full story of what Dominic Cummings got up to when he was suffering from the virus and supposedly shielding himself and his family isn't easy without using the words selfish, arrogant and dickhead.

So why even try?

Yes, we could compose what some would sniff was a far more articulate way to describe a moment in the timeline of the pandemic as remarkable as it should have been regrettable. But it wouldn't be half as accurate or as satisfying.

Because when Boris Johnson's spinweiler, the man behind the message that the nation should Stay Home and Save Lives, travelled the length of England at a time when his bosses were assuring us he was sweating bullets in his London sickbed, his actions *were* selfish, they *were* arrogant and he *was* a dickhead.

He was selfish because, while the Government message he'd helped write left tens of millions terrified *not* to Stay Home and Save Lives if they tell ill, he decided to 'use my initiative' by taking his wife and child to a bolthole nearly 300 miles away, a trip that ended with the child in hospital.

He was arrogant because, even confronted with what he'd done, he not only saw no reason to apologise, he also refused to accept — or even care — that his trip looked bad in light of his own iron-clad advice to the nation. This morning, he stood outside his London home and told a scrum of reporters: "Who cares how it looks? You guys are probably as right about this as you were about Brexit. And remember how right you were about that?"

I barely need to add that all of the above is why he was also a dickhead.

THAT morning, Saturday May 23, Cummings had been tag-teamed by the mass- and up-market press, the *Mirror* and *Guardian* both telling how he'd broken lockdown rules to visit his parents while sufferings symptoms of coronavirus.

A neighbour in Durham claimed to have had 'the shock of my life' –– how unremarkable a life has this guy *had*? –– when he saw the 'distinctive figure' of Cummings outside the house on March 31, a day after it was reported that he was infected and quarantined.

Four days before that, Government advice on preventing the spread of the virus had become a law stating:

> *"You should not visit family who do not live in your home. The only exception is having shopping or medication dropped off."*

This last proviso had got Cabinet minister Robert Jenrick off the hook after he drove from London to drop supplies off for *his* parents, even if the fact that they live 150 miles away in Herefordshire made you wonder if he might have asked someone in the vicinity to pop round with milk and aspirin.

In late March, however, Downing Street had insisted that Cummings was safely tucked up in his bed at home, this backed up on April 14 when his journalist wife Mary Wakefield wrote in *The Spectator* that, on March 27 — the day both Boris Johnson and Health Secretary Matt Hancock were diagnosed with coronavirus symptoms — her husband had 'rushed home' to care for her. A day later, she wrote, 'he began to feel weird' and then couldn't get out of bed.

"Day in, day out for 10 days he lay doggo with a high fewer and spasms," she went on. "Day six is a turning point, when you either get better or head for ICU. But was Dom fighting off the bug or heading for a ventilator? Just as Dom began to feel better...Boris was heading in the other direction, to hospital."

This was April 5, the same day Scotland's chief medical officer Cathy Calderwood was being photographed with her family at *their* second home in Fife. Also that day, a witness in Durham claims to have seen Cummings, although this was later denied. Wakefield's article does not say where they were during quarantine, but it adds: *"After the uncertainty of the bug itself, we emerged into the almost comical uncertainty of London lockdown."*

Cummings himself wrote in the same issue: *"At the end of March and for the first two weeks of April I was ill, so we were both shut in together."*

He described the experience as *'sticky...everything is covered in a layer of spilt Ribena, honey, peanut butter and play school glue'*, though whether it was stickier than the situation No10 found it in is another matter — because whatever way you look at it, whatever your allegiances, whether or not you see any of this as an issue or a nonsense, the truth is that they lied about his whereabouts, just as Holyrood had lied about Calderwood's reasons for breaking the rules on non-essential travel.

The difference, of course, is that Holyrood failed.

Calderwood was gone from her post within 18 hours of the story breaking, as was Westminster's top boffin Professor Neil Ferguson early this month after he was caught sneaking his married lover round for a cuddle while the rest of us weren't even allowed to visit our own families. Health secretary Matt Hancock described himself as 'speechless' at this and claimed Ferguson 'took the right decision to resign', while former Tory leader Sir Iain Duncan Smith said the boffin's behaviour 'risks undermining the government's lockdown message'.

Quite why they weren't quite so lost for words now and quite why they didn't feel Cummings had also undermined the message remains a mystery. All we know is that not for one nano-second was there a hint that he'd resign or be sacked.

Yet the fact that he, his wife and their son were infected is not an excuse for their 500-odd-mile round trip, even if he and No 10 tried to pass it off as one. His argument was that he feared both of them becoming incapacitated and being unable to look after their four-year-old, the inference being that no one within a 250-mile radius was able to help out. He cited a section in the Government's advice that reads:

"We are aware not all these measures will be possible if you are living with children, but keep following this guidance to the best of your ability."

It was a defence that offered more questions than answers.

•What if he'd taken ill at the wheel and crashed the car?

•What if his wife and/or child had become so 'incapacitated' they needed hospital treatment, but they were stuck in the middle of nowhere?

•Did they drive to Durham without stopping, or did they pop into motorway services for a pee and a coffee? In which case, were they ever within two metres of any other customer?

The more you thought about the potential for mishap, the more it felt like far from offering an excuse to hit the road, this situation Cummings found himsef in was all the more reason for locking the door, muting the phone and crawling under the duvet for a sweat-soaked week, just like the rest of us hadn't been so much advised as ordered to. Them's the rules. It's the law of land, something he was reminded of when, as it turns out, Durham Constabulary dropped in on Tuesday March 31 to confirm he was in fact who the neighbour had said he was and to 'reiterate the appropriate advice around essential travel'.

No further action was taken, not even the on-the-spot £60 fine we'd been warned would come with any flouting of that law brought in five days earlier.

Little wonder, then, that the cry across the land was that there was — all together now — one law for us and another for them. Little wonder that, almost in an instant, the mood of the nation towards self-isolation and social-distancing changed from a reluctant shrug that it's for our own good to a teenage sulk of *Why The Hell Should We?*

This, Dominic, is why it mattered how it looked. This shift in attitude, this erosion of trust and this loss of patience that would soon result in mass demonstrations across the nation without a thought for the risk.

To all intents, lockdown as we knew it ended the moment Dominic went for a drive. Especially when news broke of the day he got behind the wheel again and went to Barnard Castle.

THESE past few years, I've had so many eye appointments they're thinking of relocating the clinic to my spare bedroom.

They've tried everything on that dodgy right lamp. They've dished out endless drops, pills and ointments, stuck needles in, cut a lump from under the bottom lid, removed a knackered cornea and sewn in one harvested from a dead dude.

But you know one thing they haven't suggested? Strapping a toddler into the car and driving around until my sights feels better. And why? Because any doctor who prescribed this as a way to safely test a patient's sight would be struck off. While anyone who does it off their own bat deserves to be locked up.

Yet this is the reason Dominic Cummings offers us for his decision to drive 25 miles from Durham to Barnard Castle after already having driven 250 miles with his sick family in tow; that he wanted to make sure his eyesight was good enough to let them make it back to London.

He told us this during a press conference in the Downing Street rose garden on Tuesday March 26, an hour of live telly that either confirmed just how little Cummings fears media disapproval or just how scared the political lobby are of him. Because you sat there, screaming at the screen for them to get stuck in harder, to hold his feet up to Boris's firepit. You raged at his refusal to offer a morsel of remorse, to even accept why there was a fuss.

No, he didn't regret his actions.

Yes, he believes he acted reasonably and within the law.

No, he didn't believe there was one rule for him and another for the rest.

Most of all, he wasn't there to apologise — and certainly not to entertain calls for his head — but to 'clear up any confusion and misunderstandings'.

He told how, while in Durham on April 2, his son had suffered 'a bad fever' and had been whisked off to hospital by ambulance but had not tested positive for coronavirus. Next day, Cummings said he picked him and his wife up in their car 'because there were no taxis'.

As for that visit to tourist hotspot Barnard Castle on 12 April, during which time he admitted to leaving the car and walking 'ten to 15 metres to the riverbank', he said: "My wife was very worried, particularly as my eyesight seemed to have been affected. She did not want to risk a near-300-mile drive with our child, so we agreed we should go for a short drive to see if I could drive safely."

You yelled for someone to ask him whether it had crossed his mind that fatal traffic accidents can happen as easily on a short journey as a long one. Your telly was peddle-dashed with spittle and flecks of Digestive biscuit as you bawled:

> *"What if he'd started seeing double, misjudged a bend and taken out whoever was coming the other way?!?"*

It felt corrupt enough that the chancer was still employed despite making a needless 520-mile round trip from London to County Durham on the pretext that it was the good of his family's health, while spinning the message that staying home was for the good of everyone else's. If he really *is* so reckless that he thinks his eyesight's best tested from behind a steering wheel, it's incredible that he also hasn't lost his licence.

For me, that's the real scandal here. While Calderwood may

have been arrogant and stupid in making those visits to her second home that cost her the gig as Scotland's chief medical officer, at least no one could have been hurt by her actions.

Cummings? He was ill, his wife was ill, their four-year-old son was shut in a tin box with them for hours and ended up ill — and then, rather than seek medical help when he feared the virus might affect his sight, he decides to play Wacky Races.

Yet when confronted, he admits he doesn't care. When his boss is cornered, *he* burbles that if Dom says it was ok, then it was ok. When put on the spot, wet-lipped waste of space Michael Gove - who, like Bojo, seems scared stiff of the guy - stuttered that he too has on occasion checked his mincers not by reading an optician's chart, but by going for a spin.

Tory ministers who privately were raging not only at what Cummings had done but by the fact that it had been covered up for so long still felt the need to support him in public for fear of their own jackets being on decidedly shaky pegs. In short, if anyone harboured lingering doubts over whether Johnson's was a Cabinet with more than a few screws loose, this episode surely dashed them for good.

CUMMINGS looked faintly bored as he claimed in his press conference that he'd 'acted on instinct' when he decided to pack up the family and head to an empty property owned by his farming family.

Doesn't say much for a man who's meant to have his finger on the pulse of the nation, not when tens of millions have sent the past two months resisting those same instincts with all their might and against all their better judgement.

I mean, what if we'd all just done what suited us best all this time? Everyone with parents in care homes or partners living on the other side of town, all of us who long for a hug from kids living away from home or who are simply stir crazy and fancied driving somewhere leafy? It would have been a recipe for pandemic-emonium. Yet instead, the common sense and sac-rifice of 90 per cent of the population has helped the scientists and the NHS do their job in horrible circumstances.

The actions of Cummings, on the other hand, did nothing to help anyone — not even himself, as he says he drove to Dur-ham in case he needed childcare, but as this turned out not be the case he'd have been as well at home, where the chances are his kiddie might not have got ill. But you know what gets me even more than all his shrugs and his bored denials and all the rubbish about his bogus eyesight test? Hearing him excuse what he'd done by highlighting a loophole in the guidelines put there not for people afforded the luxury of second homes, but those whose *only* homes are the least safe place on earth.

During that rose garden conference — sat behind a bare trestle table, sleeves rolled up on open-necked white shirt — he quoted a clause about travel being legitimate in 'excep-tional circumstances' as if this included his situation. But he must have known this clause had been inserted to ensure vic-tims of domestic abuse could leave home without risk of po-lice action should they be stopped.

These are some of the most vulnerable among us at any time, not just during this crisis. Yet Cummings had the nerve to piggy-back their misery in a bid to justify his own selfish-ness, his own arrogance, his own downright dickheadedness.

And while we're at it, let's add one more act of deception to the charge sheet; re-writing history to cover his tyre tracks. Cummings attacked The Media™ for 'running false stories' suggesting he didn't care about Covid-19 or its death toll, when in fact he'd blogged a year ago on 'the possible threat of coronaviruses and urgent need for planning'.

Fact check: His original post of March 4 2019 didn't mention coronaviruses and was only edited in at 8.55pm on April 14, the day he returned from Durham.

So, how could Johnson still justify backing him after all of this? Simple, he wouldn't dare not, just as Gove backed him because he knows the right people to keep in with as he climbs the greasy political poll. So fair play amidst all this to full-time Moray MP and part-time football ref Douglas Ross for taking a stand and resigning from the Cabinet in protest.

A gesture as welcome as it was ironic, since the guy spends every weekend hearing strangers telling him he must be blind.

I'VE already shared my hand-knitted theory about how we should only be concerned with the things we can control and how unhealthy it is to carry the burden of the things we can't. But what happened with Cummings is a timely reminder that even if we can't control what effect our own actions have on others, we should always be aware of what *influence* they might have; this difference between control and influence being a subtle one, but no less important for it.

For instance, the main reason Nicola Sturgeon is currently dragging her feet on following Johnson's lead in loosening lockdown is her fear of a second spike in infections. And today, social media is awash with post from punters claiming that if this infection strikes, it'll be down to the likes of Cummings and Cathy Calderwood showing such a terrible example.

Yet as much as I've made my feelings clear on the unforgivable actions of both, this is a load of old bollocks.

The drivers in mile-long queues for a Big Mac or a KFC? The morons lifting barriers aside at closed countryside car parks so they can dump the motor and go for a walk? The selfish sods forcing mountain rescue volunteers to scramble because they saw they sunshine and decided they were Bear Grylls rather than a human mixed grill?

The ones crowding onto every beach and into every park, the ones having illegal house parties and raves that morph into riots? The demented drunk in Glasgow jailed last week for spitting at a cop and laughing 'coronavirus, coronavirus'?

Cummings and Calderwood didn't *make* them do it. They did it and keep on doing it because they *choose* to, because they think it's their right. Yes, clowns like Cummings have to take responsibility for being hypocrites. But as your mammy would say: If they jumped in a loch, would you do it too?

For instance, the head of the Scottish Police Federation has warned Sturgeon against turning advice on social distancing into law, because it would be impossible to impose — and while he may be right, the bottom line is that with proper *self*-policing, it would be the easiest thing in the world.

All it takes is for each of us to stop pointing the finger at Calderwood and Cummings and whoever else for what *we've* done and start remembering that our responsibilities to ourselves and each other mean more than a tan or a box of McNuggets.

For the umpteenth time in this book, I'm aware that what comes next makes me sound older than Joe Biden's grandad, but I learned about responsibility growing up in a tenement, where everyone took their turn cleaning the stairs without being reminded, where the night before pay-day all the mums pooled whatever was in the cupboard so no one went short of a decent dinner.

This has always stayed with me, it's always seemed to be the simplest of concepts that if you do the right thing, then there's a far better chance of the person next to you doing the same.

That's where influence comes in, that's where the example we set to others matters so much. That's where, for all we can't control how others react to our actions, we have to try and think two steps ahead to how those actions will resonate down the line; butterflies and hurricanes, all that stuff.

In the case of Dominic Cummings, he wasn't to know that the furore over his two fingers to lockdown would coincide with an atrocity that sent shock waves around the globe.

But perhaps if he'd had the sense and the humility to think ahead, perhaps if he'd given a second's thought to how his selfishness might influence the attitudes of millions, the scenes we saw across Britain in the days and weeks ahead might have been a whole lot less chaotic, violent and divisive.

◆ ◆ ◆

THE night before that press conference in Downing Street's rose garden, a 46-year-old black man called George Floyd was murdered in Minneapolis when a white police officer called Derek Chauvin kneeled on his throat for almost eight minutes on the pretext of restraining him.

Floyd was heard repeatedly calling out that he couldn't breathe. Bystanders begged Chauvin to let him be. Instead, fellow officers J. Alexander Kueng and Thomas Lane moved into help restrain Floyd, while colleague Tou Thao held back onlookers. As Floyd called for his mother and told Chauvin 'I'm about to die', he was told to 'relax'. Officer Thao then told witnesses: "This is why you don't do drugs, kids."

Even when an ambulance arrived, Chauvin kept his knee on Floyd's neck for a further minute. By the time he relented, he'd been pushing down for seven minutes and 46 seconds, Floyd was motionless and at 9.25pm was pronounced dead at a nearby emergency room.

Floyd was alleged to have bought a pack of cigarettes from a convenience store with a fake $20 note and police claimed that when staff followed him to his car to demand the good back, he was 'in the driver's seat and awfully drunk'.

But even if he'd stolen the shop's takings at gunpoint — even if he'd robbed Fort Knox — those police officers had no right to do what they do. The brutal truth is that George Floyd was executed without trial and the subtext is that it happened because of his colour.

That same day, a white woman called Amy Cooper had called police to Central Park in New York after a black man called Christian Cooper asked her to follow rules by putting her dog on a lead in a wooded area. She told the 911 operator: "There's an African-American man...he is threatening me..."

By now, Mr Cooper was recording the incident, footage showing Ms Cooper pointing her finger in his face. He also quite clearly says 'thank you' when she finally puts a lead on the dog. A little cameo, this, which pales beside the events in Minneapolis a few hours later, but which in conjunction with it — and added to the appearance in a Georgia court earlier this week of three white men accusing of shooting dead 25-year-old black jogger Ahmud Arbery — made racism *the* hot-button issue on the planet overnight.

Throughout May 26, tributes were placed at the spot where George Floyd died, many referencing the Black Lives Matter campaign which called for non-violent disobedience to protest police brutality against African-American suspects. Hundreds marched on the city's police HQ carrying placards and banners reading 'Justice For George' and 'I Can't Breathe'.

This one demonstration became two, three and more across the Minneapolis area, then fanned out into across the United States. As numbers grew, so did tensions; property vandalised, looting, stand-offs with armed riot police.

By May 29, a night-time curfew had been imposed across Minneapolis as a pattern emerged of peaceful daytime protests turning ugly after dark. By June 9, one local newspaper would report that more than 500 businesses had been damaged or destroyed, dozens by fire.

Inside a fortnight, protests had spread to an estimated 2,000 towns and cities worldwide. Crowds besieged the White House gates, forcing President Trump to first scramble to an underground bunker and then stage a photo-op visit to church, where he posed with a Bible held upside down in his right hand.

How the church didn't spontaneously combust is a miracle.

Yet no matter what justification anyone made for such a public display of anger, there's no doubt the sheer scale of the movement posed a huge threat to public safety through the potential spread of the virus. Yes, there were many daytime gatherings where protestors went out of their way to socially distance. But by night, all bets were off and pretty soon the chaos in some cities was going on round the clock.

In Britain, the movement would ignite on Sunday June 7, when a statue of seventeenth century slave trader Edward Colston was toppled Saddam-style from its plinth in Bristol, dragged through the streets and hurled into the harbour, a gesture symbolic of the 19,000 Africans who died in transportation by Colston's ships and were thrown overboard.

On that pivotal Sunday in Bristol, an estimated 10,000 had turned out, with social distancing on few minds. Soon, it was same story in Trafalgar Square, in Glasgow's George Square and dozens of points in between — the twist now being the confrontation in the air as those gangs of self-styled patriots gathered as defenders our heritage, sparking running battles with police and anti-racism protestors alike.

In Glasgow, there were skirmishes, but in truth these were mainly down to Celtic and Rangers supporters looking for an excuse to square up in the absence of football. On Saturday June 13 in the heart of London, though, it really kicked off — a horrible, furious, confused day where hordes of white, mostly young, mostly male and overwhelmingly angry counter-demonstrators turned up to 'protect' monuments which they revered and respected so much that one was arrested for taking a pee on a memorial to a policeman murdered in a terrorist attack out the House of Parliament.

It was a day summed up for me by two very different images.

The first was a photo of burly Black Lives Matter protester Patrick Hutchinson heaving an injured white man over his shoulder and carrying him to safety after he'd been beaten to the ground. It didn't matter to Hutchinson that the victim — shaven-headed and inked with a Millwall tattoo — was part of the mob whose methods of 'protecting' London had included pelting cops with bottles and stones and smoke bombs.

All he saw was the prospect of the cause he'd come to support being wrecked by a brainless minority battering what they saw as the enemy, so he shoved his way in among flying boots and flailing fists to get a fellow human being out of harm's way. He'd come to tell the world that Black Lives Matter, but he was demonstrating something too many of his fellow protestors had ignored — that no cause is an excuse to see yourself as being above the law.

And the second image? Ah man, it made me laugh out loud. It showed a crowd who'd come to 'protect' those statues, youngish men in baseball caps and t-shirts and shades, proudly posing behind a flag bearing a Union Jack, the head of a roaring lion...and the slogan:

BRITIAN FIRST.

They really should go on an exchange trip with that guy in the States cruising in his **NO YOU'RE RIGHT'S** pick-up truck.

FOR those of us following all of this at home, those suffering from the virus, shielding from it or simply doing their best not to spread it, these were dispiriting scenes; not just because of the anger and the violence, but because they — *we* — were being warned daily that one false move could wreck all our chances of emerging from lockdown any time soon.

We were being told we couldn't hug our parents, go for a pint or go to the football for fear of catastrophe, yet thousands were milling and marauding on our doorsteps without a hint of Westminster or Holyrood stepping in. It made no sense, until you realised the problem for politicians in London and Edinburgh was that the Black Lives Matter movement was *such* a game-changer, it was *so* important to so many, that to ban it could have backfired spectacularly, even if they imposed that ban for all the right health-based reasons.

This is why I bear Dominic Cummings so much resentment for the way he gave lockdown the finger and acted on 'instinct' by driving his sick family the length of England. Because even if he truly believed he was doing the right thing, he should at least have recognised his wider responsibility as a key fgure in a government coping with a pandemic and realised the scale of the potential knock-on from his actions.

He wasn't to know George Floyd would be murdered. But he must have had *some* idea that *something* would happen along the way to throw his selfishness, his arrogance, his dick-headedness into sharp relief, something that would make the public point and yell: *"See? This is all your fault."*

After all, we in the idiot public have been told throughout lockdown that if we don't do the right thing, the death toll will be our fault, so we were entitled to ask why those in power wouldn't grasp that it works both ways.

Why? The arrogance Cummings showed from the minute he was doorstepped in the wake of those first blaring head-lines told us exactly why.

He didn't care. He said so, straight out. He didn't care how it looked, didn't care what anyone thought. He was right and the entire nation was wrong. And sadly, infuriatingly, his is an attitude that permeates all the way along the corridors of power.

Just as the chances are George Floyd wouldn't have been murdered over a dodgy $20 note had he not been black, Dominic Cummings wouldn't have got away with driving his sick family the length of Britain had he not been powerful.

20: WE'RE JUST HAVING A LITTLE EARTHQUAKE HERE, RYAN..

Sunday June 7
·UK coronavirus death toll rises by 77 overnight, the lowest figure since lock-down began.
·No new deaths in Scotland or Northern Ireland.
·Matt Hancock denies epidemiology expert Prof John Edmunds' claim that failure to lock down earlier 'cost a lot of lives'.

TODAY, the good people of New Zealand hold their breath. Because tomorrow, their lovely little country could be officially declared coronavirus-free.

It's a joyful prospect that hangs on whether anyone among them comes down with the bug overnight. But as they're now closing in one three weeks without a single fresh case...well, fingers and toes crossed.

Our Kiwi cousins recorded their first case on February 28, two days before Scotland's. Yet while the official death toll here now approaches 2,500, theirs — with a population just 300,000 fewer than ours — sits at 22.

Think about that for a moment. Britain's losses as a whole would fill a 40,000-capacity football stadium. New Zealand's would make up two teams, with no substitutes.

Sure, there are mitigating factors, such as New Zealand's relatively remote position on the planet (it lies more than 1,000 miles off nearest neighbour, Australia) and a population density of just 48 per square mile compared to Scotland's 174. But even then, its chief medical officer Dr Ashley Bloomfield estimates that 'had we been the UK, we'd have been looking at 3,000-3,500 deaths', so they must be doing *something* right.

The most coronavirus patients in New Zealand's hospitals at one time has been 20, the last of them leaving isolation in

Auckland on May 18, meaning that if no new cases appeared within 28 days—a week tomorrow—they'd be able to say the virus has been eliminated and could hit their intending target of ending lockdown on June 22.

However, PM Jacinda Ardern is so pleased with how well her restrictions have worked she's ready to open everything bar their borders from tomorrow. This would be a triumph for good science, good sense, for patience and for co-operation, a gold star for a PM who has genuinely *led* throughout this crisis, right down to taking a 20 per cent pay cut while Westminster MPs were awarding themselves £10,000 in extra expenses.

It hasn't all been roses, of course. Thousands have lost their jobs and a priceless tourism industry is in bits. But they've rebuilt before after devastating earthquakes and you'd back them to do so again, not least because of the crystal-clear communication Ardern has with her people, day in and day out.

For me, this communication is a key reason why New Zealand is so close to eradicating the virus, while the mixed messages from Holyrood and Downing Street contribute hugely the fact that, only on Wednesday, the UK's 176 deaths were the same as the EU's 27 member states put together and to Scotland, as of today, being locked down for as long as Wuhan was, but without any sign of a return to some kind of normal.

Not that we're alone in struggling to match Jacinda Ardern's success. Over the past week, Japan, China, South Korea, Iran , Lebanon, Germany, Saudi Arabia, El Salvador, Iraq, Sri Lanka and Pakistan have all reintroduced some form of lockdown amidst fears of a second spike. Tonight, this will be uppermost in close on five million Kiwi minds. They'll know how well they've done so far, yet also how easily their efforts could be undone in no time. With Ardern at the helm, though, the good ship Kiwi seems steady as they go.

◆ ◆ ◆

IT'S the last Monday in May and Jacinda Ardern has just gone live on breakfast telly from New Zealand's government HQ, known to one and all as the Beehive.

Behind her, the stage is set for that day's coronavirus briefing, with two podiums, two national flags and a pair of pop-up banners urging the nation to unite against the bug and advising that the threat is at Alert Level 2.

Like most news anchors, Newshub AM's Ryan Bridge is used to politicians interrupting him to break the flow of the interview. Usually, though, it's down either to them not wanting to address a difficult issue or to basic rudeness — while this time, Ardern has a decent excuse:

"We're just having a bit of an earthquake here, Ryan..."

She holds up a hand and half-turns to show the props around her wobbling, but the gesture is hardly needed, since the camera trained on her has itself got the judders.

"Quite a decent shake here," she goes on, smiling, "if you see things moving behind me, it's just because the Beehive moves a little more than most buildings."

Bridge gathers himself and asks if the quake's still ongoing. The PM pauses, nods and smiles: "It's OK, I'm not under any hanging lights or anything like that. We're safe."

And the interview goes on as if nothing has happened.

Now, you might shrug that it's New Zealand and, over there, earthquakes are as common as drizzle is here. If you know your stuff, you might even be aware they get around 15,000 every single year and that, of these, only 150-200 make as much as a teacup quiver. This one hit 5.8 on the Richter Scale, not powerful enough to cause structural damage or injuries.

So, you might well say, big wowee.

But it's not the magnitude of the event that matters here, it's not the fact that the PM didn't disappear into a chasm that spread across the floor like a rip in a fat man's trousers. No, it's the way she dealt with something this unscripted that left its mark, the smile and the quip and the way she was perfectly happy to get on with doing her job and let the presenter get on with doing his.

In comparison, think back to Theresa May at the 2017 Tory Conference, how neither she nor anyone around her had the first clue what to do when she got a frog in her throat and couldn't get her speech out for coughing.

Remember how ministers sat behind her, stage-managing pointless standing ovations to buy her time? How no one had the brains or the decency to step up and fill in until she'd gathered herself, to show a bit of wit?

How, even without the excuse of an earthquake, the letters on the backdrop behind started falling off like a punchline to a joke that barely needed one?

That's what happens when the show's run by people who lack social skills, people not only devoid of the humility to admit to and deal with their vulnerabilities, but to laugh them off. Those cringeworthy minutes, which lasted for hours, summed up May's three years in charge, a tenure where she displayed a rank inability to decide on whether to have tea or coffee in cabinet meetings, never mind sort out Brexit.

The one before her, David Cameron, was no better, a chancer finally found out by his appalling handling of the In-Out EU referendum and his cowardly decision to quite the moment the result didn't go his way.

As for the one who *followed* May, the blessed Boris...well, we've all been extras in his slapstick movie. This is the class of man and woman we allow to be in charge, these are the elite who define us in the eyes of the world.

This is why, when May's conference calamity went viral, it confirmed her forever as a dud, a joke, a failure; yet the day that bit of a live TV earthquake won the internet, all it did was crank Jacinda Ardern's legend up another notch.

◆ ◆ ◆

JACINDA KATE LAURELL ARDERN turns 40 on July 26 this

year. She's been New Zealand's PM since 2017, seven months after being elected MP for the Auckland seat of Mount Albert and just seven weeks after becoming Labour Party leader.

She inherited an opposition languishing at its lowest ebb, but launched her General Election campaign with a promise of 'relentless positivity'.

By polling day, she'd rallied enough support for Labour to gain 14 seats and deny the ruling National party a majority. She approached the Greens and the centrist NZ First party to form a coalition and on October 26 became her nation's youngest PM in 161 years.

Three months later, she revealed she was pregnant and on June 24 became only the second elected head of government, after Benazir Bhutto of Pakistan in 1990, to give birth while in office. She and TV presenter partner Clarke Gayford named their daughter Neve Te Aroha.

On March 15, 2019, in the city of Christchurch, 51 died and 49 more were injured in terrorist gun attacks on two mosques. Within a month, New Zealand's parliament had passed a law banning most semi-automatic weapons and assault rifles, parts that convert guns into semi-automatic guns, and higher capacity ammunition magazines.

Almost a year to the day from the Christchurch atrocity, Ardern reacted just as decisively to the onset of coronavirus by announcing what she called 'the widest ranging and toughest border restrictions of any country in the world', first ordering anyone entering the country to isolate for 14 days and then — just four days later, on March 19 — closing their borders to 'all non-citizens and non-permanent residents'.

This brought lawsuits from two un-named parties accusing her of 'unlawfully detaining citizens for political gain' and even comparing her actions to those of Hitler during the Holocaust. The case was thrown out and, by May, her personal approval rate stood at 59.5 per cent.

From this distance, these popularity levels seem very much down to a much under-rated quality on Ardern's part; she isn't scared to be who she is, to do what she thinks is morally right and to look her people in the eye whatever the situation and however doubtful they may be of her decisions.

This seems such an obvious way to be, but look around and ask yourself how many major politician figures are capable of it. How many of them can you look at and listen and truly believe that this is them for real, rather than the person they think they should come across as? And how many of them, in putting on this front, come across at all well?

I can't think of one — not even Barack Obama, who I'm guessing would be the first name on most lips, but who for all his charm and articulacy still pretty much went ahead and did all the same things every other American president does; wage wars, make the rich richer, pander to corporate agendas. Surely if anyone was ever going to use the platform of the White House to educate millions about racism and actually *make* black lives matter, it should have been him. Yet the same old prejudices that abounded before he was elected plainly exist long after he's gone.

Ardern? She was brought up a Mormon, but turned her back on the church because she believed in gay rights and it didn't. She is openly anti-capitalist and anti-nuclear, she rails against global child poverty, wants a discussion on removing The Queen as her country's head of state, champions more rights for the indigenous Maori population and backs a two-state settlement to the Israeli-Palestine conflict.

More tangibly, she has faced down her homeland's pro-life lobby by decriminalising abortion; before March of this year, despite New Zealand's long history of promoting women's rights (both sexes had the vote there more than 30 years before it became law in Britain), terminating any pregnancy was technically punishable under law unless two specialists confirmed carrying the child posed a danger to life, physical health or mental health. Now, the decision is solely down to the woman and her GP until 20 weeks into term, after which it becomes 'subject to tests on the woman's health and well-being, gestational age of the foetus and whether it is clinically appropriate'.

It would have been be easy for anyone with high political ambitions to steer well clear of issues this prickly, to talk about them rather than act on them put career before conscience, yet Ardern prefers to be upfront and honest — a mindset which has made her remarkably popular at home and abroad.

Of course, no young, successful, feminist, opinionated, left-wing woman who's this pro-choice and anti-Establishment ever has been everyone's cup of tea. Some also like to sneer that *anyone* could have steered a country like New Zealand through the pandemic, given that they have six times as many sheep as people. Others laugh off her achievement's in office, saying that compared to, say, Margaret Thatcher she's had no genuine crises to deal with and they'll judge her once she has.

Then again, as Malcolm Tucker said in *The Thick Of It*: "There were people who saw Nelson Mandela walk out of prison live on TV and moaned because they wanted to watch *Diagnosis Murder* on the other side…"

PS…on Monday June 8, New Zealand *was* officially declared free of coronavirus, with the PM admitting she 'did a little dance' at the thought of announcing an end to self-isolation and social distancing. Eight days later, they then recorded their first two cases in more than a month; two women who'd flown from Britain via Qatar and Australia.

You're welcome, Jacinda…

21: SOMEONE AT NUMBER
TEN TO BE PROUD OF

THREE days into April and ten into lockdown, health secretary Matt Hancock went live on TV to lecture multi-millionaire footballers on how it was time they did more to help others in the nation's hour of need. I'd love him to bump into Manchester United striker Marcus Rashford sometime soon and dare repeat that jibe.

Or rather, DOCTOR Marcus Rashford.

Because on Wednesday July 15, the Manchester United striker became, at 22, the youngest recipient of this honorary title from his home city's university, a reward for his efforts in raising £20million during the pandemic to help feed kids who, like him when he was growing up, weren't guaranteed three square meals a day.

Not to mention for his courage in forcing Downing Street to U-turn on plans to scrap free school meals while those kids were studying at home.

For me, it's the least he deserved. After all, there are plenty of Sirs and Lords out there who were raised above the herd for doing more harm than good to society, people who used the privilege they were born with to feather their own nests using the rest of us to do the graft for them.

As I wrote at the time of Hancock's dig at footballers, where was the mention of tycoons, of landowners, of tax-exiles and tax-evaders in his call to arms for the rich to 'do their bit' for a struggling nation? In fact, never mind all that, let's ask what Hancock himself has done for the rest of us in this hour of need? Let's have a vote on what honour *he* should be given for his contribution to the common good.

But please, don't all rush at once, we're still meant to be keeping two metres between each other. Or is it one? Hard to remember the way our leaders change the rules more often than they do their knickers.

Time and again during this crisis, you've been left shaking your head in wonder at where the Tories get ministers like the Health Secretary from. A job lot knitted by the old ladies in the Shredded Wheat ads? There isn't one who doesn't look like a middle-manager in a photocopier company, each drippier than a dew-drop hanging from a tramp's nose in mid-winter.

For me, Hancock is drippiest of all, not only for his cheap shot at Rashford and Co., but so much more — in the space of a few days in June, he first crowed that 'only' 36 people had died from Covid-19 in 24 hours, hugged a fellow MP in the Commons after bowling on for months about the two-metre rule and presided over the debacle of introducing a workable Test & Trace system.

Plenty colleagues give him a run for his money, though. Like Dominic Raab, our Foreign Secretary, who claimed in a Radio 4 interview that the concept of taking a knee as a Black Lives Matter protest 'came from Game Of Thrones', then declaring he'd only kneel 'for the Queen or to propose to the wife'.

And then, of course, there's BoJo himself. Who, on a visit to a West Midlands building site to launch his multi-billion-pound economic recovery plan, told a workman leaning on a shovel 'when you're in a hole this big, all you can do is keep digging'.

Then people wonder why we're in the state we're in.

◆ ◆ ◆

SO it's nice for a change to have someone at No.10 we can look up to, even if it *is* only the number on his shirt.

That someone is Rashford, a young man who's made the very best of himself after growing up knowing what it's like to go without. A guy whose humble roots keep his feet on the ground no matter how far up the social ladder fame and fortune carries him.

On Tuesday June 16, after a tigerishly determined but admirably restrained campaign on social and in mainstream media, Rashford shamed the PM into going back on his earlier decision to take free meals away from 1.3 million of Britain's poorest kids while schools were closed by the pandemic.

If life was fair, the striker could have run out at Tottenham Hotspur's stadium the following night to the greatest ovation any away player ever earned, rather than into the near-silence of a closed-door return to action. In different times, fans of both teams would have been lining the streets to welcome him off the team bus and congratulate him on achieving more with his quiet, positive influence than all the braying and bluster of our entire political class had managed in months.

Then again, in different times — better, fairer times — it wouldn't have needed a 22-year-old centre-forward to make sure more than a million vulnerable boys and girls didn't go hungry in a nation with an £2.6 *trillion*-a-year economy. The kind of different times where at least someone in the Cabinet understood what it meant to go hungry, to dig down the back of a sagging sofa for the last few coins that make up a bus fare, to go without altogether; rather than every last one having been programmed since infancy to be part of those who rule the roost, whether they grew up fit for purpose or not.

And, yes, I'm sure at this point some will be sneering that *'oh aye, you say these kids go without, but they all have big tellies and Sky Sports and iPhones',* but that's a whole other economic argument. If anyone wants to get into how the ease of getting high-interest credit has sucked millions even deeper in debt and often into poverty than previous generations who only had what was in their pocket, let's do it once all this is over.

For now, though, we all know deep down what Rashford's Law is about; a Government who decided that, because schools were closed, it stood to reason that there were no school meals and therefore no need for *free* school meals. A Government whose skewed take on life made them believe the same parents who couldn't afford to feed their kids during a normal school day — or, before anyone says it, who'd spaffed their dole money on fags and drinks and drugs instead — would suddenly be willing and able to feed them at home three times a day.

It's also, lest we forget, about every opposition politician who didn't have the guts to scream so loud about this injustice, this affront to human dignity, that *they* forced Johnson to change his addled mind. Oh sure, they're all over Marcus like a rash now, Sir Keir Starmer and Nicola and the rest. But what the hell are they *there* for, why do they get two and a half times the average UK salary and the whopping expense account, if not to hold the PM's feet to the fire on issues like this?

Today, it seems their role is to bask in the reflected glory of one dedicated young man's passion and determination and, ultimately, his victory — and, in Nicola Sturgeon's case, to show herself at her most opportunistic by nipping in minutes before Johnson was about to announce his U-turn to let the world know *she* was making sure 175,000 vulnerable Scottish youngsters were fed this summer.

An action that, in the week when Rashford and his mates returned to action in the English Premier League, makes it tempting to label her with that old playground term of being a poacher; the one who lets everyone else do the work then taps the ball between the jumpers with the goalkeeper beaten. But then again, at the end of the day Brian, all that really matters is those 175,000 boys and girls on our doorstep having access to proper meals as an economic catastrophe looms.

Plus, truth be told, Holyrood can't be accused of neglecting the weakest, not when Scotland gets free prescriptions, free further education, free sanitary products in all schools and colleges and free boxes of essentials for families of new-borns.

Again, some will argue that all of this largesse is paid for out of Westminster's kitty and that, one day soon, we'll be handed an almighty bill for what came down to an SNP bribe to voters.

But it's beyond argument that Westminster could do the same for the whole of the UK; if the money's there to bail out banks, it's there for them to scrap tuition fees, make medicines free and spare teenage girls the shame of not having enough change for tampons.

They just choose not to.

And that should tell anyone with a soul everything they need to know about what cloth they're cut from.

5.55pm, Wednesday June 15
HIGH up in the soaring, deserted stand they call The Holte End, a steward's hi-vis jacket bearing the initials of Dean Smith's late dad is draped over a sky blue plastic seat.

A poignant a reminder at this pivotal point in lockdown of what so many have lost since the last time a ball was kicked, because Dean Smith is the manager of Aston Villa, born and bred in Birmingham and a fan all his days and Ron Smith was his dad as well as a matchday worker at home games.

Ron was already in a care home suffering from dementia when he contracted coronavirus and died on May 28, aged 79. Six weeks earlier, Dolores Salas Carrio, 82-year-old mother of Manchester City manager Pep Guardiola, had passed away from the virus back home in Barcelona. Her son marked her death by donating €1 million to help buy emergency medical equipment for his home city.

Tonight, both grieving sons returned to the dugout as the world's richest league re-emerged after what became known as Project Restart, a massive operation involving strict testing of players, coaches and club officials for symptoms, of players being kept in hotels before matches and travelling to matches with a little time to spare as possible, of stadiums being closed to fans and with no more than 300 workers allowed inside; teams, backroom staff, stewards, press, TV crews.

As the tannoy blared music to no ones and Villa and Sheffield United emerged from separate tunnels to blink in the teatime sunshine for a 6pm kick-off, it was at once an exciting and an eerie occasion. Here was the national sport, returning from a shutdown during which time enough men, women and children had died to fill Villa Park's 42,785 capacity with only a few hundred spaces to spare. Here were two teams gathered around the centre circle, black bands around their biceps, standing silent for those who hadn't lived to see them play.

And then, here were those same teams, hearing the referee's whistle to start the action — and, before the first ball was kicked, dropping to one knee in support of the other global event whose impact had spread like a pandemic. The eight seconds they held the pose will live in the memory forever.

After that, it really didn't seem to matter that the game itself was so poor you wouldn't have been surprised had the camera panned up to old Ron's seat with 20 minutes left to find the jacket had sneaked off early to avoid the traffic.

A sterile 0-0 draw would be overshadowed by the fact that not only was football back, it had made an instant statement which would go on being made in every match in every league in every country from that evening on. These two sets of players had obviously agreed with each other to take the knee and had clearly got the referee's blessing, as he and his team of assistants joined in, as did both sets of coaches and subs. Yet it appeared to take the Sky Sports commentator as much by surprise as it did the armchair audience and was all the more powerful a statement for it.

Black Live Matters had also replaced the names on the back of every player's shirt, as would be the case with every Premier League game in the first round of fixtures, before the logo was reduced to a patch on their sleeves. The day after Marcus Rashford had taken on Westminster and won, it was clear that the guys who earn the biggest bucks and who have the greatest clout had taken the fight against racism into their own hands.

Maybe for the second round of fixtures they should have had UP YOU HANCOCK *printed on their shirts.*

As for the game itself, Sky would have prayed for a goalfest to raise the curtain on a month-and-a-bit when they and BT Sport would be showing every single top-flight English match between them. Just in case, though, they and the host clubs had moved heaven and earth to distract the world from the fact that the most important element of all was missing.

Football without fans is nothing, said Manchester United's legendary boss Matt Busby. So in an attempt to fill that void, marketing bods had draped huge banners across acres of empty seats, erected screens where a select few supporters could tune in via Zoom, sold cardboard cutouts with faces of season ticket holders stuck on them.

The broadcasters, meanwhile, had the lightbulb moment of offering viewers the chance to listen either with the naked soundtrack of the shouts from the pitch and the thwack of boot on ball, or to switch channels and pretend there was an atmosphere thanks to a backdrop of interactive crowd-noise technology nicked from the FIFA video game, fake oohs and aahs that sort-of followed the flow of the action.

> *"If you want to hear that crowd noise, tune to Sky Sports Main Event — but if you prefer your football au natural, stick with us here on Sky Sports Non-Event..."*

And, one moment of controversy when high-tech gadgetry let the ref down and he disallowed a perfectly good goal for the away team, it really *was* a non-event, petering out into a draw and leaving you begging for better from the second half of the night's double-header; live and direct from the Etihad Stadium in Manchester, where it hosed down on Guardiola, his City side and visitors Arsenal, who looked every bit like a squad who'd flown up from London three hours before kick-off and had the pre-match meal in mid-air.

This time, at least, there were goals; all three to City, who were more entertaining than their visitors, Villa and Sheffield United put together and in all honesty could have beaten them in a game of 11 versus 33. Yet no matter how slick and quick their attacking play was, it still didn't feel right. Maybe in a few days it would, once it became the New Normal™, but right now the bells and whistle were somewhat lipstick on a pig-esque.

But at least our cousins down south had managed to get some games back on. While up here in Scotland, we still couldn't decide who'd be playing in what league next season, never mind sort out who was at home to who and when.

Take a knee? We'd been down on ours for three bloody months.

Since all the aforementioned bickering and back-stabbing of latte March and April, nothing much had happened; or, at least, nothing positive. And definitely nothing that wouldn't bore the average non-football fan into a catatonic state. Since they're now planning to start the 2020-21 Premiership season on August 1, though, it felt like it was maybe coming close to the time when they need to sit down and finally put all their differences behind them. Yet today, this seems unlikelier than ever now that Hearts and Partick Thistle, relegated from the Premiership and Championship respectively, have decided to take their grievance over the way it happened to the courts.

To recap, 'it' happened like this; a majority of the Scottish Professional Football League's 42 member clubs voted to end the season, calculate final tables on the basis of points won per game played, declare the top teams in all four divisions champions and relegate the bottom teams in the top three of those divisions, while allowing the bottom side in the fourth to stay up and postponing play-offs that might have allowed a club from the Pyramid System to replace them.

That was on Monday May 18. By then, Hearts chairwoman Ann Budge had been appointed to run a working group which would come up with a proposal for revamped leagues that did away with relegation, allowed for promotion to take place and let two Pyramid clubs - Kelty Hearts (no relation) and Brora Rangers - into the senior ranks.

Her proposals were roundly rejected. So, on Wednesday June 17 - just as English football returned with a fanfare of trumpets - Hearts and Partick Thistle lodged court papers challenging their fate. The day after that, they threatened to delay the new season if need be. They day after *that*, they put out a further warning that if they weren't allowed to stay up, they'd fight to make sure divisional winners Dundee United, Raith Rovers and Cove Rangers weren't allowed to *come* up.

The whole situation was now messier than a junkie's bedsit.

We'd gone three months without one person coming up with one properly thought-through, innovative, forward-thinking, workable idea acceptable to a bulk of members. We were drowning in a swamp of self-interest, vindictiveness — and, most damning of all, stupidity.

Yes, I'd written from the off that it was horribly unfair for anyone to be relegated without the chance to get themselves out of trouble via the full complement of fixtures, just as it was unfair on those denied the chance of promotion for the same reasons. But the bottom line is both Hearts and Thistle had the chance to be off the bottom of their respective divisions when lockdown came had they won their final games — and had they done so, I'd bet my last two bob that we wouldn't have heard another word from them on the subject.

They wouldn't have been fighting in the courts for whoever they'd leapfrogged to be spared the drop, that's for damn sure.

What a truncated season had come down to, rightly or wrongly, was a game of musical chairs. And the first rule of musical chairs? When the record stops, don't be the one left standing around like a spare one at a wedding.

That's all that happened to Hearts, to Partick Thistle and to League One stragglers Stranraer when the plug got pulled on Scottish football's jukebox. They'd played the game by the same rules as everyone else, they just weren't good enough at it; between the three of them they'd won two league games since November.

Might they have got out of trouble had they been allowed to complete their fixtures? Of course they might. But then again, I'm pretty sure Craig Levein and Gary Caldwell made that very argument when they'd faced the sack as managers of, yes, Hearts and Partick Thistle earlier in the season and a fat lot of good their hypotheses did them then.

So you have to ask why either of those same boards who wielded the axe then would think it would wash with their rival clubs now. Desperation, most probably. And no one can blame them for feeling it, because the future's uncertain enough without facing the drop into divisions that — for all anyone knows — might not even see the new season. Hearts are meant to start their Championship campaign in October, but by the time June was limping to its conclusion there was still no clue when or if Leagues One and Two might kick off.

When those 42 SPFL clubs met via video link on Monday June 22, had they voted to do away with relegation after all, it would have been to their credit. The fact that they didn't, however, shouldn't be held against any of them, because despite the rhetoric being flung around by Budge and Thistle chairwoman Jacqui Low, no one's been 'wronged' in all of this.

Well, no one except those of us who just want to get on with the game.

STILL, all of the above might well be rendered redundant soon enough, what with North Korea having blown up the building where their peace talks with the South used to be held and 20 Indian soldiers having died during hand-to-hand battles with Chinese forces in the Himalayas.

Roll on the pubs re-opening so we can blot out the world

22: PEAK BRAINLESSNESS

Wednesday June 24
·UK coronavirus death toll rises by 154 to 43,081.
·Pubs, hairdressers and cinemas in Scotland to reopen from July 15.
·Health experts warn No10 to prepare for second wave of infections.

IT'S easy to mock Nicola Sturgeon - I should know, it's a staple of what I do. But today offered a reminder that, now and again, it's worth tuning into First Minister's Questions live from Planet Holyrood to remind ourselves of something important about the woman who runs Scotland.

That compared to the leaders of what might loosely be called the Opposition, she's an FM-ing colossus.

Her Tory oppo, ex-car salesman Jackson Carlaw, is such a satire of today's Westminster gammonati, a man with such a look of a golf club bar bore he'd have been rejected by *The Thick Of It* for being too unbelievable. As for Richard Leonard? Scottish Labour's floppy-haired, Yorkshire-born drink of water is the kind of personality vacuum who walks into a room and makes you feel like two people just walked out.

Today, as Sturgeon treated the nation to her latest, ever-so-cautious tip-toe towards maybe sort of exiting lockdown sometime in the near-to-mid future, her twin oppos offered a command performance in time-wasting and grandstanding when they should have been contributing.

Carlaw was the time-waster, offering nothing more than a string of questions that boiled down to: "Yes, First Minister, but what about..?" That's all he brings to the party. If she says it's sunny, he demands to know what she's going to do about the farmers who need it to rain. Worse than this, though, not only doesn't he have anything constructive to say, he doesn't even have the wit to produce the killer line that destroys her policies. Everything's a cliché.

Leonard, meanwhile, was the grandstander as he put on his sombre face and brought up the ongoing scandal of care home deaths; a subject that, without doubt, needs thrashed out when this crisis is over and fingers pointed at those who got our handling of it so badly wrong. But, like Carlaw, it seemed his only purpose in raising the matter was to put Sturgeon on the spot, push her onto the back foot, buy himself a headline.

No ideas, no solutions, just accusations. Is that really what being an Opposition leader is all about? Because if so, we should all get a turn for a week.

It speaks volumes that it took LibDem chief Willie Rennie (and for readers unaware of his work, this is like suggesting it took a song written by Ringo to rescue a Beatles album) to ask a question that meant a damn thing, one about whether teachers would get a break before the schools return and what support they'd be offered to help deliver full-on lessons by mid-August after weeks working flat-out on the SNP's abortive Blended Learning plan.

Now *that's* an issue for the moment, a problem that needs dealt with immediately. Those teachers were already on their knees after months of trying to home-school their own kids, run hubs for the children of key workers and prepare for classrooms re-opening before John Swinney's remarkable u-turn on Tuesday, a kick in the guts that must have made plenty feel like quitting, a decision that confuses skilled educators with childminders.

Scientific and medical experts had advised Holyrood to go with reduced numbers and staggered timetables. But then businesses started demanding the economy got cranked up, so Holyrood flip-flopped, because if kids aren't at school then armies of mum and dad can't get to work.

A huge risk to take? Definitely, though then again we've all been asking Sturgeon to take more risks, so she's damned if she does and damned is she doesn't.

If schools going back is a success, Carlaw and Leonard will

toss a coin to decide who tells her she should have had the balls to do it earlier. If it's a failure, the other gets to call her useless. And all they'll prove, yet again, is that they care about nothing more than the sound of their own voices. The fact that, even at a time like this, they can't put ideologies aside and work as one to help beat this menace we're facing is shameful.

Do I think Nicola Sturgeon's played a blinder during the pandemic? Far, far from it — and, yes, I'll keep on caning her whenever she gets things wrong. But at least she puts herself out there to BE wrong.

You doubt if the time-waster and the grandstander would have half her bottle if they were handed the reins of power, something we should all pray never, ever happens.

❖ ❖ ❖

THE best social policy ever created is a decent job.

If ever there was an inspirational message as we teeter on the brink of economic calamity, this one from Sir Tom Hunter is surely it. After a lifetime of investing in Scotland, the 59-year-old entrepreneur — he started with a loan from his dad, selling training shoes from the back of a van, before growing Europe's biggest independent sports retailer — doesn't argue with predictions of bad things might get post-pandemic.

But where he differs from so many other experts is in his positive mindset, his desire not to wallow in self-pity, but to pull together government, businesses, charities, educators and more in a bid to build a viable future. In his words, it's vital that we decide what we need to get ourselves back on track, to work out how we're going to achieve it and to do both fast; no protocol, steering committees or long-winded reports.

Half the country's workforce told a survey this week they fear for their jobs and even this fear in itself is, as Sir Tom says, bad for mental health, which makes it all the more urgent for Holyrood and Westminster alike to gather in the smartest minds available and to get them working on a plan as of now.

Especially as the longer this all drags on, those smartest minds seem vastly outnumbered by people among us so dense that light bends around them.

People like the bigots who, at a football match between Manchester City and Burnley, few a banner reading White Lives Matter banner above the heads of footballers taking a knee before kick-off. People like the scumbags who've taken to robbing residents of Scotland's care homes.

Seriously, what do we do with creatures this stupid? How do we educate any kids unlucky enough to have been brought into the world by them?

I'm not going to explain why the White Lives Matter banner was so provocative. If you don't get it already, get someone to Google it and read the results to you. All I'll say is that the stunt was depressingly inevitable in the wake of an incident down in Reading last weekend, when three white sunbathers were stabbed to death in a park by 25-year-old local man Khairi Saadallah in what police described as a terrorist attack.

It was a stick-on that the hard of thinking on the hard right would use this senseless crime to muddy the waters, to turn a struggle for equality into an exercise in division. As for the gang who've carried out a spate of raids on care homes across Glasgow, Lanarkshire and West Lothian? Jesus, just when your hoped and prayed that life couldn't get worse for residents and staff alike left bereft by a horrifying coronavirus death toll, along come creeps like these, sneaking in to around a dozen premises and snatching whatever came to hand.

Police have called the thefts 'shameful', but somehow the word doesn't seem nearly adequate.

After all, shameful suggests that those responsible might be capable of feeling shame.

ALL of which kind of brings us to back to where the book opened up: Our moment of Peak Brainlessness.

Those murders in Reading happened on June 20. Chapter One is set on June 25, as sirens blared across a Britain whose every spare inch of sunlit grass and sand had been crammed by crowds who got too drunk and too loud and, in too many cases, too violent.

Now here we were, three months into lockdown and four into our battle with the virus itself. And no one seemed to have learned one damn thing.

Back then, we could excuse our leaders for not knowing what to say or do for the best. Back then, we could kind of understand the panic buying in supermarkets, even if it made us shake our heads in despair.

Yet here we were all this time later, with our leaders still bumbling and stumbling, still sending out constantly mixed messages.

Here we were, still growling at each other in Asda, except this time not for taking the last of the Andrex, but for not wearing face masks; face masks, by the by, which we were under no pressure to wear at the peak of the pandemic, but which are somehow compulsory now that we're told that the infection rate's under control. Nothing about this crisis is joined-up. From public safety to education to business to sport, nothing fits, nothing flows.

From yesterday, for instance, we could get our hair cut in a salon, but not get our toenails done. From yesterday we could go into a pub without a mask, but we had to wear one in an off licence. We've been allowed to mass in parks for picnics and city squares for demonstrations, but fans won't be allowed in when football restarts and theatres can't open at all.

Still think we're smart?

These months of lockdown that feel like years should have been a challenge which, while pushing our politicians and doctors and boffins to the limit, also proved the most exciting challenge of their lives, because it offered the chance to be part of something incredible, a pulling together of the human race and its mammoth resources to see off a deadly enemy with as little damage to lives and jobs as possible.

But the longer the bug lingers, the more we seem loathe to pull together, the less willing or able politicians are to pool their abilities. More depressingly still, it appears they actively prefer to work against each other, to scramble for a moral high ground that doesn't exist.

This politicisation of it all turns my stomach, the idea that we should either be on Team Nicola or Team Boris, the thought that Holyrood's handling of the crisis should be seen as a dry run for the ability to run an independent Scotland.

That we've put the reopening of pubs before that of gyms gives lie to any weasel-words either Sturgeon or Johnson ever dare utter about wanting a healthy population, about taking pressure off our poor, creaking NHS.

That chancellor Rishi Sunak is chucking £1,000-a-head bribes at businesses to keep furloughed staff on the books not only when many of those businesses neither need nor want the money, but also when millions of self-employed workers haven't had a penny since March proves how little planning has gone into our fiscal recovery.

More than anything, though, the intransigence of those in charge, their inability to think outside the box and refusal to admit weakness, has now worn the public down to the point where way more than us than is healthy hear the latest rules written on the back of a fag packet and shrug: *Why Should We?*

Enough among us are now pretty much doing what we want — deciding how much distancing we think is necessary, how many friends from how many households we can meet up with — to make a second spike pretty much inevitable. The guidelines have changed so often and so randomly that most of us don't even listen any more. In football terms, Nicola and Boris have lost the dressing room.

See, when those scientists mentioned way back in this

book's introduction realised their theory of everything was wrong and there was 96 per cent of a universe out there to re-discover, they reaction wasn't one of despair, but of excitement. But that's because scientists never dare believe they're smarter than the Universe.

It's only us dimwits who think we know it all.

Friday June 26

THE speed with which our emergency services react when it all goes off is matched only by their courage.

That's why, on a rainy morning in the heart of Glasgow, they had a bloodbath in a hotel crammed with asylum seekers under control in no time.

It's why a 42-year-old police officer called John Whyte didn't flinch in putting his life on the line when he walked in on someone a knifeman running amok. And it's why they really, *really* don't need a repeat of the scenes they'd faced a mile or so across the city the night before.

Kelvingrove Park on Thursday had been a human zoo from lunchtime to sundown, swarming with drunks ignoring the risk of spreading the virus in the name of what they called a good time. What started out as a giant picnic and a few beers with pals degenerated into punch-ups, the sound of afternoon laughter drowned out by the howl of late-night sirens.

Sure, it was all a big laugh to those involved. No one died, only a couple even got lifted. But just imagine what happened next morning a mile or so away at the Park Inn on West George Street had happened at the height of their partying.

Imagine the strain on police and ambulance crews, imagine the potential loss of life had they not been able to respond as quickly to the hotel emergency call because they were too busy rounding up pissed kids. Just like Dominic Cummings when he went on his self-isolation tour of England, those bawling, brawling masses weren't just being stupid in risking infection, they were being unbelievably selfish too.

That's the land we live in now, though, as witnessed in at beauty spots from Glasgow's west end to England's south coast yesterday the minute lockdown was eased and the sun came out. Cops run ragged, paramedics overworked, neighbours kept awake late into the night and council litter-pickers sent for weight training sessions to prepare for the next morning's Herculean clear-up effort.

Days like these signal our decent into Bamageddon, they make me despair for the generation today's halfwitted Love Island-wannabes will spawn. Once more, I realise this makes me sound older than coal. But I'd rather stand accused of being a dinosaur than stand for the bawling and the brawling, the mob mentality we've seen all too often these past few weeks and which we see too often these days full stop.

Yes, we've been cooped up for way too long, but that shouldn't mean we have to go tonto every time we step outside our front doors. Except that it appears that's the only way too many know how behave these days, the ones who've forgotten the meaning of moderation, who have no Off switch.

Every picnic turns into a rave, every rave into a riot, every beach into a rubbish tip. In Glasgow, on Edinburgh's leafy Meadows, in Manchester, down the Tyneside coast, all across London and down as far as normally sleepy Bournemouth — where three bodies lay bleeding from stab wounds sustained on that mad, mad Thursday — the concept of emerging from self-isolation to meet and to celebrate has been swept away on a tide of anger, of abuse, of violence, all fuelled by a belief held by way too many that only they themselves matter.

Somewhere, we crossed a line between enjoying ourselves and spoiling things for everyone else; where and when is one for the sociologists to debate. All I know is we sure don't look like retracing our steps any time soon.

WE'LL never know for sure what finally pushed 28-year-old Sudanese refugee Badreddin Abadlla Adam into the abyss of madness that saw him stab three fellow hotel guests, two workers and PC Whyte.

Word is he snapped after complaining about meals served during his stay, something many might see as a flimsy excuse for stabbing everyone within arm's length. But this seemed merely the final straw, because the camel's back had been buckling ever since he and many more like him were rounded up and transported from the security of their homes to a series of hotels and guest houses across Glasgow back in March.

The afternoon before Adam's rampage, Mears Group chief operating officer John Taylor - in charge of a £1billion contract awarded by the Home Office in 2019 to manage accommodation for asylum seekers - had admitted to *The Independent* that they failed to carry out assessments before placing clients —including trafficking victims, children and pregnant women — in premises that put them at risk. He said a 'blanket decision' was made in late March to move these clients to hotels, that no checks were made into individual needs before transfer and that it soon became 'obvious' this setting 'wasn't appropriate' for some people, with many complaining that social distancing was all but impossible. Mr Taylor went on:

> *"In hindsight, would we have had time to do this assessment as lockdown came in? Maybe, maybe not. But it's certainly one of the learnings and one of the issues we've taken on board, and hopefully we'll never have to repeat it again."*

Within hours of this interview, however, Mears contacted the paper to say Mr Taylor was 'wrong to state assessments were not carried out' prior to moving asylum seekers to hotels, though they confirmed it took four weeks to transfer all the pregnant women back to Mears accommodation.

An updated statement said: "Our staff had discussions with

everyone affected prior to moves and a number were identified as needing Mears, rather than hotel, accommodation. There was a small number of pregnant service users and families initially moved to hotels who, after further health and welfare discussions, were moved on quickly."

Not quickly enough, however, to save Adnan Wasid Elbi, a 30-year-old born in Libya but who found his way to Glasgow from Syria via Denmark and Ireland - and who, on May 5, was found dead in the Glasgow guest house to which he'd been decanted by the Mears Group.

He had spoken previously of his terror at being sent back to war-torn Syria and of his despair at being forced to live on an allowance of £5.39 a day. He had also hinted previously that he could take his own life. Like Badreddin Abadlla Adam, he had had arrived in Glasgow with the image of it being a place of freedom and of opportunity. Sadly, as with so many refugees, asylum seekers, immigrants — call them what we will — the reality turned out to be very different.

As Robina Quereshi of pressure group Positive Action In Housing put it, so many have been treated more like Amazon parcels than people; lifted and dropped, stockpiled, seen by the system as little more than numbers on a spreadsheet drawn up by a company who saw them as ways to generate profit.

At a time when the world's getting all bent out of shape about the slave trade of 300 years ago, we really need to ask ourselves what's so different about some of the offences to human decency happening right here and right now.

People are still dying in bondage.

We just can't see their chains.

Tuesday June 30
But hey, the good news is that Primark's open.

Today, the 100th day since lockdown, rain-soaked queues

snake along high streets across Scotland as stores shutters clatter up at long last. It appears what we've missed most all this time is cheap summer frocks.

Let's just hope it doesn't turn into a case of shop till we drop the way it has 310 miles south Leicester, where a series of mini-spikes have forced Westminster to close non-essential stores as well as schools, bars, restaurants and cafes until at least July 4, ten days after restrictions are due to ease across the rest of England.

Until yesterday, the East Midlands city had been easing back to business, its battered economy able to operate under new guidelines about distancing and reduced numbers. But this is an area with two petri-dish elements to its make-up; rows of tight terraced houses and a 49 per cent Asian population who, as with many families in China and Italy, often live in multi-generational households; and so, with the shutters barely back up, one population of 300,000 was suddenly accounting for ten per cent of England's current cases.

And wouldn't you just know it? They even had their own Cathy Calderwood in the form of Mayor Sir Peter Soulsby, a one-time Labour MP who had preached self-isolation for the masses while sneaking off do to visit his girlfriend.

As ever, part of you was left slack-jawed at the affront of someone in a position of such responsibility giving so little of a toss for their own rules. Yet another part could only shrug and sigh: "Well, what else do we expect any more? Which of them *doesn't* behave this way?"

As much of a generalisation as this may be and as unfair as surely is on the vast majority in power who do play the game, it would be a fool who didn't believe even one among those masses didn't hear of Soulsby's selfishness and decide: "Sod it, if he can do it, so can I."

Just as it would be a fool who imagined Leicester would go down as an isolated case as we came to realise just how much of a gamble of easing back towards some sort of normality had been.

Wednesday July 1
•Nightingale hospitals to be repurposed as cancer testing centres to cope with increasing backlog.
•Bank of England says UK economy recovering faster than May predictions.
•UK Covid-19 fatalities up 155 to 43,730; overall deaths below normal for time of year.

HARRODS. Top Shop. Upper Crust. TM Lewin. Virgin Money. Accenture. Clydesdale and Yorkshire Bank. Airbus. EasyJet. WH Smith. Bensons For Beds. Steelite International. Wright's Pies. The Adelphi Hotel. Norwich Theatre Royal.

Just some of the companies who, in the past 48 hours, have announced more than 12,000 job losses between them. More and more hammer blows to the economy, yet which still feel merely like the overture to the symphony of suffering to come once October arrives, the furlough scheme ends and the dole queue *really* starts growing.

It's a situation serious enough to make Boris pull on a hi-vis jacket and hard hat today to hit a building site and announce where the first £5billion of a £640billion rebuilding package would be spent. Roads, bridges, hospitals, schools, prisons, makeovers for High Street. Projects slated to start yesterday, if not the day before.

We've seen and heard it all before, of course. Politicians have always thrown money at broken economies, even if it only begs the question where this flying pile of cash was when people needed it in the first place.

If it wasn't already in the budget, why not? And if it was, what other projects will have to suffer to allow it to be distributed?

That's what Johnson's being asked right now — and from no louder source than his sparring partner Nicola Sturgeon, who used the opportunity to launch into a round of her favourite game: Fantasy Budgets.

THE rules of Fantasy Budgets are simple.

Think of a number. Quadruple it. Chuck in a VAT reduction and a National Insurance rebate. Call it £80billion for cash — and there you have it, simple as that; the glue to stick the Humpty Dumpty that is battered Britain back together again.

The FM's been in her element this week, telling Boris exactly how much is needed to get the nation up and pumping again while knowing full well there's not a snowball's chance of him coming up with it. But that's the best bit about the game; the meaner you make the guy who actually has to come up with the money look, the more heroic *you* look.

So, on Tuesday, 24 hours before Boris signed off on his spend-a-thon, Nicola came out with a blueprint demanding 16 times what he then came out with, which allowed her to label him 'woeful' and her supporters to cheer her to the rafters.

Seriously, when running a branch office is that much fun, you wonder why she'd want the burden of a management buyout that would mean having to balance her own books.

Not that I'm arguing that her figure for kickstarting Britain post-lockdown is far off the mark. Not only does the £5billion downpayment promised by the Prime Minister seem way too little, but it also strikes you very much like some cosmetic deckchairs-on-the-Titanic shuffling of the existing kitty.

All I'm suggesting is that not only is it the easiest thing in the world to be generous with another Government's cash, it's also a complete waste of everyone's time. So if I was Sturgeon's opposition in Holyrood today, rather than it being led by men with all the backbone of a tomato, I'd be asking her politely to stop playing to the Nationalist gallery and putting a tad more of a shoulder behind economic issues she CAN control?

Like finally making a decision on whether Scotland's crucial tourist industry can open for business properly or not. After all, it's worth £10billion in a good year. It attracts 15million visitors. But right now, it's on its knees.

Hotels, restaurants and bars are scheduled to re-open their doors 13 days from now. Yet despite customers from England, Wales and Ireland contributing 70p of every Scottish tourist pound, owners can't take bookings with any security, because they can't get a definitive answer on whether the First Minister intends to impose quarantine on visitors from around the UK.

As with everything relating to us coming out of lockdown, all we can do is wait and see. All she'll say is that she 'won't rule it out', which is about as much use as a face mask made out of a string vest. So, how do companies who've already made every penny a prisoner commit investment to a summer that may yet be a financial wash-out? How do our English, Welsh and Irish cousins commit to a holiday here if they can't be sure it won't end in yet more self-isolation that costs them wages?

The simple answer in both cases is they can't. Yet rather than taking positive action to avert impending disaster, the FM would rather meddle in an issue which, although we all have a vested interest in it, is outwith her control, while dithering over one which is much within it.

Here and now, with situations like the re-emergence of our priceless tourism and hospitality sectors, is when she had to earn her money, her reputation, her legacy. Here and now, she had to stop with the wait-and-see and take a stand: Either we plough ahead and face up to the possibility of a second spike or we hang back and watch our economy implode.

There's no middle ground, no either or. Either we commit to getting Scotland off its knees and or we accept the prospect of being flat on our backs.

And, yes, I get the irony of me criticising the FM for telling the PM how to do his job when I'm then telling her how to do hers. Difference is, though, our futures don't depend on 7,500 new houses being built on West Midlands wasteland or the A1 being widened as far as Carlisle; but they DO depend on hotels in Hawick, pubs in Perth and restaurants in Rothesay getting back to full steam.

Billions of pounds, millions of tourists, thousands of jobs. They all hinge on Nicola Sturgeon drawing on all her courage and making a decision.

This isn't fantasy, FM, it's the harshest of realities.

Friday July 3

PUBS in England can re-open from 6am tomorrow in a move Downing Street hopes will avoid a rush to the bar.

You know, because the earlier they start pulling pints the less likely drinkers are to want one after spitting feathers for 100-odd days.

Just another dollop of logic, Boris-style. And if that makes it seem like I couldn't wait to dish out another dollop of abuse to a leader under mammoth pressure...well, what does anyone expect? Not a day seems to go by any more without the guy saying or doing something that would even make Donald Trump go: "*What the absolute f...?*"

There's no question he's even more desperate to get the boozers open again than most punters are to storm the doors. He's made it a higher priority than getting kids back to school or getting gyms and swimming pools up and running safely.

It's like he thinks that if we're sedated with a few lagers and a tray of Sambucas, we're less likely get stroppy about all our other crap.

Once more, you wonder if he's even *met* anyone British.

Sun 5 July

HERE'S a top tip for any shop worker who's forced to demand customers wear face masks once it becomes compulsory.

Don't get mad.

Get rich.

It certainly worked for a Starbucks coffee-wallah called Lenin Gutierrez after a woman shamed him on Facebook for enforcing company policy about covering her coupon.

Because today, the jammy barista's $100,000 better off, all thanks to strangers launching an appeal to compensate him for the hurt she caused. The kind of fortune to make angry punters a whole lot easier to put up with, I'm sure you'll agree.

For example, if anyone's feeling generous, some twonk emailed this week calling me a Unionist scumbag who should be deported. I filed it alongside a string of love letters from a regular who wants me sacked for being wee Nicola's poodle.

Got to be worth enough for a a new car at least, yeah?

No, you're right, it isn't; mainly because this is Britain, where that kind of abuse is generally the nearest we get to polite conversation. Wheras Lenin Guttierez works in San Diego, California, where they'd sue Mother Nature for a pigeon pooing on their favourite sweater. So it's kind of a given that, come Friday and the latest new regulations, the best *our* shop staff can hope if not everyone masks up is that the cops turn up to dish out on-the-spot fines as promised by the FM.

Sixty quid a time it'll cost if we don't do as we're told, even though we're led to believe coronavirus is on the run and even though we were allowed to breathe all over each other when the pandemic was at its peak.

This makes no sense. Though then again, what does when it comes to Holyrood's handling of this crisis? They're making it up on the hoof and all we can do is try and keep up. If this is how it's to be, though, at least let's try to create some good out of it by giving all those £60 penalties to charity. We could maybe even let shops nominate their own good causes:

> *"Failure to wear a face covering in Danny's Dry Cleaners will increase the risk of infection, but will also mean a donation to Macmillan Cancer Support. Your call, people…"*

Because the good news is that whether we're talking about

California in the US of A or the one near Falkirk, there will always be indignati like Amber Lynn Gillies, the git who threw that stroppaccino in Starbucks. She was all 'I know my rights' and 'next time I'm bringing a cop and my medical exemption' — so if I was a fundraiser, I'd be praying for loads like her to come out of the woodwork over the coming weeks.

Not only has every charitable event from your local garden fete to the London Marathon bitten the dust, but let's remind ourselves that, for some reason, we as a nation have taken the collective decision that the NHS, already paid for from our taxes, is the only good cause worth supporting.

So, in the words of Mr Tesco, every little helps. Sixty quid here and there from stroppy sods is better than nothing; for just the price of a twataccino, a child in Africa could have clean water for a week.

Maybe Nicola could then ramp it up by charging £20 a head to attend demos or get into public parks. Better still, why not crank the scheme right up by imposing £100 fines on anyone who drops litter in those parks?

Which judging by the mess left behind after every sunny day this summer would pay for a Scotland-sized perspex bio-dome by late August.

Monday July 6
·Chancellor Rishi Sunak is to lift the threshold at which people start paying stamp duty on house sales from £125,000 to as much as £500,000.
·Delays to appointments because of Covid-19 could lead to 35,000 excess cancer deaths in the next year.

TODAY, a panel of 239 scientists have written to the World Health Organisation demanding more straight talk when it comes to explaining why face masks are crucial in the fight to halt the virus.

A good shout this, but one which at the same time makes you ponder on why we need to be told in the first place. I mean, we knew from the off that the virus was carried on droplets of water from our noses and mouths; or, at least, there was no reason for us *not* to know. Yet here we are, just about seven months on from the first case being recorded and scientists are still hitting their heads off brick walls, still having to ask why politicians whose job it is to keep us in line seem so unwilling to scream: *"Wear a mask, you dolts!"*

And there's no doubt they *are* unwilling, as the shilly-shallying from Holyrood and Westminster over making face coverings compulsory in public places proves. Both the FM and the PM have seemed terrified of our response if we're made to put a little bit of cloth over our coupons for the length of time it takes to buy a loaf and a pint of milk.

As Donald Milton, a professor of environmental health at Maryland University and a co-author of the open letter to the WHO, put it: "The best vaccine against fear is knowledge."

So let's get ourselves some:

·The virus is carried on droplets emitted from human mouths and noses. Larger droplets fall onto surfaces and can be picked up, then carried to the eyes, nose or mouth. That's why regular hand washing and surface cleaning is crucial. Smaller droplets, however, can stay in the air for longer and be inhaled deeply into the lungs.

·The virus can survive in the air for three hours and up to three days on some surfaces. Virus-laden droplets are released not just by sneezes or coughs, but also by talking and possibly even just by breathing. Shouting, singing and panting during exercise are thought to release higher amounts of droplets.

·A lot of people crowded close together indoors where it is poorly ventilated — say, a gym — drives the pandemic. Masks block water droplets at their source.

But as the song almost goes: If we don't know this by now...

OUT on the bike this morning, 40 miles rolling to Drymen and back with my pal Carolyn McKeown, stopping halfway for coffee and a roll. The miles are racking up now that the knee's properly better and the weather with it.

Carolyn's a natural coach, a leader, a motivator. Her gentle cajoling out on the roads got me confident enough to make it over the Pyrenees last September and it's been the same again during lockdown, when the boost I've needed has been as much mental as physical.

It was warm today, the breeze doing that thing it loves doing to cyclists by getting in our faces on the way out before rotating to batter us on the way back as well. Yet the miles still flew by, a perfect morning.

After lunch, time for a walk with Sherlock, the four-legged wonder who has made the past couple of months as doable my two-wheeled pal. He's growing like a weed, starting to lose his razor-sharp baby teeth, developing a personality all of his own. Most of all, he's transformed Sonia's mood at a time when she's still fretting over getting back to work. Before he arrived, I was genuinely worried for her. She wasn't quite in despair, but too much time to think and no money coming in were chipping away at her in tandem. Now, though, she's so much more like herself, she's loving playing mummy, loving bathing and brushing and blow-drying the wee fella.

His puppy-daftness has her laughing again, that out-loud, raunchy laugh that had been silenced for too long. She's no longer thinking out loud non-stop about why she can't re-open the salon, why English hairdressers are back at work and ours aren't, how she's going to keep paying her way in the world.

Shez takes all those worries away.

And the beautiful thing is, he doesn't even know it.

Thursday July 9

AND so begins Downing Street's answer to the DFS sale. A £30billion giveaway to kickstart the economy, designed to dovetail with the impending return of live gigs, tattoo parlours, five-a-side football, gyms and outdoor swimming pools.

Except for viewers in Scotland. Where we're still suffering from our very own satellite delay on all of these leisure-time pleasures. And where, this morning, Nicola Sturgeon has also banned holidays to Spain; with Serbia, one of two countries on a list of 57 the FM believes too risky to visit without 14 days of quarantine on our return — even though the English, Welsh and Northern Irish wouldn't have to — piling yet more misery on a tourist industry which had prayed the worst was over.

Still, never mind if you have to cancel your holiday, because the Chancellor of the Exchequer, Rishi Sunak, is inviting us all out for a half-price slap-up meal. To the value of £10 and not including alcohol. Mondays to Wednesdays. From next month.

His scheme's called Eat Out To Help Out and the idea if that cafes, restaurants and bars take 50 per cent off our bill then claim it back from the government. A good shout, on the face of it. And yet it doesn't feel right, because although the basic premise of encouraging us to eat out will help local businesses get back on their feet, what the Chancellor is suggesting is that we all *need* half-price meals, which we plainly don't. There are plenty of us who've been on full pay during lockdown, yet we get the same discount as the family left without an income.

Maybe I'm thinking about it too much. Maybe this is all just some sort of guilt trip about not having been badly affected. But I'm left wondering why Richard Branson should get 50 per cent off a coffee and a toastie the same as an office worker he's just sacked.

So, pain in the arse that I am, my plan is to tell cafes on entering that I'm paying full price, though mum's the word if they want to claim the discount back anyway. Chances are it'll cause way more bother than it's worth, since they're more than likely to have programmed the new prices into their tills, but it's the principle — especially as we're not really saving in the long run, since the estimated £500million cost is coming out of the public purse.

We're paying for each other's half-price pie and chips, folks.

The other headline of Sunak's economic kiss of life is a plan to pay firms £1,000 for every worker who's been furloughed but is still on the books at January 31. But (and again, maybe this is just me hitting cynicism critical mass) doesn't this just feel like a bribe aimed at delaying the inevitable?

Instead of bracing ourselves for an unemployment tsunami when the furlough scheme ends in October, aren't we just bunging bosses to hold off another few months? Delaying the unemployment tsunami until the first of February?

Suppose that's why I've never been headhunted as a No10 spin doctor, given the Chancellor's take is that these £1,000 bonuses will 'protect 12 million jobs and create hundreds of thousands more'. With 9.4m workers across Britain currently on furlough, we're talking another £9.4bn of taxpayer's money if every company takes up the offer. On top of this, Sunak promises to shell out:

•£3.1bn in grants for energy-saving home improvements;

•£3.7bn to pay new starts aged 16-24 for six months;

•£3.8bn to eliminate Stamp Duty on the first £500,000 of homes bought before March 31 next year;

•£4.1bn to cut VAT on all hospitality, accommodation and attractions from 20 per cent to five per cent, and;

•£5.6bn for 'infrastructure projects to stimulate growth'.

It helps take the cost of coronavirus to around £188bn — and, according to Sunak, 'the task has only just begun' after '18 years of economic growth were wiped out in two months'.

It's a head-spinning amount of money. Yet to add a tad of context, it's still less than a quarter of what you and I had to cough up to bale out the banks back in 2008 - and we didn't get a half-price bacon sandwich in return for *that*.

Saturday July 11

"DEAR First Minister. Thank you for taking the time to read this email. I would like to express my unhappiness at being forced to wear a face mask at the shops. However, I understand you have a tough job and that not every decision you make will be universally popular.
All the best to you and yours,
Mrs Mary McTwonkerty."

IN an ideal world, this would be the kind of polite response Nicola Sturgeon got to her insistence today that anyone upset with new rules on covering up in public should complain to her rather than giving shop staff grief.

But it's not an ideal world, it's one where those who shout the loudest tend to be the least polite, most narrow-minded and — not unrelatedly — the least grammatically proficient among us. So you can only presume the FM has a very large team of staff who read this kind of stuff on her behalf, as well as a very large team of counsellors to deal with the stress it induces.

It's all part of her Everywoman schtick, though; I'm one of you, my inbox is always open, feel free to pop in any time. And I'm guessing loads *will* pop in after Sturgeon's announcement on day one of masks becoming compulsory in shops that we'd better get used to them for the long haul.

She compared this situation first to the 2006 smoking ban - — 'people said it would be a nightmare, that the police would never be able to enforce it' — then to the seatbelt law, saying: "I wear mine because I know if the car crashes, it could save my live and those of others too."

Today, 18 new cases were recorded in Scotland, three times as many as the previous day and the highest 24-hour total in the past three weeks. No deaths were recorded for the second day in a row, but 12 patients were in intensive care. The UK death toll, meanwhile, rose 48 to 44,650.

In this weird weird stand-off period of the pandemic, with infections and fatalities back down around where they were at the start of lockdown but the virus still lurking, the FM's analogies about smoking and seatbelts held water. Yet even when she says something anyone with half a brain can get on board, along comes a couple of guys with half a brain between them to muddy the waters.

Because today, Boris Johnson finally admitted that 'opinion is shifting' on facemasks and that it may well be time to make them compulsory, while Donald Trump last night wore one in front of the White House media pack for the very first time.

So maybe it's time for the rest of us to throw ours away.

For the avoidance of argument, that last sentence is only a joke. But, as with so much over the months, it's not a million miles from reality, since no matter how obvious something seems these days, the minute either of these buffoons does it we can't help but question whether or not it's right.

Still, at least both are easing towards some sort of belated understanding of the situation, even if they're having to be dragged kicking and screaming. And the trouble with this is that, along the way, their dragging heels have sparked off an atmosphere of confusion and distrust against something which is, when it comes down to it, frighteningly simple.

Sticking on a mask around strangers just in case should be no big deal. Yet instead, we hear more reports than of shopper-on-shopper stand-offs, barneys on buses and in train stations, staff in all sorts of business being abused for enforcing the rules; and all because those rules have been imposed with a mumble and a shrug rather than a fixed stare and a pointed index finger.

Had masks been sold to us as a temporary inconvenience that there was no way around, had they maybe even been turned into some sort of Junior Dragon's Den contest where the kid who came up with the funkiest design saw it rolled out in its millions, it really *would* have become as natural in no time as wearing a seat belt or not smoking in pubs.

Instead, though, the same leaders who don't think twice about hitting us with bad news like a tax hike or the closure of a cancer ward seemed terrified to tell this one like it was, with the result that shopkeepers down south have united to tell No 10 it's not their responsibility to enforce the new rule, which will mean cops being called to disturbances over non-compliance when they have neither the bodies nor the will to add it to a To Do List longer than a telescopic truncheon.

So what are we meant to do if someone's wandering round Sainsbury's au natural? Make a citizen's arrest? Hold them down and forcibly mask them? Because chances are we'll then find the reason they weren't wearing a mask was asthma or claustrophobia, they'll call the cops — after they've dialled a No Win, No Fee lawyer, natch — and it'll all goes nuclear.

And, ps, this is before we consider the absolute nitwittery of those among us who have conceded they need to wear a mask, but haven't worked out how to do it properly.

You see them everywhere, mouths covered up but noses flopping free like wedding tackle from the waistband of a pair of Y-fronts. What's up with these people? Don't they get that air and water come out of nostrils as well as cakeholes and that both are connected to our lungs?

If not, how they've managed to make it this far through life without bursting into flames is remarkable. While the fact that one of them made it to be Prime Minister of Great Britain and another President of the United States?

Wow.

◆ ◆ ◆

Monday July 13
THE locals knew him as Patient 91.

Across three long months fighting for breath and for life itself in a Covid ward, he became a symbol of a nation's desire not to record a single death from the disease.

And today, as he was finally declared well enough to fly home, no one was happier than Stephen Cameron himself that his Vietnamese hosts are still on course to achieve that goal.

Stephen, a 42-year-old pilot from Motherwell, had travelled to Ho Chi Minh City in February to take up a new job with the national airline. A few weeks in, a night at the busy Buddha

Bar resulted in him testing positive for coronavirus.

He got the worrying news on March 18, but within days his condition had deteriorated and a week or so after that he was in an induced coma, kept alive by a life support machine called an Ecmo, which extracts blood, infuses it with oxygen then pumps it back into the body, but Stephen's complication was that his blood became sticky and clotted, leading to kidney failure, dialysis and a lung capacity down to just ten per cent.

The severity of his symptoms and their knock-on effects were so rare in Vietnamese terms that he became a staple of nightly news bulletins. Dozens of intensive care specialists were pictured holding regular conference calls to discuss his condition — and there's little doubt that without this level of care, this stranger in a strange land wouldn't have made it.

As it was, May had dawned before he came round, just strong enough to offer a thumbs-up for the camera and to hold show off his beloved, claret and amber Motherwell football scarf - and it was only today that he finally left hospital to fly back to a ward in Wishaw, a few miles from home, saying:

> *"I'm overwhelmed by the generosity of the Vietnamese people, the dedication and professionalism of the doctors and nurses. I go home with a happy heart because I'm going home but a sad one because I'm leaving so many friends."*

A COUPLE of weeks before, still confined to bed, Stephen had been blunt about his situation in an interview with the BBC:

> *"Almost anywhere else on the planet I'd be dead, they'd have flicked the switch after 30 days. I'm humbled by how I've been taken into the hearts of the Vietnamese people. When it came out in the press that I needed a lung transplant, loads of people offered theirs, including a 70-year-old Vietnam war*

veteran. But it would have been a double transplant so that wouldn't have ended well for him. Most of all, I'm grateful for the bloody-mindedness of doctors in not wanting me to die on their watch..."

And that's the key to a wonderfully uplifting story; the fact that this country of 95 million was utterly determined not to lose one, single Covid sufferer.

Way back in January, when most of the world still regarded coronavirus as an illness causing panic a remote corner of China rather than a pandemic revving itself up to invade the entire planet, Vietnam's government warned 'drastic action' would be needed to protect its people.

When, on the 23rd of that month, a man who had travelled from the bug's epicentre in Wuhan to visit his son in Ho Chi Minh City was confirmed as their first coronavirus patient, that 'drastic action' was taken without hesitation.

Travel curfews imposed overnight, stringent checks brought in at the Chinese border, schools shut until mid-May — and, most relevant to our own experience, a massive tracing operation introduced. By mid-March, everyone who entered the country plus anyone already there who'd had contact with a confirmed case had to spend 14 days in a State quarantine centre, often as basic as a mat and a blanket on the floor of a dormitory. Professor Guy Thwaites, a Ho Chi Minh City-based Oxford University clinical researcher working with Vietnam's infectious disease programme, said:

"They very quickly acted in ways which seemed extreme at the time but were subsequently shown to be rather sensible. This is a country that has dealt with a lot of outbreaks in the past. The government and population are very, very used to dealing with infectious diseases and are respectful of them, probably far more so than wealthier countries. They know how to respond to these things."

HAVING spent time in Vietnam in 2015, cycling from Ho Chi Minh City through the heartland of the ramshackle resistance who held off America with homemade weapons, across the Mekon Delta and into Cambodia, the professor's words come as no surprise.

Because even from the snapshot we got over a couple of weeks, it became tangibly obvious that both nations were simply overflowing with hugely resourceful, hard-grafting, relentlessly infectious optimists whose attitude boiled down a cheery smile and a shrug of: "*Sure, why not?*"

At the time, I wrote that had we in Britain endured the hell they both have in the past half century — in Vietnam's case, a war when America vowed to 'bomb them back to the Stone Age', in Cambodia's the genocidal regime of Pol Pot, who tortured, executed and start half his own four million population — we'd currently be making Mad Max look like a documentary.

Yet travel across these lands, less than half a century on from unspeakable carnage wreaked from both abroad and within, and you'll find countless towns and villages bustling with men, women and children taking responsibility for their own futures, using whatever skills they have to make each other's lives better and to make their local economies work.

This can-do spirit is what appears, from this distance at least, to have inspired the level of care and of determination that got Stephen Cameron through the worst.

The irony being that while our leaders tell us ever more gravely that our rising toll of victims are not mere numbers, the people of Vietnam will forever remember their greatest success as Patient 91.

Tuesday July 13-Friday July 17
TIME off. Laptop closed. Not interested in the papers, in football, even in the pubs re-opening. Just in walking Sherlock, getting out on the bike and seeing the happiness on Sonia's lovely face as she finally gets back to work.

Can we just stay here forever?

Saturday July 18
SADLY, no we can't. Because after five blissful days of relaxing and eating and knowing next to nothing about what's been going on in the news — except to catch Captain Tom becoming a Sir in a historic outdoor ceremony at Windsor Castle - there's a column to write for tomorrow.

And the very first story that catches the eye is one about how — *guess what?* -- Edinburgh and London can't agree on something, in this case when spectators will be allowed back into sporting events.

Down south, they'll be trialling cricket matches with very limited, socially-distanced crowds from this time next week. Yet when the new Scottish football season (hopefully) gets underway the week after that, it will be behind closed doors.

Who's right and who's wrong on this one is something we could argue all day long, but what's not up for debate is the fact that Holyrood and Westminster still have no intention of even pretending to present united front on one single thing.

How can sitting outside at Lord's be more or less risky than sitting outside at Tynecastle? Who knows?

All I know is that it's surprising one of them hasn't reverted to the Gregorian calendar by now, just to be awkward.

◆ ◆ ◆

Sunday 19 July

IMAGINE the entire population of Aberdeen turning up at the same time to sign on the dole. Then imagine the whole of Oban joining the end of the queue.

Allowing for social distancing of two metres between each of them, the 215,000 men and women waiting in line would stretch back from Union Street to Prestatyn in North Wales.

That's how many people in Scotland are claiming benefits right now. That's the scale of the economic disaster we're facing up to. Yet give it three months and these will look like the good old days, because come October, bosses at countless companies left potless by the pandemic will have to decide whether to bring staff back from furlough and onto 100 per cent wages — or cut their losses and let some go.

Even if one in ten of the 737,000 Scottish workers on the 80 per cent pay lockdown job retention scheme are shown the door, we'd be close to 300,000 on benefits. And let's face it, one in ten would be a result and a half. Chancellor Rishi Sunak has paid lip service to this chilling prospect by offering £1,000 for every worker kept on until January at least, while Holyrood economic secretary Fiona Hyslop has promised £100m to tackle joblessness, with half aimed at young people — and I'm sure both mean well, that they're both doing their level best.

But both plans are, like so many others thrown at us these past few months, a sticking plaster on a broken leg; what they don't get is that this is too complex an issue to put a price tag on. It's not dry rot in the spare bedroom, we can't just get three estimates and pick the cheapest.

We have businesses out there who lost contracts the likes of they might never see again.

We have businesses who don't know when or if they'll ever be able to work at full capacity again.

We have businesses whose owners have used the last few months to step back and ask themselves what it is they want, whether they've spent too long running flat out to stand still, whether this might be the ideal time to downsize and spare themselves a heart attack.

We have businesses who've run themselves ragged trying to keep going despite coronavirus, the ones who've provided our essential services in the toughest of circumstances.

We have businesses who've thought outside the box, who couldn't do what they usually do and so who diversified into products the emergency demanded.

Let's be blunt, we also have business which weren't really businesses at all; the ones who pressed the panic button about 20 minutes after the shutters came down and who will take any free cash that's now going.

And we still haven't even mentioned the 200,000 and more self-employed souls who've been forced to scramble for grants or loans or Universal Credit to survive on. Put all this together and we see just how complex our economy really us — and surely we can, from this, see how pointless it is just con-nfusing money with Elaptoplast.

Listen, I'm no fiscal genius, but it seems from the viewpoint of an ordinary bloke with ordinary budgetary issues that this is no time for a one-size-fits-all attempt at a solution, no time for patronising families with money-off pizza vouchers.

No, this is a time for offering individual firms — corner shops, hair salons, restaurants, factories, you name it — tailored help to survive, whether that's rent holidays, tax breaks or subsiding the cost of gas, electricity and fuel.

This is, to hark back to a previous story, the time for our leaders to treat all these individual economic victims of the pandemic with the same level care the Vietnamese showed Stephen Cameron. The UK is the world's sixth-largest economy at £2.25 *trillion* per year; that's more than two million *million* pounds, more than enough to see us through. All it takes is the will and the wit to work with every employer in the land and nurture our nation back to health.

Bet your life we'd find the cash and the will if it was a war.

Monday July 20

BORIS JOHNSON compares it to 'a nuclear deterrent'.

In which case, Nicola Sturgeon seems more than ready to press the button.

We're talking a second national lockdown here, a possibility which today is being seriously discussed for the first time by Downing Street and Holyrood.

A new report from the London-based Academy of Medical Science claims a winter where the traditional flu outbreak could be made worse by the onset of what it calls coronavirus-like symptoms which could 'overwhelm' any track and trace system and calls for a nationwide increase in vaccinations to help avoid the worst. The report said:

> *"This winter, it will be a priority to increase the uptake of the influenza vaccination programme for high-risk groups vulnerable to influenza, such as the elderly and clinically vulnerable, young children who can amplify community spread and health and social care workers. A generalised increase in respiratory infections over the winter could rapidly overwhelm test-and-trace capacity. The usual number of winter respiratory viruses, with symptoms similar to early SARS-CoV-2, will lead to a very rapid rise in testing and potential quarantine requirements."*

The Academy warned that while homes with temperatures below 18 °C can reduce immunity to viruses, turning up heating could actually backfire if it causes humidity levels to drop. It claimed a winter second peak of the pandemic could be worse than the first, as more time indoors means a greater likelihood of direct person-to-person transmission, airborne transmission due to poor ventilation and lower temperatures allowing the virus to stay alive on surfaces:

> *"In more modern, well-insulated homes, central heating may reduce levels of relative humidity below 40 per cent, which can dry out the nasal mucosa and reduce muco-ciliary clear-*

ance that increases susceptibility of Covid-19 and influenza infection."

It then referred to a scientific paper published last month by Croatian scientists which claimed transmission of Covid-19 'is more efficient in a cold and dry climate than in warm and humid locations' and advising we stay constantly hydrated to stem the flow of germs.

A Scottish Government yesterday reiterated that Covid-19 is 'the greatest public health challenge of our lifetimes' and said: "As long as people continue to act responsibly and follow advice, we would hope to avoid impose national restrictions. However, we have always made it clear that if necessary, we will impose restrictions again."

This after Johnson downplayed the prospect of ordering people to stay home a second time, saying: "I can't abandon that tool any more than I would abandon a nuclear deterrent. But it is like a nuclear deterrent, I certainly don't want to use it.

"Nor do I think we will be in that position again."

Well, that's my mind put at ease…

Tuesday July 21

THE good news today is that Oxford University scientists could have a vaccine available for mass use by Christmas. Amidst a welter of optimistic headlines - **Hope Hope Hooray, A Shot In The Arm, Gift Of The Jab** - it's being reported that ChAdOx1 nCoV-19 triggered 'a strong immune response' in 1,000 healthy volunteers and that half a million more — many in Brazil and South Africa, where infection rates are currently far higher than here — will be signed up for further trial.

The UK is said to have secured 100 million doses, with the first 30 million predicted to be delivered this autumn. If trials are successful, vaccinations could start within a month. Data published by the Oxford team in medical journal *The Lancet* claimed the most common side-effects fatigue and headache, which were treated with paracetamol.

Meanwhile, a Southampton lab has reportedly developed what 'a game-changing drug' which could 'drastically cut the death rate among Covid-19 patients'.

Trials involving 101 hospital patients found the inhaled drug, which uses an anti-viral protein called interferon beta, cut the need for intensive care treatment by 79 per cent and that patients were also twice as likely to recover during the two-week treatment period.

NONE of which is happening a moment too soon for sufferers all around the world; take the Americas, where close on 22,000 deaths and 900,000 new cases were reported last week alone.

Mexico's toll today passed 40,000, with infections beyond 356,000. Deaths from the virus in the United States topped 1,000 today for the first time in two weeks, but the 59th time in 202 days since its first infections. Colombia suffered 239 more deaths, taking its total over 7,000. On average, Brazil is recording 33,000 new cases and 1,000 deaths every day.

Even the arch-doubter and mass-hypnotist himself, The Great Trumpino, admitted today 'it will unfortunately get worse before it gets better', provoking Nancy Pelosi, Democrat and Speaker of the House of Representatives, to snarl:

> *"He is recognising the mistakes that he has made by now embracing mask wearing and the recognition this is not a hoax. It is a pandemic that has gotten worse before it will get better because of his inaction and in fact it is clearly the 'Trump virus'. If he had said months ago 'let's wear a mask, let's socially distance' instead of having rallies, then more people would have followed his lead. If it's important to wear a mask now, it would have been important to wear it in March*

- instead of telling us that by April, we would all be going to church together. I wish that were the case, but it was never going to be. He is President of the United States."

Cheers for the reminder.

Wednesday July 22

GOODNESS knows how many times we had the conversation during those months when she was off work, the one about how once she was back it would all be different.

Time to take the foot off the pedal, to pick and choose her clients, to stop driving herself to exhaustion and start enjoying life before it was too late. She meant every word, too; just as she had the time it landed her in hospital with sepsis, just as she had every time she came home so tired all she could do was eat, sleep and sometimes weep.

But how long did it last? About as long as it ever lasts — just about long enough for the first woman tormented by a head like a burst couch to text late at night and for an appointment. And off my beautiful Sonia went, back on a treadmill moving faster than she could ever run.

She's a people-pleaser. She lives to give them haircuts that make them happy, new colours that give them confidence, to listen to all their problems without trying to fix them, to hug them and bring them coffee and make all their worries disappear for a couple of hours at least.

That's why her own health and happiness have always come last and why, just a few days out of salon lockdown, her appointment book's already chocca until October. To be fair, she's no happier about it than I am. Trouble is, she doesn't know how to change it, how to say no. All she knows is that, somehow, she'll have to learn.

It's the same for everyone in her profession right now; the entire country's either been waiting four months for a cut and blow dry or counting the days for emergency repairs on the home-made attempt they made at giving themselves a trim. Chances are it's the same for hundreds of thousands of others in countless other professions too, anyone providing a service that we as customers took for granted until it was taken away.

Everyone's under pressure to make up for lost time, for lost income. No one wants to turn anyone any in case they don't come back — after all, no one knows if and when the shutters might have to come clanging back down again.

We've done sums proving that, without the overheads of a salon weighing her down, Sonia could work four days a week and come away with more in her pocket than when she was grafting six or seven before the virus hit. The closer her return to work loomed, though the more it dawned that this change wouldn't work unless she came to the decision herself.

So she went to her old premises on Saturday, complete with sand sanitising station and monogrammed partitions between all the cutting positions, but it didn't feel right from the off. That buzz I wrote about earlier, the six clients in at once, music, Prosecco, cakes, laughter; all of it replaced by one in and one out, not being allowed to wash or dry their hair, having to re-sanitise the whole place before next one arrived.

On top of this, her room was within a physiotherapy clinic whose owner was clearly uncomfortable with the risk of his clients and hers coming in contact. So that night, she came home and announced that she was giving the place up, there and then. Instead, she'd go out to people's houses, sit out when the weather was nice and do their hair in the garden. This, thanks to travelling time, would cut down how many appointments she could take on, even if it didn't reduce her hours.

Or, at least, it *should* have cut down how many appointments she could take on. In reality, a few days in, she's already shoehorning in the odd extra client because they're just round the corner from the one before and she can put the ones after that back by an hour. So it was synchronicity that she walked into a beauty salon near the flat, a little place called Soul

Space, where they asked whether she'd fancy working out of there a couple of days a week. I hope she takes them up on the offer.

Two days in there, two more out and about? Rest of the week off? That would be ideal. It would be hugely ironic if, after nearly 40 years wielding the scissors, it took a global health crisis to bring her to a place where she finally began working to live.

She won't be alone in having this revelation, that's for sure, because after four months of forced leisure, of more family time than most had been afforderd in four years, of all that headspace, you meet more and more friends and neighbours who have slowly begun to realise that life really is too short to graft ourselves into an early grave.

Yes, put 100 percent into whatever job you do, but within a framework that allows us to rest, recharge, be close to the ones we love. But please, give yourself a break, because if you don't then no one else will.

That's all I want for Sonia - the gift of time, something we might all come to realise is among the most precious we have.

Sunday July 26

A GORGEOUS, sun-kissed 30 miles solo out to Bishopton and back last Saturday morning, 30 more up and over Queen's View on a warm Monday teatime, 30 more on the sweat-dropping indoor bike on Wednesday afternoon, 37 out to Drymen and back once more today.

And just like that, I'm one-third of the way to the Champs Elysees. *Well, virtually.*

Because, like a whole load of charities, Myeloma UK are shoring up the hole in this summer's finances by recreating lost fundraising adventures around our local streets. In this case, the London to Paris bike ride that would normally have been the centrepiece of their entire year. A bunch of pals were supposed to be doing it come September, the same time I was meant to be climbing Kilimanjaro with our Macmillan Cancer Support crew, but both — like most things so many of had been looking forward to this year — bit the dust.

Back in May, the good people behind the 85-mile Etape Caledonia cycle led the way by asking entrants to cover the distance wherever they happened to be and even posted out medals to those of us who did. This time, for Myeloma, it's 317 miles, though we've until August 17 to do it in.

Our big pal Ewan Ogilvie has this nasty form of blood cancer, but it didn't stop him entering for the real thing, so doing the virtual version is the least the rest of us can do. As summer turns to autumn, I'm pretty sure tens of thousands will end up doing something similar when — not if, because it seems inevitable — the London Marathon, having been shunted back from April to October, is scrapped altogether.

And why not? Why shouldn't be recreate these wonderful events in our own streets, even in our own spare rooms? After all, if commuters are finding they can do their jobs just as well from home rather than sitting in traffic jams or departure lounges, why can't fundraisers do their bit up and down their own streets rather than travelling the length of the country or even crossing continents to do pretty much the same thing?

There's a question I've often been asked across 20-odd years of charity events around the world: Why incur the cost of flights and hotels and when you could just give that money to the cause in the first place?

It's one worth asking, but it's one easily countered by the effect on fundraising of experiencing somewhere like, say, The Great Wall of China, of sharing that experience with people back home and seeing donations rocket far higher than they would if we merely replicated the trek on a machine in a gym. Telling the story of how your ageing frame hauled itself up and over the Pyrenees against its will has a far more positive effect on the grand total than doing it on a spin bike.

Plus, being their doesn't take any money out of the chosen charity's funds. Wpay our *own* flights and hotels because we want to see these places; these are holidays that do other people some good. I've climbed volcanoes in Ecuador, pulled a sledge across the Arctic Circle, cycled across the Killing Fields of Cambodia, expanding my mind more than I ever did in school while helping people at the same time.

This year, though, it can't be done, simple as that. We won't get to Kilimanjaro in September, nor in all likelihood come the stand-by date in February. It's a pain, but the mountain will still be there this time next year. *Won't it..?*

Wednesday July 29
•Tokyo's Governor, Yuriko Koike, says containing the spread of coronavirus in the Japanese capital is the first step towards the postponed Olympics and Paralympics going ahead next summer.
•New cases in Japan top 1,000 for the first time since a new wave of infections spread beyond Tokyo.
•The owner of a venue which staged a trial socially distanced gig by singer Frank Turner claims it 'can't be the future' after failing to cover costs.

RIGHT now, I'd do anything for a few days in Lisbon.

Hole up in the Hotel Pessoa, dinner at Bairro do Alvarez, port and sardines in one of the huddle of cramped bars off the Rua Misericordia, a train down to the sands of Cascais.

But it's not happening, that's a given. This point in the pandemic's progress is so delicate that it just doesn't feel worth the gamble of booking up, not when infection rates could spike overnight and wreck the whole shebang.

So there's a big part of me that finds it hard to sympathise with the armies of Brits currently throwing the stuffed donkey out the pram at either being told they'll have to quarantine on their return from the sunshine or having to cut stays short for fear of their tour operator going out of business. It feels like they must have more money than sense to charge ahead with holiday plans when they didn't have a clue what the virus was going to do next.

Yet the little part of me that's left over *is* kind of on their side, because there's no doubt the infuriating inability of those in charge to make a decision on quarantine and stick to it has encouraged tens of thousands to waste collective fortunes.

Over the course of this month, for instance, Spain has gone from safe for us to visit without going into quarantine on our return to unsafe, to safe again and now back to unsafe. Understandable, this, in terms of the unpredictability of the situation — but not much use if you're looking for clarity on whether or not to travel there. Take the latest advice from Westminster culture secretary Oliver Dowden, yet another one of those cabinet identikits hand-knitted by the Shredded Wheat grannies and a man whose statement on the situation made him seem so far out of touch he might as well have got his butler to hand out the press release on a silver salvers.

He told his subjects that 'as long as people are aware of the risk that quarantine could be imposed, they should continue to book holidays'. You know, because we can all afford to lose a grand or two on a fortnight in the sun. We can all afford two weeks off work to self-isolate once we're back.

What does he think we all are? Trust-funded loungers who wouldn't miss the price of a fornight's holiday if we dropped it running for a bus?

It's like he neither knows nor cares that there are people who only found out about the latest rules for visiting Spain once they touched down last weekend. That there are people who had to cut breaks short and fly home because they couldn't afford 14 days off work in quarantine. There are hordes still fighting to get cash back for cruises, honeymoons, stag and hen weekends and more, all cancelled without compensation because of lockdown. Yet now he wants us those same hordes to gamble again, just when the job market's about to go into terminal meltdown? No wonder people stop listening and just do what the hell they fancy.

Then there's Nicola Sturgeon, whose latest folksy address told the nation that if was her, she wouldn't be having any foreign hols malarkey; no, she'd be giving it a fortnight in Granny's Heilan' Hame.

Makes you think that a whole lot of people who hang on

her every word could have done with this advice before they booked up for Magaluf and Torremolinos, not once they were already out there. And also whether her advert for our tourist industry maybe comes with a splash of hypocrisy, since three weeks ago thousands of our hotels and B&Bs couldn't take bookings because she couldn't decide if the English, Welsh and Irish would have to quarantine on their arrival.

In truth, the lack of common sense and consistency being shown by, leaders and punters alike, over travel kind of sums up where we've been from the start of lockdown; constantly guessing at issues that call for definitives.

Both the FM and PM should have said from way before the summer holiday season kicked in that all trips to all venues were taken at the traveller's own risk and that quarantine on our return was always an option. This might not have made some people think any straighter, but at least they would have had no one to blame but themselves for the consequences.

Amidst all this confusion, leading tour operator Tui is to close 166 shops in the UK and Ireland - almost a third of its total — because of a drop in demand and a migration to online bookings. This comes after it announced plans in May to cut 8,000 jobs in a bid to reduce overheads by 30 per cent.

Tui restarted its overseas holiday programme on July 11, but in common with others in the industry they were badly hit by the Spanish quarantine situation. So too rival Jet2, who over the past few days have contacted customers in Balearic and Canary Island resorts to tell them they had until Monday August 3 to return home on rearranged flights or risk having to get back at their own expense, as they can no longer afford to operate with near-empty planes. EasyJet is already in the process of shedding a third of its staff, Ryanair around 3,000 workers and British Airways was warning as early as April that 12,000 of its 42,000 workers would have to go.

Smaller tourism firms - Shearings, Hays, Barrhead Travel - have made several thousand redundant between them, while more than half the operators who bring visitors to the UK - a

£24 billion-a-year market — fear they won't survive another six months without government financial aid.

The doomsday prediction is that 120,000 jobs in the aviation industry alone could be lost by next spring; a collapse on the scale of the coal industry's demise in the early 80s.

Friday July 31

AND so, as a long, tough month crawls to a close, Scottish football finally returns. Come noon tomorrow, Aberdeen meet Rangers in the opening game of a new Premiership season, what seems several years — and a million pointless arguments — since the last one was stopped in its tracks.

What's more, just for once, our top division is the only game in town. The English leagues don't start until the middle of September and even though there's still a welter of knock-out matches to be played in the Champions League and Europa League, none clash with any of our fixtures. After a lifetime of all but nine out of ten live games from up here being tagged on to the schedule to fulfil a contractual obligation, the exception being Celtic versus Rangers (or vice versa, before some numbskull accuses me of bias) we're the top banana.

For once, the world really is watching.

A thought that leaves me issuing once simple plea in my preview piece for tomorrow morning's paper:

Don't fuck it up, chaps...

23: F FOR F****** FAILURE

WELL, no one can say they didn't give it their best shot. We made it eight whole hours into the season before the first halfwits made arses of themselves and everyone else involved in the game.

Which by Scottish football's standards isn't a bad effort at all.

Just after quarter to two on Saturday August 1, Aberdeen's players trooped off after losing their opening match 1-0 at home to Rangers. By mid-evening, eight of the squad were in a city centre bar, breaking every known coronavirus rule.

The Premiership had only been cleared to start if its 12 clubs tested all employees twice a week, stuck to iron-clad regulations on how many could be in one dressing room at one time or travel in the same car, how close coaches could get to players during training sessions. Come matchdays, rival teams weren't allowed to emerge from the same tunnel; plus, most jarringly visible of all, no fans were allowed into stadium.

So why, in a city already on the brink of being plunged back into lockdown after the reopening of its nightlife brought a spike in new cases, right experienced professionals — because none of the eight are kids — thought none of the above applied outwide Pittodrie Stadium is beyond extraordinary.

Yet off they popped, sitting down together to eat before heading for Soul Bar, a former church on the city's main Union Street which, come Wednesday, would be closed after a punter who'd caught the virus in the nearby Hawthorn Bar nipped in for a pint. On Thursday morning, Aberdeen manager Derek McInnes had to cancel training after routine Covid testing showed two of the eight up as positive. They were instantly put in quarantine, with the other six ordered to self-isolate.

By Friday, the following day's match at St Johnstone was postponed, Nicola Sturgeon describing the team night out as 'unacceptable. Then, on Saturday, the players put out what was labelled an 'unreserved apology' but which was as unreserved as a restaurant table with a Reserved giant sign on it:

> *"First and foremost we would like to apologise to every AFC fan, the manager, everyone at the club, the football authorities, the First Minister, all healthcare workers along with everyone else that has worked tirelessly around the clock to get the country, and in particular football, back up and running again. We, as a small group of players, made a huge error of judgement last weekend by thinking it was ok to visit a city centre venue together. None of us could have foreseen the escalation of Covid-19 cases in the Grampian area, nor did we deliberately attempt to flaunt or disobey government guidelines which we all must adhere to, or indeed the clear guidelines set out by the club. This was by no means a team night out as has been portrayed and while we attempted to comply with Government social distancing guidelines, we now recognise that our group of eight exceeded the number of households permitted to meet up. This was a genuine error on our part as professional football players, and in doing so, we have let our manager down. As players we appreciate our club has gone above and beyond to put protocols in place to protect us and it was never our intention to put that those jeopardy, or to put our team-mates or football staff at risk. As a player group, we once again apologise unreservedly to the fans, the manager, the board and all the staff at the club."*
> **Jonny, Michael, Scott, Matty, Sam, Dylan, Craig, Bruce**.

JONNY, Michael, Scott, Matty, Sam, Dylan, Craig, Bruce.

That's the bit that got me, they way they signed off like members of a boy band employing a squad rotation system. So sure of their own fame that they didn't even need surnames.

Well, if I was paying their wages there's only One Direction this bunch would be headed — and that's out the door.

In just about any other business under as much financial pressure as football clubs are right now, the HR wallahs would be scouring the small print for a way to sack the lot of them.

Gross misconduct? Endangering the health and safety of their colleagues? Bringing the game into disrepute? Being a selfish shower of self-entitled muppets? Take your pick. All I know is that if they were joiners or bus drivers or call centre workers rather than sporting (ahem) heroes, their feet wouldn't have touched the ground. Their gaffers wouldn't have hesitateds in putting the company's reputation first and emptying them.

But joiners, bus drivers and call centre workers don't have agents. They don't have a transfer value. They don't have the status and power that comes with being able to kick a ball around better than most.

So what happens when Jonny and Michael and Scott and Matty, Sam and Dylan and Craig and Bruce extend a middle finger to the rules drummed into them, when they choose to put themselves and everyone around them at risk of a disease which has killed twice as many in Britain as their stadium holds, when they force their club's next match to be postponed and the entire Scottish season to be jeopardised?

They get away with a club fine that's donated to charity, a suspended three-game ban from the SFA then with issuing a half-arsed apology for going on an illicit team night out.

Sorry, let's re-phrase that last bit; because it *wasn't* a night out, was it? At least, not a *team* night out. Sure, it was at night and they were out and they're members of a team, but it wasn't a team night out. This was made crystal clear in that statement issued by Aberdeen FC on behalf of the Covid Eight, not so much an unreserved apology as a grudging admission that they'd now been made aware of all the reasons why they shouldn't have been where they were, when they were, in the numbers they were.

This despite all those reasons having being drummed into

all of us day after day after day. Makes you think that any of these eight who wasn't aware of the rules either hadn't been listening or reckoned they didn't have to. Whichever is the case with Jonny and Michael and Scott and Matty, with Sam and Dylan and Craig and Bruce, they don't come out of this well and that excuse for an apology only makes them look even worse than their initial actions had – as is the case with the club itself, since it didn't feel the need to suggest a few teensy-weensy changes to the statement.

Like all of the words.

At very least, someone should have told them to them sign it from Jonny Hayes, Michael Devlin, Scott McKenna, Matty Kennedy, Sam Cosgrove, Dylan McGeouch, Craig Bryson and Bruce Anderson; a little respect, an ounce of gravitas.

Yet not only were they happy with the boy-band motif, the in-club Red TV then streamed an interview with Hayes to 'clear the air' in the way a donkey fart would have.

"We thought because we were together every day that maybe we were part of one big household," he said.

Seriously? You can't car-share and only three players can be in one dressing room at a time, yet you don't get the difference between being part of a squad and part of a squat?

"At any one point there were seven households together," he said. "We didn't know that was unacceptable."

Seriously? Then why not check first, maybe with Michael Devlin, who as vice-chairman of the Scottish Professional Footballers Association presumably has some vague idea of pandemic protocols and who was with you.

"We have to isolate for two weeks," Hayes went on. "That in it-self is punishment."

Seriously? So now THEY were the victims?

"We shouldn't have gone out for dinner, we shouldn't have gone to a bar. Hindsight's a wonderful thing."

Seriously? Is meant to make the world feel better about you?

Sorry, Jonny. If you'd stopped at 'we shouldn't have gone

out' it might just about have washed. But once you throw in the line about hindsight being a wonderful thing, this whole 'unreserved apology' schtick falls flat, since an unreserved apology means saying sorry for doing what you did, full stop.

Saying you're sorry but you didn't know any better, that it's not how it looks, that you didn't mean any harm? That stinks of apologising because someone's advised you to — and that's the sort of hypocritical rot we hunt politicians out of office for.

Just as well footballers don't have to put themselves up for re-election...

BY the time all this was playing itself out, word had emerged of a surprise house party thrown by Celtic striker Leigh Griffiths for girlfriend Caitlyn Melville's birthday.

Pictures she posted to Instagram - and later deleted — showed groups of pals seemingly breaking social distancing rules and although there was no suggestion that anyone caught the virus at the event, the club 'warned the player of his responsibilities'.

It was a warning you'd have thought the rest of the squad would have taken on board if they knew what was good for them, yet one which one in particular ignored big style. And once he did, the season that had barely started was in grave danger of being over.

After their 5-1 home win over Hamilton Accies on Sunday August 2, manager Neil Lennon gave his squad a couple of days off, with the strict instructions not to stray far from home and to stick to the rules.

Boli Bolingoli, a left-back signed from Austrian club Rapid Vienna on a four-year contract for a reported £3m transfer fee 13 months ago, clearly believes the world to be a very small place indeed, though. Because his take on 'not straying far' was to catch a plane to Malaga first thing on Monday with a Belgian model in tow.

Not only did he not let his bosses know he was jetting off for an overnight at the five-star Hotel Don Pepe Gran Meliá resort in Marbella, not only did he decide not to admit his offence when they got back and to go straight back to training with the rest of the squad, he then travelled with them to Kilmarnock on the Sunday and came on as a substitute for the final three minutes of a 1-1 draw.

If his club bosses and Scotland's footballing authorities had been none the wiser, they soon found out how badly they'd been duped when *The Scottish Sun* broke the story 48 hours later. It's a toss-up which was more furious, Celtic manager Lennon or Nicola Sturgeon, who each went into full-on rant mode within half an hour that lunchtime. Lennon fumed:

> *"I am livid, it's a total betrayal of trust — once for going and twice for not reporting that he went. He took a flight to Spain on Monday and flew back on Tuesday - one day in Spain, no logic to that — and decided to keep it to himself. We couldn't have done any more as a club to maintain standards. This is a rogue player who has gone off tangent and decided to do something very, very selfish. He trained all week in this bubble, was part of the squad for Sunday and put everybody at risk, Kilmarnock players and staff as well. We were livid and appalled. We've been bitterly and sorely let down by the selfish actions of one individual. He blatantly disregarded instructions. The players are angry, disappointed and frustrated. It's just not good enough, simply not good enough. He put everything at risk and never told a soul. The players didn't seem to know anything about it. The behaviour of the individual is just baffling."*

It was a filleting that came right up from the soles of the Irishman's shoes, not to mention one that must have made the Aberdeen Eight realise just how lightly they'd got off in the way *their* gaffers had tip-toed around the issue.

The First Minister, meanwhile, very publicly put Scottish football on 'a yellow card' and it was hard to blame her:

"Every day I stand here and ask members of the public to make huge sacrifices on how they live their lives. The vast majority are doing that and it's not easy. We can't have privileged football players just deciding that they're not going to bother. This can't go on. Consider today the yellow card. Next time it will be the red card because you will leave us with absolutely no choice."

Her mood had clearly been made all the darker by news of the wally Bolingoli's jolly having broken right in the middle of a summit between her clinical director Professor Jason Leitch and the managers and captains of the 12 Premiership clubs.

Her reaction was to tell the league — well, she said it was their decision, but believe it if you like — to postpone three matches; Aberdeen at home to Hamilton and Celtic at St Mirren the following night and, irony ironies, Celtic against Aberdeen on the Saturday. It would have been hugely unfair on 99.9 per cent of footballers had she shown the Premiership a straight red there and then. But make no mistake, one more fly pint, one more illicit barbecue and that card would be out so fast she'd make Billy The Kid look like the Venus di Milo.

And the house of cards that is fragile, dysfunctional Scottish football would surely collapse.

In a calendar packed tighter than an Aberdeen boozer, even a fortnight in mothballs would make it impossible to complete the Premiership, the Championship, Leagues One and Two and the League Cup might not even start, last season's Scottish Cup - still to be completed this winter — would be at risk, along with Scotland's Euro play-offs and Nations League fixtures.

There was now no chance of punters being back inside stadiums by mid-September and planned and the longer stands lay empty, the greater the risk to clubs already relying on handouts from charitable tycoons for their survival. As with Dominic Cummings and his countryside capers, we were talking butterflies and hurricanes, every indiscretion playing its part in causing mass chaos.

It's not just football, either. As Jason Leitch made clear today, the Premiership became a test case for *all* sport when it allowed to restart, so its every cock-up affects rugby, golf, swimming, horse racing, you name it. These are just some of the ripples that spread from the selfishness of nine numpties, the kind of ramifications that didn't even cross their minds as they charged about as if they were immune to the virus.

There's a saying we have up here about a particularly poor game that goes: "This would get fitba' stopped."

Boli Bolingoli, Jonny Hayes, Scott McKenna, Craig Bryson, Sam Cosgrove, Michael Devlin, Dylan McGeouch, Bruce Anderson and Matty Kennedy are damn lucky they only managed to make it happen on a temporary basis for a few clubs clubs.

◆ ◆ ◆

STILL, call me an old cynic. But even in her obvious anger, the FM must have allowed herself a private sigh of relief at the headlines these nine numpties were making and the spleen it allowed her to vent. Because right then, she really needed something — anything — to deflect from a different kind of scandal engulfing her government.

The Great Exams Fiasco.

◆ ◆ ◆

BACK on March 19, the day after we learned that Scotland's schools would close within 48 hours, Education Minister John Swinney declared that this year's National 5 and Higher exams would be cancelled.

A month later, he announced grades would be awarded on the basis of course work over the entire year, saying: "Teachers and lecturers are being asked to make important decisions about how learners may have otherwise performed in the exams. Their insights means they are best placed to make judgements on learners 'performance."

However, it then emerged that grades would in reality be adjusted according to previous performances of individual schools, leaving opposition politicians predicting those from deprived communities — their words, not mine — would be disadvantaged, with Scottish Labour's education spokesman Iain Gray saying: "Pupils deserve to be graded based on merit and should not be penalised for the past record of their schools. This will hit pupils in deprived areas hardest."

Gray's claims were flatly denied by Fiona Robertson, chief executive of the Scottish Qualifications Authority, who said: "The assertion that we will fail a young person because of the school they go to feels like an unfair statement. We are looking at whether there is a professional dialogue we can enter into with a school, if the shape or distribution or indeed the volume of attainment looks very different to how it has historically."

That was in early June, but by July 1 she was admitting: "We have considered the matter carefully...and have concluded it will not be possible to include engagement with schools and colleges within the moderation process."

On August 1, Iain Gray said: "Thousands of Scots will get their results on Tuesday, but real concerns remain that some will have their teachers 'assessments reduced based on the basis of their school's previous performance and that would be most unfair."

AND so it came to pass.

Or to fail, depending on your school's postcode.

The SQA had looked at the results thousands of teachers predicted for 124,000 pupils — more than one in five of all those sitting National 5, Higher and Advanced Higher exams — and marked them down. Why? Well, the First Minister said it was so 'this year's results have the degree of credibility that means that they are not so out of sync with previous years'.

What she *meant* was that it was if you're at a school which has traditionally turned in bad results, you were being given results bad enough so it didn't look like they were fiddling the figures. And let's be honest here, if the Tories had done this, we wouldn't be able to move for protestors.

Wee Nicola's Tartan Army would be marching 20-deep on Westminster as we speak, shoulder to shoulder and to hell with social distancing. A fortnight in quarantine would be well worth it for the chance to barrack the toffee-nosed clowns who'd decided our kids weren't posh enough for good grades.

Except that it wasn't Boris and his buddies who marked down those 124,000 papers simply because they came from schools in the 'wrong' areas. It was a Scottish Qualifications Authority under the control of our SNP-controlled Scottish Government. And they should be ashamed, every single one of them involved in a scandal that they must have known was never going to be swept under the carpet.

For me, this had the potential to become the SNP's Poll Tax. This was their reminder to ambitious, hard-working families up and down the land to know their place.

As for all those teachers who'd been asked to make in-formed judgements on young people they'd worked with all year? They should have been lobbying their unions to defend their reputation and their judgement, even if it meant hitting the cobbles. That's how serious an issue this was.

At a time when the FM wants us to believe an independent Scotland would be a fairer nation than a Britain run by the Old Boys Network, she'd shot herself in both feet by admitting it's more credible for a kid in Bearsden or Morningside to get straight A grades than one in Ferguslie Park or Wester Hailes.

That's the word she used — credible. The results predicted for pupils in so-called 'deprived' areas were, she said, so good as to be 'unprecedented and therefore not credible', by which she was also pretty much telling teachers working in those 'deprived' areas that their judgement on the abilities of pupils they work with every single day can't be trusted.

So much for that old Scottish saying about us all being Jock Tamson's Bairns. Seems we'd have a much better chance if our father was Jonathan Thomson Esquire.

It hasn't been an easy year for the SQA; how could it be when schools were shut down and exams scrapped for the first time in 130 years? But the way they'd dealt with this unique set of circumstances deserved as best a D for dunce. Downgraded to F for fucking farcical. Not that the Nats saw it this way, of course. They made it immediately clear that they were more than happy with how the numbers looked — and so, after four months of lockdown when the FM had been at pain to tell us that virus victims are people and not statistics, suddenly that's all our youngsters were to her: Numbers.

The opinions of teachers who know them as individuals had been disregarded, because the percentage pass-rates these individual judgements would create didn't look good on a graph. They'd shown 'deprived' pupils closing the gap on the 'better-off' far too quickly, which neither the Nats nor the SQA would be able to explain. So the 'deprived' pupils had to suffer.

By the way, please forgive the repeated use of quote marks around the word 'deprived', but it's merely to make clear the fact that it's not one I would use. After all, who's to say the kid from the big house whose parents are too busy to spend proper time with him isn't *more* deprived than the one in the council scheme whose mum and dad encourage her non-stop?

In fact, let's not piss about — *deprived* is shorthand for *poor*. And if there's one place on this earth where being poor only makes us more hell-bent on punching above our weight, it's surely Scotland; if America is the Land of the Free, we're the land of *Is That Yer Best Shot, Big Man?*

It is, of course, nothing new for Scots to find their chances of getting on in the world depend on the answer to one simple, insidious question: *What school did you go to?*

Difference is, Nicola Sturgeon would be the first to tell us that those who for generations routinely asked it on the basis of religion were dinosaurs.

So the fact that she seemed to thinks it was OK on the basis of income? See me after class...

◆ ◆ ◆

IT pretty much goes without saying that the FM got it from all sides as soon as the results plopped on the mat.

Even firebrand SNP MP Mhairi Black, who like me grew up in Paisley, a once-thriving industrial town scarred by decades of job losses, said she was 'deeply distressed' by the news and called on Holyrood to 'address the issue'.

Education Minister John Swinney, however, was gamely trying to pretend there was nothing to see here as he chirped:

> "Our young people who have achieved qualifications this year can be confident they will stand the test of time and have been awarded in a fair and robust manner such that will allow progression on to the next step of learner journeys or into employment."

Tell that to the young people who marched on Glasgow's City Chambers come Friday to chant for 'fair grades'.

Asked whether she'd have joined the protest had her own results been downgraded because of her school's past, Nicola Sturgeon herself said it was 'very possible', before claiming that 'if we get a situation where lots of appeals are awarded, then it will show that that process has worked as intended'.

So, they marked 124,000 papers down *hoping* the results would be overturned? Sorry, but that's maybe the most bizarre thing about this shambles so far.

As for Swinney, he wasn't quite as sure of himself by the Sunday as he had been a couple of days earlier, admitting:

"I have heard the anger of students who feel their hard work has been taken away from them and am determined to address it. These are unprecedented times and, as we have said throughout this pandemic, we will not get everything right first time."

A statement that left you asking *why* they couldn't get it right first time, given that just about everyone outwith their political echo chamber had warned them it was all going to go pear-shaped. You were forced to question the motives of an administration which blankly ignored anyone and everyone — opposition politician, schoolteacher, pupil, parent, journalist, anyone — and ploughed on with am unworkable, unfair plan.

Then you de-coded his words and realised that the sub-text read: "OK, we cocked up. But let's blame the pandemic."

NEXT day, Monday August 10, Swinney issued a statement to the Scottish Parliament in which he revealed he was directing the SQA to reinstate all downgraded results to those originally recommended by their teacher. He apologised to all those affected, paid tribute to those who had protested on the streets or written complaints to him and announced an independent review into the handling of this year's awards.

"It's deeply regrettable that we got this wrong," he said, "and I'm sorry about that."

Step forward the FM to add: "Despite our best intentions, I acknowledge we did not get this right and I'm sorry for that. Ministers asked the SQA to apply an approach that delivered a set of results comparable in terms of quality to last year's. The view ministers take now is that it didn't take enough account of the individual circumstances."

As apologies go, it was as unreserved as the one made by the Aberdeen players she'd so recently caned. But such is politics.

And now, the SNP faced a major test of its integrity in the shape of the vote of no confidence in John Swinney brought before Holyrood on the afternoon of Thursday August 13. An exam paper with only one question: *Does loyalty to the party mean more than your duty to Scotland's next generation?*

That's what this boiled down to. Nationalist MSPs had the choice to accept that the SQA results fiasco was the final straw for Swinney as Education Minister, or to put the wagons in a circle and save his skin; agreeing with heavy hearts that he had to go would resonate with public opinion, clubbing together to allow him to cling on would be the kind of thing they'd usually sneer at the Westminster old boys' network for.

Well, we all either know by now which way the show of hands went or we can guess. The wagons went in a circle and Swinney survived, a decision that can only be seen as a stamp of approval to a man who's spent lockdown flailing around like a drunk man chasing a balloon.

It shouldn't be forgotten that, even before the exams fiasco, he'd made schools sweat bullets to get classrooms ready for a part-time, socially distanced return, only to tear up all their plans five minutes before the bell went and announce that they were fine to go back full-time after all.

Not a shred of mea culpa was expressed for this waste of everyone's time and effort — not to mention a wad of public money — and now, even as he was forced into an excruciating climbdown over those 124,000 downgraded results, he still couldn't take responsibility like a grown-up.

In his statement to parliament, he claimed 'we' set out to ensure the system was credible, but called it regrettable that 'we' did not get it right for all young people. Then he revealed that 'I' am directing the SQA to re-issue those awards based solely on teacher or lecturer judgement.

In other words, getting it wrong is a collective thing, but putting it right's all his own work.

And as if this wasn't cringeworthy enough, Sturgeon then attempted to deflect attention from her own government's mess by pointing out that a carbon-copy of the exam marks fiasco was now happening across the rest of the UK. As 40 per cent of English, Welsh and Northern Irish results came back lower than teachers had recommended, the FM crowed that her party 'own our mistakes'.

As an encore, she then described Swinney — her deputy as well as the minister loosely in charge of education — as 'the most honourable man I have ever known'.

To which all I can say is that Eddie The Eagle came across as an honourable kind of guy too, but he was hopeless as an Olympic skier

24: THE NEVER-ENDING STORY

Saturday August 15
•New Zealand records 13 new cases after two months virus-free.
•England's education chiefs waive fees of £9-£150 for appeals against downgraded exam results.
•British tourists rage at the 'shambles' of a last-gasp decision to quarantine anyone returning from France.

TO BE honest, I didn't expect to still be writing this book by now. And I'm pretty damn sure you'd hoped to be done with reading it long ago so you could get back to sticking forks in your eyes

Three months, maybe four? That sounded about right. End to March until the end of June or into July at worst, then it would all close out into a perfect circle, with Boris staring down the lens the way he had right back at the start and telling us lockdown was finally over.

Yet not only doesn't that blessed official release appear to be happening anytime soon, it feels more likely that the PM's next big live show might be to clang us back into full lockdown.

It's a week now since rules on wearing masks were extended to England's cinemas and funeral homes, Scotland's banks and beauty salons and all Northern Ireland's enclosed public spaces, as well as since Belgium, Andorra and the Bahamas were added to the list of countries from which those arriving have to self-isolate for 14 days and quarantine was reimposed on passengers from Spain and Luxembourg.

It's six days since the daily figure of confirmed new COVID-19 infections passed 1,000 for the first time since June - rising by 1,062 to 310,825 - though no one seems sure whether this is down to a higher infection rate or a hike in the volume of testing. By yesterday, that daily figure was 1,441.

There's a Dunkirk-style flotilla bringing platoons of British holidaymakers back across the Channel before France tackles a sweeping second wave with draconian new restrictions on movement. And don't get me started on the poor sods trapped in Draconia itself.

Here, conspiracy theories gather pace about the 'sinister agenda' behind making us mask up, along with scare stories of Government mind-control plans and even parallels drawn with Nazi Germany. All nonsense, but unsurprising all the same; when people are confused, when they feel let down, when they can't understand instructions from leaders they perhaps didn't trust in the first place, some get scared. And in this era of social media, fear shows itself in endless streams of consciousness that spread like mini-viruses of their own.

So the ones who don't believe masks make a difference to the spread of infection — or who deny there's even an infection to spread — start labelling the ones who do as sheep; the irony of which most seem too dim to appreciate, given that they're generally only cutting and pasting someone else's rants for want of the wit to construct their own.

There's an uneasiness in the air, a huge level of uncertainty. Everyone seems to be having the same conversation, the one about how none of the rules make sense, how the latest lot contradicts the last, how the FM and PM are clutching at straws, how neither knows what do next and how all their faffing around proves they're desperately buying time until a vaccine's ready or the virus gets bored and gives up.

A perfect case in point is Nicola Sturgeon's decision to ban back-ground music in pubs, restaurants and cafes.

Sure, we'd long since accepted that crowding in to watch live bands or take a turn on the karaoke were on hold. Even we, the idiot human race, got that shouting and singing in each other's faces was a sure-fire way of upping the R rate. But still and all, to be told that a little low-level tuneage was a risk to public health...well, it felt more than a little straw-clutchy.

◆ ◆ ◆

I'D been sitting in the window seat of Nic's NYC Deli on Byres Road for maybe ten minutes on Thursday morning when it dawned that something wasn't right.

The coffee was good, my breakfast was excellent as ever, the girls behind the counter were on their usual top form despite the encumbrance of their perspex visors.

So what was it? What was missing? Then the lightbulb pinged; it was the *silence*, that's what was wrong.

"Your Spotify not working?"

"No, it's this new rule — we're not allowed music."

I had to admit this latest tweak had passed me by.

"Yeah, apparently having music on makes customers lean in to hear conversations and this spreads germs. Or we'll sing along and that'll spread germs as well."

A real tipping point for me, this. The moment when my last shreds of faith in our leaders began to evaporate.

See, for maybe 15 years now, most of my writing's been done in cafes because otherwise work would be a solitary affair and that's never good for the mental health.

This, as much as serving food and drinks, is the role of the cafe in our communities, places where an awful lot of people who often spend a lot of the day on their own come to be part of something — and music is a key component of that.

In all the countless hours I've spent in this environment, fellow customers have annoyed me by eating with their mouths open, slurping their tea, talking too loudly, letting their kiddies run wild or not paying close enough attention to personal hygiene and personal space and I'm sure they've been equally annoyed by me just being me.

But never has it felt like any of them posed a public health risk by singing along too loudly to a bit of Smooth FM.

So, are we seriously to believe switching the radio off will make a genuine difference to the pandemic? Are we to believe that having lost more than 40,000 poor souls in this country alone, all but a few taken at a time when the less-than-smooth FM and PM alike thought it wise for us to wear masks, a bit of tuneage with our bacon sandwich is now a potential killer?

By the by, I use the example of Smooth FM pointedly, as later that same day I had a hospital appointment for the dodgy eye and it was playing in the background. So it's healthy to sing along in an NHS waiting room, but not in a cafe? No wonder so many conspiracy fantasists are running around in tin-foil hats.

Listen, those deluded twunts can go play with the buses. There *is* no hidden agenda in decisions like these, just as the Illuminati didn't set up Eat Out To Help Out so they could sneak sedatives into our fish and chips. We're just dealing with people in positions of power who are at the end of their tether, who are floundering way out of their depth.

Like me — like pretty much everyone — the politicians and the scientists and the docs thought lockdown would have a natural shelf-life and that soon enough they'd get back to shouting Yah-Boo at each other across the benches.

Yet here we were, spring long since been and gone, drifting through summer and not so far from the nights beginning to draw in. Starting to wonder if we might still be in this God-awful mess come the depths of winter.

SO, how *do* you finish a book when the story has no ending?

You can't just fade to black like it's the last episode of *The Sopranos*. Yet you can't just keep writing and writing until Amazon need a flatbed truck to deliver each individual copy.

The cover's been ready to rock for a week now. With online print-on-demand being the miracle it is, if I pressed Send on the manuscript right now it'd be on sale within 48 hours.

Yet how *can* you press Send when every instinct tells you that the second you do, something huge will happen and you'll have missed it? It'd be like covering the World Cup Final and sending the match report ten minutes from time at 0-0.

Truth is, I'm scared to hit the button, because I know the second the words have whizzed off into the ether something huge *will* happen. So days go by and still it sits here on the screen, me tinkering with this bit and adding to that, but mainly distract myself by riding the bike or walking Sherlock, hoping one time I'll come home and the loose ends will have magically tied themselves in a net, lockdown-ending bow.

Our little cycling crowd have been stepping up the miles week by week; a 50, a 60, a 70. Over the past month we've been joined by Gus MacPherson, one-time St Mirren manager and, until the virus, in charge of the club's recruitment. He bought a bike to fill the days when they put him on furlough and now that he's officially redundant, it's become a priceless purchase.

That's been one of the few major positives of these past months, the huge upsurge in cycling and the benefitds to both mental and physical it has brought so many.

Gus is living proof of this. He comes alive out on the road, using the freedom of the countryside as his space in which to think, as well as making himself two stones lighter thanks to the miles mounting up on his Strava app.

I can't remember ever seeing as many bikes on the road as there have been these last few months, as well as so many different sizes and shapes and ages of rider. Add to this the numbers who've bought or hired indoor cycles, getting in the saddle has clearly a key ways for us — in Britain, the States, across Europe and even, as I read only the other day, in India — to remove ourselves from the feeling of being shut in.

A happy thought rendered all the more ironic by the news Sonia greets me with on my return from a glorious teatime scoot with the troops on this first day of September.

We're going back into lockdown.

◆ ◆ ◆

OK, so it's not quite full-on lockdown, the 23-hour-a-day kind we were faced with as March ended. But for 800,000 of us in and around Scotland's biggest city, it's not a kick in the backside off it. On a day when 66 positive tests were recorded in the area, the FM has barred all households in Glasgow, East Renfrewshire and West Dunbartonshire from visiting each other as of midnight. It's a decision which even affects the FM herself directly as her home is in the curfew zone, as well as one she calls 'unwelcome' but 'essential', saying:

> *"We could see thus virus run out of control again. If the numbers we are seeing continue, more people will fall ill from Covid and more people will go into hospital."*

Once upon a time, home was where the heart was; but it now appears to be where the threat is. Which might just be the most demoralising thought of the entire pandemic.

Because to order almost a sixth of Scotland's population not to cross each other's doorsteps for fear of causing a potentially disastrous second wave of infections...well, it's hard to get past the thought that it's either a massive over-reaction on the part of our leaders or a sorry indictment of our individual and collective stupidity. Either way, it breaks your heart.

On one hand, when we look at the situation in our schools, where absenteeism is rocketing and confusion over face masks and distancing reigns, we see *prima face* evidence of the failure of government to lay down clear messages on a crucial issue.

Yet on the other, there's no doubt too many among us are making life even harder for those running the show by plain refusing to keep themselves and others safe. And, in many cases, the simple reason appears to be that unless we're *ordered* to whay's right, we're incapable of working it out for ourselves.

That's why when Labour MSP Monica Lennon reacted to this step backwards by claiming to be 'puzzled' that we can still meet in pubs but not 'in the safety of our homes', she was at best being mischievous and at worst thick as a rhino toastie.

Fact is, as I'm sure someone of her intelligence is well aware, pubs and restaurants and cafes were only allowed to re-open once they'd slashed capacity, partitioned off their tables, put serving staff behind perspex, scrubbed every surface to within an inch of its life a dozen times a day and even stopped playing background music. One breach and their shutters would be back down before you could say pie, beans and chips.

How many of these precautions do any of us take when visitors come calling? Do we stay a metre away from them, with some sort of barrier between us? Do we muffle conversation behind masks, do we sanitise everything they've touched once they go?

I'm sure many do, but certain many more don't, because... well, it's our home, isn't it? We keep it clean, don't we? And they're our family, our neighbours, aren't they? Yet it's this sort of domestic complacency we're told is to blame for the fresh spike in cases, with the FM claiming that most of the 314 recorded in the first two days of this week took hold in the home. My mantra from the off has been that we'd get through the worst if we all considered our own home and family to be our personal bubble and that if we all maintained standards within those individual bubbles, the danger would pass in time. These new rules, however, suggest the country's divided between those who look after their own house first and those who see it as someone else's job to keep the world safe.

We know what we're doing. We're not daft. It's other people who cause the problems.

That's been the mindset of way too many who want to be allowed back to work, to have the kids back at school, to have a normal social life, yet who also demand to be kept safe when the bottom line is that we can either have one or the other.

The wants and needs of the masses have taken over from our logic every bit as has been the case with the people in charge of the country, which I'm guessing is one of the reasons the FM imposed this new curfew — not only to stem the spike, but also to scare us into remembering that easing restrictions isn't the same as declaring every night party night.

Yet we all know someone who'll already be counting the hours until that curfew's lifted so they have the whole street round for a bevvy. These are the numbskulls our leaders must despair of.

Those leaders might have made a million mistakes these past six months, some of which have most definitely cost lives, but at least they've always tried their best.

Sadly, that's something not all of us can say.

Thing is, nobody's asking anyone to do any *more* than their best. All we're being asked to do is think clearly, remember our responsibilities to ourselves and to others, to do our bit so we can help see this virus off the premises once and for all.

Because if we're not bright enough to get that, we might as well cancel Christmas right now.

Wednesday September 2
•Tory MPs criticise plans in Rishi Sunak's so-called 'Covid Budget' that could cost millions of self-employed taxpayers £200 each.
•UK education secretary Gavin Williamson was told 'weeks before' exam results came out that copying Scotland's marking model would backfire.
•English schools go back after six months of home studying.

THIS morning, I read back over those words written last night and wonder if they might be a little too emotional.

Christmas? Cancelled? At the start of September?

It feels like the kind of knee-jerk reaction I'd promised myself—not to mention you, my several million devoted readers —this book would shy away from.

And yet...and yet...

That's a phrase Sherlock - the detective, not the puppy — uses whenever he drifts off into a muse about some idea he at first dismissed as too fantastic to be true, but which with a second rumination begins to make sense. And this, the more I think about it, is how the thought of a locked-down Yuletide season begins to feel. A prospect no one wants to believe is possible, but which is no more than one decent, late-autumnal spike of infections harnessed to a few big nights out away from becoming reality.

Let's just say that, within the two weeks 800,000 of us have been ordered to spend without visiting each other's homes, there's a surge of cases in another area — and then another — and that they both find themselves subject to new restrictions.

Suddenly, we're heading into the second half of September with a third of the country walking on eggshells to try and head off a second wave. Next thing, 250,000 students are flooding back for the new term, criss-crossing the country or flying in from all parts of the globe. When they're not cooped up in halls of residence with their communal dining areas and shared bathroom facilities, they're out giving it major yeehah for Fresher's Week and, before we know it, there's a whole new raft of positive tests to cope with. As October then dawns, the high streets and the shopping malls start to get busier. The weather turns iffy and traditional flu symptoms kick in. Old folk are into the season where they're at their most vulnerable, schoolkids start sharing every germ that's doing the rounds.

In short, none of us needs to be what Dr Watson describes as the greatest reasoning machine of all time to work out that the potential is very much there for us to be confined to barracks long before Santa starts packing the sleigh.

The student thing really worries me. My daughter Georgia's going into third year at Glasgow University and I'm delighted she and her pals Kat and Alex decided in late spring to get out of halls and into their own flat. But had the pandemic struck two years back, the dilemma would have been whether she moved to the city at all or studied at the kitchen table.

Except that, by the time we learned face-to-face teaching had been scrapped, we'd more than likely have already booked her accommodation, the best digs go months in advance.

So, health risk or not, the undergraduate hordes with their rucksacks and guitars and boxes of Ramen noodles and 12-packs of cider will be here before we know it — and odds of them not adding to that second wave are longer than the queue for Mars Bars at a Pink Floyd laser show.

Saturday, September 5
ENGLAND won a football match in Iceland today, 1-0 thanks to a 90th minute penalty from Raheem Sterling followed by the home side missing one of their own deep in stoppage time.

These are the bald facts of a turgid match which will be live far longer in the memory for its *oo-er-missus* aftermath, when English starlets Mason Greenwood and Phil Foden celebrated their senior international debuts by sneaking a couple of leggy local models back to their rooms in a hotel which was meant to be a bio-bubble hermetically sealed off to all visitors.

That the guilty players, from Manchester United and City respectively, were instantly dropped for Tuesday night's trip to Denmark and packed off home to face the music was no surprise in itself; had he not taken action, England manager Gareth Southgame would have been caned from all sides. But what *did* take me a little aback was his claim that 'we'd have sent them home even if their actions hadn't been broken our Covid protocols'.

Seriously? Young international sportsmen in sex-is-wrong shocker? The ball's burst, Brian, the ball's burst with the groundman's best pitchfork.

Because while Greenwood and Foden might now wish they'd thought twice before risking the health of everyone around them for the sake of a leg-over, part of them must also yearn to be young and successful in a different era.

One where they'd have been shunned if they *didn't* pull

post-match...

Tuesday, September 8
·UK coronavirus deaths now stand at 41,584.
·30 new deaths recorded in the past 24 hours.
·Overall, 352,550 cases have been confirmed.

TODAY, France and Spain brace themselves for a potentially lethal second wave of Covid-19 cases which doctors say started among those aged 20 to 29, the ones told at the start of the first wave that they were the least vulnerable to infection.

But who, let's not kid ourselves, would still have believed themselves invincible even if the virus had been specifically grown in a CIA lab to affect them and them alone. Meanwhile, in England, cases among the same age group have tripled since early July and quadrupled in those from ten to 19. Within these figures, the country's deputy chief medical officer homes in on 17 to 21-year-olds, urging them to 're-engage and realise this is a continuing threat to us all'.

It seems clear as a day that this is not the moment to flirt with the issue of how young people are influencing infections. We simply don't have time to wait for the penny to drop.

And yet...and yet.

When, just about a month ago, that bunch of highly paid footballers hit the town against all pandemic protocols, Nicola Sturgeon read them the riot act — and quite right too. A raft of matches postponed, an entire sport famously put on a yellow card. She couldn't have made it any clearer that one more blip would see the season binned.

Yet now that global evidence suggests an entire generation has the potential to push Scotland back into total lockdown? She's tip-toeing around them. Picking her words extra-carefully. Giving them the benefit of the doubt. The FM's attitude to the armies of youngsters who don't give a monkey's about social distancing couldn't be more different from when those nine Aberdeen and Celtic numpties stepped out of line.

Compare these statements:

•August 11, after Celtic left-back Boli Bolingoli flew to Spain without informing his club and eight Aberdeen stars went a crowded bar after a match: *"Every day I stand here and ask members of the public to make huge sacrifices on how they live their lives…we can't have privileged football players just deciding they're not going to bother. This can't go on."*

•September 8, as evidence mounts that young people are the primary source of a spike in new cases: *"If transmission becomes established in the younger population, it will eventually reach the older and more vulnerable population. So, to younger people — please think about your loved ones as well as yourselves, which I know everybody does."*

What a line that last one was, the one about how she 'knows everybody does' think of others and not just themselves — seriously, she *knows* that *everybody* thinks of others? That's an opening line for a therapy session, right there, a distortion of reality if ever there was one.

Yet even without the qualifications to be that therapist, it's not only obvious that neither she nor any of us can possibly know what *everybody* is thinking, but also that five minutes on any street in any town will show her good faith to be very much misplaced.

Because at the risk of sounding several zillion years old, it's felt recently like most kids have never heard of coronavirus; or, at least, believe they really are immune to it they way they swarm to and from school shoulder-to-shoulder, crowd into bus stops, pile in groups to pubs and pizza joints.

So, why no yellow card for the mobbing schoolkids, the teenage squads packing houses the length and breadth of the land for illicit parties? I'm guessing the answer's as simple as it is cynical: Those teens and twentysomethings will have a far bigger say come IndyRef2 than nine footballers who might not even be living here by then.

If the Nats are going to turn a 45 per cent share of the vote into 51 next time round, they need as many youngsters onside as possible, so sending them to bed without any supper, even over something as serious as this, won't help those ambitions one little bit.

If I'm wrong, why *else* won't she give it to them straight? Why, so soon after putting all of football on probation because of the actions of a tiny minority, is she leaving whole armies of kids to work out their own mistakes? It's hard to come up with any other reason than that she doesn't want to fall out with them. Yet at a time when Scotland is mourning its first Covid-19 losses in three weeks, as new cases accelerate daily and as new figures show the bug was responsible for 83 per cent of all excess deaths between April and June, you'd have hoped a leader who has — broken record alert — told us that 'politics mean nothing' during the pandemic would have dealt with the issue in front of her, not a theoretical one away in the middle-distance.

It's a risky policy. And, on the eve of universities and colleges returning, that risk increases the longer she continues without telling it like it is.

If the FM claims to know that our kids are thinking of others as well as themselves, she's either lying to herself or she's out of touch with the state of the nation. And of all the things I've criticised her for, being out of touch is definitely not one.

THE bold Boris, meanwhile, is making it illegal for any group larger than six to meet in England from Monday.

So at least he'll still be able to hook up with everyone who thinks he knows what he's doing with Brexit, with a couple of spares seat for Jacob Rees-Mogg to put his feet up on.

This week, Whitehall's top lawyer quit in protest at the PM's latest bid to rewrite a withdrawal deal from the EU he'd been celebrating a few months back. Jonathon Jones became the sixth leading civil servant to walk away from an increasingly shambolic process, the final straw being a trade bill which even Tory ministers admit breaks international law.

That's our Prime Minister, people. A man who isn't merely

content with pulling ip the drawbridge and turning Britain into an island socially as well as geographically, but who seems hell-bent on pushing buttons in Brussels so they lose their rag, tell us to take a flying you-know-what and he gets to blame them for the consequences of the whole, horrible mess he and his chums have created. Give it a few months and Britain might not have six friends in the world, never mind one room.

BUT wait, there's yet more mind-boggling news from the world of weird-haired, empty-headed world leaders.

Donald Trump's been nominated for the Nobel Peace Prize.

I repeat.

Donald Trump has been nominated for the Nobel Peace Prize.

A man who threatened to nuke North Korea, called neo-Nazi protestors 'very decent people', defended a teen vigilante who last week gunned down two anti-racism campaigners on a Wisconsin street. A man who, a few days ago, mocked North Carolina's order to wear a face mask during a campaign visit and urged followers to do the same.

A snapshot, this, of Trump's calming effect on the planet. And yet, to repeat, he's up for the Nobel Peace Prize.

It's surely only a matter of time before the judges throw in the Literature gong too for his services to Twitter.

Monday September 15

WOKE up this morning on the beautiful island of Arran; a start to a sentence which, if written about birthdays long past, might have prefixed an anecdote about how a quiet pint in downtown Paisley ended with a midnight crossing adventure in a stolen rowing boat.

(Remind me to tell you sometime about the one that starts with how we woke up in Brussels, it's a belter.)

Today, though, I'm 58 and Arran was planned well ahead, just me and Sonia and Sherlock - and the truth is that I couldn't be in a better place. That's not some sort of new-age-bollocky nonsense about having found myself, by the way. It literally means there could not be a better place to celebrity a birthday than right here, looking out onto Brodick's chocolate-box bay with its glass-still waters, beautiful wife snuggled in by my side and our fabulous fleeceball still zonked out on a blanket at the end of the bed.

We've had a fantastic few days, so good it makes me want to scream at the thought that I've never been here before; not just at this the B&B, but on Arran itself. It took us just over two hours door to door — drive to Ardrossan, queue for the ferry, across before we knew it — yet I've been to Australia more often. I've done wee David Smith's spin class based on a ride round the the island a dozen times, but never the real thing.

Talk about knowing nothing about what's on your own doorstep? Talk about wasted time? Seriously, I've spent many inside-the-head hours this weekend beating myself up about being such a dolt. But we're here now and it's been amazing, rain running down your neck or not. It was yesterday before it finally dried up and the sun came out, yet even at its greyest and wettest the scenery was properly breathtaking.

We've taken Shez to a different beach each day — the one across from our digs on Friday, north to Lochranza early on Saturday then south to Lamlash yesterday, all so different they could have been in different countries rather than within half an hour's drive of each other.

For the first time since he came into our lives, we could let the wee fella off the leash and the joy of seeing him run and splash until he was done in was total.

Friday night, we ducked out in between deluges and dashed a couple of hundred yards to a little bar called The Crofter's, where Sherlock made new pals and we struck gold with a menu put together by the kind of chef you could only guess once worked in the fanciest of big-city restaurants, only to get burned out then come out of semi-retirement to enjoy his art under less intense pressure.

Or maybe he was just a really talented local dude.

Anyway, the food was so good we booked to go back again the next night and ended up going on the Sunday too. There are plenty more places to try the next time we're back and the next after that.

For now, it's Monday morning and I'm 58. Sonia gives me cards from herself and from Sherlock, as well as a Taggart box set, aftershave and shower gel. Tonight, we'll drop the wee fella off at his big sister Georgia's flat back in Glasgow and pop off for some precious alone time at Ingliston Country Club, our wedding venue and all-time favourite bolthole.

Before then, though, one last awesome breakfast courtesy of Tess and Mitch at Hunter's Guest House, complete with a novelty that wouldn't get old if we ate here every morning from now until I turned 158. On the table, there's the usual bowl of sachets of sauce, vinegar and mayonnaise. But in also in there sits a pair of blunt-ended craft scissors whose purpose it takes me a while to suss out, but which Sonia gets right away.

"They're to cut the corners off the sachets," she says.

Now, be honest. Isn't that the most genius thing you ever did come across? Simple, yet brilliant. No more trying to rip plastic with your teeth, no more getting condiments all down your front when the mission goes wrong. All these years of putting essentials in tiny little bags and no one ever thought of this before. It makes me very, very happy that a guest house owner on a tiny Scottish island finally has.

I must be getting old.

Wednesday September 16
GOT up to make coffee this morning and the kettle went phut. Sonia went to vacuum and Mr Dyson he said No.

Worse still, I put the telly on and the Sky box wasn't working.

Thank goodness, then, for Amazon. A few clicks of an app and the electrical goodies were already being packaged up for delivery some time tomorrow, until when we could boil water in a saucepan and get Sherlock to lick the floors clean.

As for the Sky box?

That's the interesting one, today's little Thought For The Day moment. Because to put *it* right, all we had to do was push the tip of a pen into the tiny Reset button on the back of the box and wait. Screen goes blank, then a message flashes promising us all will be well in a minute or so. Screen goes blank again, system re-boots and, sure enough, all *is* well in a minute or so.

And you know, as every vicar who ever shoehorned religion into an everyday situation on Radio Four's morning God-slot would begin his key transition sentence, wouldn't it be perfect if we could do the same with today's world?

Oh yes, it very much would. If only we had a cheat code that took away all the din, the confusion, the stupidity and — most of all — the hurt of the crazy six months gone by, the white noise you can't hear yourself think for. Maybe, like me, it feels like you're trapped in a room full of strangers gabbling without listening, except the room's the size of an entire planet and the gabbling could shift the tectonic plates from beneath our feet.

How did it come to this? How did we lose our cool and our reason so completely? How did we end up at each other's throats when we should be pulling together?

Most crucially of all, how do we drag ourselves back into some sort of semblance of sanity? Seriously, I'm asking for suggestions from the floor; to hell with asking those running the show any more, because they've proven time and again under pressure that they've no more idea than you or I.

This week, plenty in positions of power must wish there really was a Re-set button, not least because of their part in the shambles of what's become known as The Rule Of Six, which gives police the powers to disperse meetings of more than that number — both indoors and outdoors — and dish out fines if they see fit.

Of all the bureaucratic bread those in charge have popped in the toaster to see if it comes up golden, this brainwave (collapsing metaphor alert) takes the biscuit, since not only have they explained it so badly you'd think Boris had translated it from Swahili, it has holes in it big enough to drive a seven-seater car through.

Nicola Sturgeon's already had to backtrack on how the rule affects children, after it was pointed out that exemptions covering organised sport meant they couldn't have more than five friends round for a birthday party, but they *could* go 20-strong for a day's grouse shooting. Not a good start, this.

Next we heard from Priti Patel, smirking on TV that she'd happily shop her neighbours to the cops if they broke the Rule Of Six by mingling too much and demanding the rest of us do the same; a stance that should come as no surprise from a Send-'Em-Back-Home Secretary who piloted an immigration policy that would have prevented her own parents coming here from Uganda.

Then came Matt Hancock, with the air of a supply teacher on the verge of a nervous breakdown yet somehow the UK's Minister for Health, blaming the rip-roaring failure of his Covid-19 testing regime on too many sick people demanding to use it. A statement you really need to swill around for a bit before it sinks in. And leaves a taste of Marmite-flavoured Listerine. No wonder so many have given up on listening, are doing exactly what they feel like doing and bugger the consequences. No wonder social media channels are clogged with lies and half-truths, with bigotry and with brainlessness. Without clear thinking from the top, without a message we can understand, chaos reigns. Without a working democracy, there's anarchy. Society splinters. Everything falls apart.

Today, the worrying reality is that we're hanging together by our last few threads.

No one knows what to do next. Go back into lockdown and kill the economy stone dead? Get that economy back up and pumping and risk a deadly second spike? There's as much of an argument for one as the other, but our leaders lack the strength of character to decide. So here we stand, caught in the middle of all their mixed messages, their muddled thinking, their deluded desperation to be all things to all of us.

Stop the world, we want to get off?

We thought that's what was happening back on the evening of Monday March 23, when the PM put us into lockdown. We trusted our leaders to know what came next when they shut schools and shops and offices, pubs and football grounds and gyms. We presumed it was all was based on years of thinking the unthinkable and they'd have a plan to get us moving again.

Yet from ordering us to Stay Home And Save Lives one day then to Stay Alert the next, from rushing to re-open boozers before gyms then ticking us off for getting fat, right through to this hazy Rule Of Six and the ludicrous Operation Moonshot - Downing Street's plan to test tens of millions a day, as long as we all close our eyes and click our heels three times — they've really just been playing pin the tail on the donkey.

The blindfolded leading the blind.

IT'S the tweaking and tinkering that grinds you down most of all. An hour's less drinking time here, a few more kids allowed to play together there.

Thumbs up to visiting your best pal today, thumbs down tomorrow unless you're there to rewire their house. Meet them to watch the big game over a couple of pints in the pub, but not a few cans in the living room. Work from home if you can, go back to the office if you can, now do us all a favour and work from home again. But stay tuned, because it could all change again by lunchtime.

Like any of it really makes a difference.

Like the virus really gives a toss.

I'm tired, dear reader, and I'm guessing you are too. When Sonia spoke to our GP this morning about feeling weary, sore and blocked up, she was given antibiotics and steroids to help her feel better, but to go with them a chat about just how many others have been reporting the same symptoms.

"It's just the way this situation is getting to us", the doc said, "an inevitable side-effect of how long we've been quarantined from normality. Mental strain is contributing more and more to physical pain."

Weirdly, it helped Sonia to hear this, to realise she wasn't alone. It actually gave her a lift. She'd cancelled today's client list to give herself a chance to recharge the batteries, but I could see a difference in her the minute she was off the phone.

The doc was right, of course. The mental strain really *is* as prevalent as the physical, the messing with our heads that comes with the never-ending fears over jobs and homes and relationship, not to mention this never-ending twiddling with the rules, the information overload as we're bombarded with teeny-tiny measures to tackle a gigantic problem.

In the unlikely event of me ever being invited to offer my thoughts on solving this problem to the FM, the PM and their respective collectives of advisers, the one thing above all others I'd ask — no, *plead* — for would undoubtedly be that they stop dithering and make a decision: Either put us back into lockdown or set us free and let the bug puff itself out.

Either does me. If we're told to stay home 23 hours a day once more, if the boozers and the cafes close once more, if we're back to meeting each other on Zoom and FaceTime, if this what spares us a second wave of infection, then I for one will toe the line and reckon nine out of ten would do the same.

If the other one in ten end up in the nick? Their problem.

If, however, the politicians and scientists and doctors agree that a crumbling economy is of greater danger to society than a virus, if they let life return to normal and trust us not to be stupid, I'll do my best to repay that trust and would guess that nine out of ten will, again, do the same.

But while the tweaking and the tinkering drags on? Sorry, but that's when the one in ten goes rogue, when a combination of the human race's innate flyness and bottomless capacity for stupidity makes everything go pear-shaped.

That, as we keep on proving, is when it becomes blindingly obvious that we really do know - all together now - *nothing*.

Thursday September 24
•*The Times* says London faces lockdown if new measures fail to curb a spike.
•Major employers including HSBC pause plans to return workers to offices.
•One in five asked in University College London study fears side-effects of a Covid-19 vaccine.

YET the tweaking and the twiddling goes on, this week in the shape of the decision to make pubs and restaurants close at 10pm rather than the standard one hour later.

Why? I'd have thought it was obvious — that's when the virus goes to bed; I certainly can't think of any other reason why it might make a bawhair's difference. The idea appears to be that the earlier we clear the licensed premises, the sooner we clear the streets and everyone's home in time for cocoa and sleepy-byes. All of which makes perfect sense apart from one inescapable fact:

That logic and alcohol tend not to mix.

You think nightclubs are crowded with people who want to dance, rather than who want to keep bevvying into the early hours? If so, it's surely only a matter of time before you're a Cabinet minister.

So even if we accept with our sensible heads on at seven o'clock that it's game over come ten, just wait till 9.59, when we're draining that double round shouted up at last orders and deciding who's house to head back to. That's the reality of this latest pointless potter with the regulations, that it simply won't work. It's more mouth music, another pretence of taking affirmative action against the virus.

As it goes, I like the way pubs are operating post-lockdown.

A week or so back, I went for a beer with my daughter for the first time in forever and it was something of a joy — no crush at the bar, everyone sitting around having a chat and a laugh, table service, lovely clean loos. Very continental, very civilised. Give us back a little low-level music and it would have been pretty near perfect, but even then the absense of bumping and banging and yelling almost made up for it.

I left hoping it catches on once we're back to whatever our normal becomes; one major reason why, for me, it seems far more practical, not to mention safer, to let restaurants and bars stick with their normal opening hours as long as they also stick to the new social distancing rules, while making house parties a criminal offence for the duration.

One thing or the other. No grey areas. No wiggle room over drinking, eating, wearing masks, any of the issues that have caused everyone such a headache. Because like it or not, we're a species who need firm direction — and anyone who wants to argue with that only needs to witness our reaction every time we're given a countdown to the next restriction.

"See the pubs are closing early from Friday?"

"Aye, so we'd better kick the arse out of it on Thursday."

Why we're given these countdowns baffles me. Surely if the new regulations are as urgent as our leaders tell us they are, then there's no time to waste? These are the questions that drive us mad. This is the conversation we've all had with each other, one that goes round and round and leaves us utterly frustrated. Most of all, these are the weaknesses in leadership that let the Covidiots and the conspiracists flourish.

Yet again this week, for example, Nicola Sturgeon's briefing podium performance as she delivered her latest set of rules made Boris Johnson look like the burbling heap of candy-floss he is. She pleaded with us to 'be strong, be kind and continue to act out of love and solidarity', a line clearly as heartfelt as her admission that 'I will never find the words to thank all of you enough for the enormous sacrifices you have made so far and I am truly sorry to be asking for more'.

Meanwhile, what was the best BoJo could muster? That 'a stitch in time saves nine', whatever the bejeezus that meant.

Yet no matter how unanimously the FM wins the rhetoric contest, as she invariably does against the PM, memorable soundbites won't control the infection rate any more than they'll save the countless business staring into the abyss.

Only the courage to make an informed and unambiguous choice on which is more controllable offers us even an outside chance of winning one of the these battles, because the truth is that we cannot possibly win both.

◆ ◆ ◆

Thursday October 2

WHATEVER Sonia had last week, I have now.

Sore joints, tight skin, blurry vision, headaches, no energy, no motivation to exercise. Is it Covid? Part of me wouldn't mind if it was, because without wishing to sound flippant, two weeks at home with nothing to do sounds at this moment like the next best thing to a holiday in the sun.

I've been doing too much, pushing myself too hard. The summer cycling season peaked with a gloriously sunny tour of Scotland's heartlands alongside — or, more accurately, panting in the wake of — Carolyn and Gus, 100 miles as magnificent for the soul as they were draining on the body.

The last 30 were torture, legs limp as lettuce, shoulders burning. I remember punching the air in sheer delight when the Garmin ticked over to the magic three figures as we finally rolled back towards where we'd started that morning in Kirkintilloch, yet in that same moment the last dregs of juice ran out and all I wanted to do was sleep.

Which is pretty much all I've wanted to do since.

There's always something to do, though; a column to write, Sherlock to take walkies, shopping to do, this bastarding book to finish. Saturday will be the first of seven long days on the Neuro-Linguistic Programming course postponed from May, then Scotland have three qualifying ties for two tournaments in six days. Plus, we're looking for a new place to live, a house rather than a flat, with a garden for Shez.

Thing is, Sonia's just as busy with work, so no wonder it never feels like we never get proper time. No wonder there are nights when we almost have to re-introduce ourselves to each other. Yet there's no doubt we're far from alone in this sense of fatigue and detachment.

This time in all our lives was supposed to be a blessing in disguise, a pause in the madness of our old normal that we wanted to believe would let us put our affairs in order, offer us the space to clean out our closets. Yet instead, it's messed us all up, it's turned us inside out; as I've read back over six months of work, proof-reading till my eyes cross but probably still missing a hundred stupid mistakes, it's astonishing just how many ways humanity has set about justifying this book's title through an endless catalogue of catastrophic decisions.

From stockpiling loo roll to transferring sick pensioners from hospitals to care homes, our response to the pandemic has been an individual and collective omnishambles.

Key figures who'd lectured us on how to saves lives — Cathy Calderwood, Dominic Cummings, No 10's scientific whizz Neil Ferguson and more — have believed in their arrogance that they could get away with breaking their own rules.

Footballers afforded freedoms you and I were denied risked the game's future by abusing the privilege — only a few days back, Dundee United player Mark Connolly, who'd given me a terrific post-match interview two games into the season about how it was the duty of his fellow pros to 'live boring lives' in the name of public health, has just been suspended for refusing to wear a mask in a taxi after the kind of night out he'd claimed he couldn't have.

Even as I'm writing these closing pages, news breaks that one Margaret Ferrier, a 60-year-old SNP MP, had travelled to London from Glasgow by train despite having felt so unwell she'd been for a coronavirus test, before speaking in a House of Commons debate—

ironically on coronavirus —before making the return journey despite said test having come back positive.

This would have been a selfish and a stupid thing for any of us to do, never mind a public servant in such a position of responsibility — and even more so one who had been hugely vocal in her demands for Cummings to be sacked for *his* selfishness. Ferrier grandstanded that situation big time, yet if anything her aberration is even worse, because she travelled by public transport. That it was Wednesday before she told anyone in her party and tonight at 5.50pm before she coughed to any of it was reckless in the extreme.

That her resignation didn't follow at 5.51pm suggests an awful lot about the character of a politician whose behaviour on this has been as two-faced as it is uncaring. We'll presume that by the time you read this she will have quit, but whenever it happens — as I say, presuming it does — will be way too late.

Like so many in pubs and in parks and on beaches, in shops and on buses and trains and taxis and even in their own homes who have consistently and catastrophically proved incapable or simply unwilling to follow simple rules that might just have helped eased the spread of the bug, Margaret Ferrier seemed to believe those rules only applied to other people.

Yet for all that we make our own choices, what chance is there of us mere mortals getting it right when we're led by the immeasurably nonsensical Boris, who set the tone even before lockdown by deciding he had better things to do than attend the first five emergency Cobra sessions to formulate a response to the virus and who right down to this, the day I finally finish the book, still manages to have the reverse Midas effect.

As in, everything he touches turns to shite.

For across today's newspapers, from the ones on the right which have backed him to the hilt to those on the left who feed off his every blunder, we find wall-to-wall open mockery of a speech yesterday in which he got his own most recent rules on meeting up with our friends wrong.

As a fresh clampdown on socialising was introduced across

North-East England, the PM reminded those living there that they could meet 'six in a home, six in hospitality but, as I understand it, not six outside. That is the situation' — except it *wasn't* the situation, because as the twit then had to Tweet, 'you can't meet different households in social settings indoors, including pubs, restaurants and your home...you should also avoid socialising with other households outside'.

Not that he'd got it wrong, of course. No, like all politicians, he had merely 'mis-spoken'. To which all I can say is that it's a crying bloody shame so many people mis-voted at the election.

Friday October 3
·UK High Street betting shops fall by almost 500 to 3,338 since lockdown.
·Boris Johnson claims virus is spiking because people got 'blasé' about risks.
·Parents face £200 fines for letting kids go Trick Or Treating at Hallowe'en.

THOSE last words about our idiot PM were supposed to finally close the book.

But then we awoke this morning to the news, Tweeted by the man himself, that Donald Trump has tested positive.

Proof that even coronavirus has a sense of humour.

Last Saturday, the President had hosted a ceremony in the White House Rose Garden to announce Amy Coney Barrett as his nominee for the US Supreme Court, an event at which many guests mingled without masks.

Later that night, the pumpkin-dyed 74-year-old flew to Pennsylvania for an outdoor campaign rally. From there, he went to Cleveland for Tuesday's first live TV election debate of three with 7,777-year-old opponent Joe Biden, during which he openly mocked the Democratic candidate for 'wearing the biggest masks you ever saw, even if he's 60 yards away'.

Trump had pre-empted this dig by explaining that the reason he, all of his family — apart from wife Melania - and most other members of his entourage had not masked up as the fact that everyone had their temperatures taken on their way into the venue, which made it unnecessary. However, by Friday, debate moderator Chris Wallace was telling Fox News that Trump *wasn't* tested pre-show as he'd turned up late and organisers decided to deal with his group on 'an honour basis'.

Ladies and gentlemen, please be upstanding for the dictionary definition of Irony.

On Wednesday, Trump flew to Minnesota for a fundraiser and outdoor rally, during which close aide Hope Hicks felt unwell and decided to isolate on board presidential plane Air Force One en route back to Washington. Hicks tested positive yesterday, but Trump still flew to an indoor fundraising event in New Jersey at which few wore masks and where the concept of social distancing was something for other people; sheep, snowflake Democrats and other un-Americans.

That night, after Hicks' test results were made public, Trump admitted during a phone interview with Fox News that he and Melania had 'been tested and are awaiting results' and praised Hicks for 'working so hard without even a small break'.

Finally, shortly after 1am this morning, Trump tweeted that he and his wife had both tested positive:

"We will begin our quarantine and recovery process immediately. We will get through this TOGETHER!"

After lunchtime, the White House announced the President had been given experimental drug cocktail Regeneron and said he was 'fatigued but in good spirits'.

He was then helicoptered to Walter Reed Army Medical Centre, his personal physician releasing a letter saying he had received his first dose of unapproved antiviral remdesivir, that his earlier fever had subsided and he'd been given additional oxygen to help saturation rates recover from 94 per cent.

All of which left you thinking: How unlucky can a man be?

He's on statins for heart disease, he's kept his weight down to a manageable 17st 4lb on a diet of McNuggets and cola, he mixes with all sorts of strangers without him or them wearing masks, he turns up too late at a TV studio for the coronavirus test everyone in the building was meant by law to get, then he takes a flight on a plane despite having travelled on it the day before with a staff member who'd since fallen ill with the bug.

All of this after predicting that America would get five cases of the virus, max, that the non-crisis would be all over in time for church on Easter Sunday, that states which chose to go into lockdown were guilty of repressing the Land of the Free and, of course, that if shining a bright light on a sufferer didn't cure them, a shot in the arm with disinfectant would.

I mean, what were the odds..?

Tuesday October 6

AFTER a weekend when his oxygen levels fell to 93 per cent, doctors called his symptoms 'concerning' then declared him to be 'not out of the woods', Trump left hospital this morning.

As a White House spokesperson promised the 'finest possible medical support', he himself issued one Tweet urging America not to be 'afraid of Covid', then a second calling it 'less lethal than flu!'; a post soon deleted by Twitter, yet if this reprimands hurt Trump, it sure as hell didn't show as he waddled towards his office, turned to the cameras and ripped his face mask off.

Armando Ianucci, creator of political satire *The Thick Of It*, later described Trump as having 'internally directed his trip into hospital' and of 'looking for the shot'. Guesting on Frankie Boyle's *New World Order* TV show, Ianucci said:

> "He released film of his exit which was edited into some kind of miraculous reverse of Apocalypse Now where good was somehow coming back to America…and you think, everywhere you go now, he's just breathing out toxic fumes."

Those live pictures of Trump's dramatic self-unmasking, like the reveal on the world's tackiest home makeover show, synched perfectly in split-screen with the briefing his chief medic, Dr Anthony Fauci, was giving in which he warned:

"If you have a problem wearing face masks and a problem avoiding crowds, then we have a serious problem this fall going into winter."

The soundbite flew higher over Trump's head than his combover in a hurricane.

◆ ◆ ◆

THIS morning, as England's football squad gather for the first time since kiddie lotharios Mason Greenwood and Phil Foden were sent home from Iceland for popping the bio-bubble, three more stars face the axe for...popping the bio-bubble.

Chelsea striker Tammy Abraham got home from Saturday's 4-0 win over Crystal Palace to find a surprise party arranged for his 21st birthday, where among 'more than six' guest, were international team-mates Ben Chilwell and Jadon Sancho.

All three have apologised for 'being naive' and 'letting people down' and all that Aberdeen Eight-style bollocks. All three have been told to stay away from training pending tests. All three will miss Thursday night's game against Wales because results won't be back in time. The three lions on their shirt may soon be replaced by a new Downing Street-style slogan:

Stay Inert.
Stay Out Late.
Stay Stupid.

◆ ◆ ◆

MEANWHILE, in our own little bubble, we broke for coffee on morning four of the Neuro Linguistic Programming course in a Glasgow city centre hotel conference suite just as phones pinged with invites to the premiere of *Lockdown 2: The Sequel.*

Tomorrow, we were being told, Nicola Sturgeon would announce a new raft of restrictions from Friday in what was described as a 'circuit breaker'; a short, sharp, total shutdown to try and halt the ever-increasing second wave of infections.

The sub-plot was that the story had been broken by *The Scottish Sun* on the basis of information that the NHS was braced for this proper lockdown-lockdown, a story shot down by Holyrood and followed up by the First Minister announcing the measures she *wouldn't* be announcing in the next day's briefing; no ban on leaving home, no school closures, no closure of public transport.

Question was, why leave us dangling for 24 hours? Why allow rumour and confusion to percolate and permeate for what, in social media terms at least, is a longer time than the messiest week in politics? On the surface, it made no sense. But then, given the ever-more-mixed messages of these past weeks that have melded into muddled months, maybe it should have made perfect sense.

Maybe this is just the way we're communicated with now.

So we waited. And, come Wednesday lunchtime, we were finally let in on the big secret that pubs and restaurants across central Scotland — from islands off the Ayrshire coast in the west, through Paisley and Glasgow and Falkirk to Edinburgh in the east — would close from 6pm on Friday, with cafes allowed to open only if they didn't have an alcohol licence.

The new rules would affect 3.4 million of us, more than half the population, and stay in place until October 25 at least. Snooker and pools halls, indoor bowling alleys, bingo halls and casinos in the same area would also be closed. Contact sports for anyone over 18, barring professionals, would be cancelled along with indoor group exercise and outdoor live shows.

Say whatever you like about the science behind it all, but this was an unmitigated disaster for thousands of businesses and their workers. The light at the end of the tunnel our bars and bistros and hotels and gyms had seen turned out to be an oncoming juggernaut.

Friday October 9, 6.35pm.

AND so, here we are, just over half an hour into the newest of our never-ending collection of New Normals.

An hour earlier, we'd come to the tearful, joyous end of a life-changing, mind-expanding, friends-for-life-making, qualification-gaining week learning ways to reprogramme the mind to deal with traumas, phobias, relationship issues, lack of confidence, insomnia — you name, I can now help it go away, see website for details — and all we wanted to do was raise a glass to each other's future happiness and success.

But we weren't allowed to; at least, not with alcohol. Yes, the hotel said, we could order as much booze as we liked, but the curfew came in at six. So, we asked, could we have it at 5.59 and keep it for when the food we'd ordered came around half past? No, they said, because although we could eat beyond six, alcohol had to be finished and removed *before* six.

Now, toasting each other with Coke or orange juice rather than G&T or beer made no real difference. It's the sentiment that counted. But still, it was a downer to have something as symbolic as a proper toast taken away for...well, for *what*?

Thirteen of us had been in the same room as each other ten hours a day for seven days, we'd worked in twos and threes and fours — the groups switching from morning to afternoon and day to day — we'd all used the same coffee machine and the same loos. Yet having a pint together in that same room was illegal because it could only happen once we'd finished work, which wouldn't allow us to drink those pints before six o'clock.

I'm not saying it should have been fine for us to break the rules and not for punters in pubs. Just that it would have made absolutely no difference to our chances of catching the bug.

This is the kind of anomaly so many can no longer grasp

and are less and less willing to accept, the arbitrary nature of the rules, the way they are what they are just because they are what they are. We're back to being kids again, being told that grown-ups don't need to give reasons; just do as they say, even if they don't always do it themselves.

And the sadness is that this doesn't only apply to something as ho-hum, as throwaway, as a quick drink at the end of a course. Tonight, it resonates across Britain in so many ways that threaten life, limb and happiness.

Across the North-West of England, whole cities are being primed for the same kind of restrictions central Scotland is now experiencing. Northern Ireland's spike is so worrying that politicians and health chiefs are considering declaring a unilateral national circuit-breaker lockdown. Same goes for Wales. Sources close to No10 suggest the PM is desperately trying to come up with a new model to simplify the rules and head off a rising tide of public disobedience.

To say it's not looking good is like suggesting BoJo's hair could maybe do with a quick tidy-up.

AROUND quarter to eight, we say our goodbyes and start for home on journeys ranging from ten minutes on a bus to four hours in a car, back to partners and kids and dogs and cats and jobs and dreams. I leave the hotel, turn right onto Cambridge Street, right again down the alley by the multi-storey, past a cluster of kids armed with slabs of beer for a *fuck-yer-curfew* night in someone's flat or some darkened park, bear left onto Renfrew Street, left again onto Hope Street and wait for the next No6 to arrive.

There's no one else at the bus stop, a rarity the LED board says will offer seven minutes of headspace, during which so much of what I've tried to write about begins to crystalise. It's been that kind of week, one where an awful of lot of stuff has made sense after so long feeling like a hopeless jumble, like finally finding the patience to detangle that bag of old cables to decide which are still usable and which are for the bin.

And as the metaphorical cables of six pandemic-stricken months come apart, a question that's been trying to form for weeks presents itself like a neon billboard.

What about all the other pandemics heading our way?

The million women across Britain who've missed out on mammograms that could save their lives. The one in five of cancer patients whose treatment is on hold because vital NHS resources are diverted elsewhere. The countless sufferers from illnesses and injuries which aren't life-threatening but which are debilitating all the same and who either can't get a hospital appointment or who soldier on in silent discomfort because they don't want to be a burden on the system.

The growing number of vulnerable men and women dying from overdoses in hotels where they'd been shipped for the duration, supposedly to keep them safe from the streets; think back to the bit in the book where this had been seen such a positive move for all concerned.

Those six victims of the Park Inn stabbing that terrible day a stressed-out asylum seeker snapped over the conditions they were forced to live in. Again, when they were taken from their homes and packed off in busloads to hotels that became prisons, they'd been told it was for their own good.

The soaring cases of depression and anxiety, the massive hike in reports of domestic abuse, the problem drinking, the comfort eating. All side-effects of life in lockdown, all creating countless invisible victims of coronavirus, the ones who never rate a mention in the briefings, aren't factored into the stats.

Best guess, there are way more among us whose lives have been affected by this crisis without ever testing positive than there have been fatalities or there are poor souls who've had to quarantine — and that's before we mention the charities facing up to mass redundancies, the theatres and nightspots who might never open again, the football clubs unsure if they'll ever kick another ball.

On this last front, matches being forfeited because one club or other has been hit with multiple positive tests is becoming commonplace. The sport's elite level risks being reduced to the status of a pub league where The Dog & Duck can't rustle up 11 sober men on a Sunday morning. I genuinely fear we won't get this season finished and that clubs will go bust as a result.

OVERALL, the big, dark, Van-Gogh-At-His-Most-Introverted picture is that way too many have been left confused, angry and sometimes even to perish by leaders simply not cut out to cope with the scale of greatest public health crisis in a lifetime.

Most accepted for months that fighting the virus came first, who were prepared to be patient above and beyond the call of duty if it meant we got to see the bug off the premises.

Yet we *haven't* seen it off. More than six months on, we're *still* stumbling and bumbling from one set of guidelines to the next, *still* waiting for an efficient test and trace system, *still* no clearer on when a vaccine will become available. So who could blame any of those women who've missed mammograms, any of those cancer patients left living in pain and fear, the hotel workers who've had to deal with all that death and bloodshed, the everyday sick and injured, the fundraisers, the factory owners, the theatre impresarios, the football club chairmen and way more besides for refusing to be patient any longer?

Who could blame them for yelling as one: When's OUR turn?

It's a question they have every right to ask and keep asking. Most have held their tongues for half the year, have tried to do their bit for the cause by not making a fuss, but it's got them nowhere. Each one is, for me at least, now well entitled to demand of our leaders in Edinburgh and London whether it's time to remember coronavirus isn't the only problem in town.

Yes, cases are rising again and we'd be crazy to downplay the dangers. But it would be just as crazy not to balance these dangers against the pandemic's indirect effects; on jobs, on physical and mental health, on sport, on good causes, on…well, on LIFE.

A death toll which, at its peak, was way out of proportion to our infection rate suggests that the way both Holyrood and Westminster have played things, demanding our unflinching support as they throw all their eggs into one basket, simply hasn't worked anywhere near as well as they'd hoped. Maybe even more than this, though, the way one half of society is at the other's throat these days screams of policies unravelling like so many jumpers caught on nails.

Doesn't matter that few of us are qualified to understand the issues we're arguing about –– masking up or not, how to protect our old folk, the dangers lurking in our schools and unis, the role of The Media™ in the public's mood, the economy versus the health of millions –– our first class degrees from Twitter University and The Facebook College of Cobblers allow us to take swipes at each other for as long as these issues keep on dominating our day-to-day existence. And as much as this might be pointless and irrational and endless irritating, who can blame anyone for expressing their confusion and their helplessness and their panic in this way?

Who could blame those whose health, living conditions and job prospects have suffered these past six months for losing the plot altogether?

Fact is, the people in charge of the UK and its constituent parts haven't communicated well enough with us and they haven't listened to our worries and our complaints. At best, they've backtracked on this issue or that off the back of public outrage, but if they think that's the same as listening then they really *do* need therapy.

It takes courage to lead.

It takes strength of character to accept the responsibility that goes hand-in-hand with power.

And never more in our lifetimes was that courage needed than right now in finding a way to deal with those millions of invisible victims of coronavirus. Never more than today was there a more urgent need for those who run the show to take responsibility for everyone in their care, rather than just those with one particular set of symptoms.

Yet so much forensic and anecdotal evidence available to us points to both Westminster and Holyrood having long since crossed a line from focussing their energies on the pandemic, as was undoubtedly their duty at the outset, to suffering from a tunnel vision that ignores all our other ills.

Today, the UK's death toll from Covid-19 sits at 42,679 deaths. But if, once the pandemic is finally over, we find that 42,680 have passed away from other untreated ailments or have missed the boat on vital surgeries, what will lockdown have been good for?

As I write this, it's 199 days since the first morning our of new normal, that morning when we awoke to working and learning from home, to no pubs or shops or gyms or holidays or hairdressers, the morning when we all dreamed of writing that novel or promised we'd re-set our moral and material compasses. And it feels like we haven't taken one step forward, grown one ounce stronger.

It feels like we really have learned absolutely nothing.

Dominic Cummings has chameleon-ed himself back into No10's wallpaper, the dickheadedness of his adventures in Covidland having done his career no harm. Those Aberdeen and Celtic footballers whose selfishness almost wrecked the season for everyone carry on as normal, even if one or two have had to change clubs to do so.

Matt Hancock remains in stressed-out supply teacher mode, but also remains the UK's minister for health. Ditto the battered and bemused John Swinney in his role attempting to control Scottish education. Priti Patel still can't count and we still can't count on Priti Patel.

With Donald Trump a month away from an election which

will either give him another four years in the White House or turf him out and turn him into the most powerful man on Earth, almost 20 per cent of Americans surveyed admitted to cleaning themselves or their food with bleach, only slightly fewer report using disinfectant on their hands and/or skin and four per cent say they have inhaled, gargled or swallowed household cleaning products as a way of killing the virus.

Jesus suffering fuck, Margaret Ferrier has even dug her heels in and refused to resign as an MP, claiming SNP spin doctors forced her into an apology she wasn't ready to make yet then also insisting that once she'd made it she held the moral high ground over Cummings.

And amidst all this madness, a pandemic of needless cancer deaths is coming. A pandemic of unemployment is coming. A mental health pandemic is coming. A pandemic that will wipe out a massive slice of our hospitality, tourism, entertainment and sporting industries is coming.

Do we go into lockdown as each of these in turn does its worst?

Plus, let's not pretend that if this coronavirus has been able to come from nothing and wreak such death and sickness then other, possibly even more resistance versions won't follow in its chaotic wake.

So, do we lock down as each of these in turn does it worst?

Is that the future? Hiding from every problem rather than solving it, running scared of our own shadow?

As the No6 pulls up and my face mask goes on, it feels hell of a like it.

But then, what do I know..?

Love & Peace.

ABOUT THE AUTHOR

BILL LECKIE is 58, has been a local and national newspaper journalist for 40 years, has worked on and off on radio and TV, hosted events here and there, spoken at dinners with varying degrees of success, interviewed some big names in various places, won a few awards he shouldn't have and missed out on a few he deserved to go home with. He sometimes teaches indoor cycling to blindingly good music. He messed up at marriage twice but looks to finally have got it right third time since la bellissima Sonia De Rosa turned his life around. His son Kenny and daughter Georgia are awesome. His puppy Sherlock fills him with love. He's spent a long time starting a lot of things without having the patience to finish them — though he intends to start changing this — forgets a lot of stuff as quickly as it comes into his head and lives in a permanently anxious fug about losing his job and being deemed unemployable. At the same time as finishing this book, he finally did something about this fear of losing everything by qualifying as a Neuro Linguistic Programming practitioner and is now available to sort out your phobias, insomnia, confidence issues and nail-biting habit.
Most of all, though, he knows nothing.
And it suits him.

PS: Is it just me, or does this bit look like Bridget Jones's pants?

Printed in Great Britain
by Amazon